AF323716

George Oppen's Poetics of the Commonplace

This book is part of the Peter Lang Humanities list.
Every volume is peer reviewed and meets
the highest quality standards for content and production.

PETER LANG
New York • Bern • Frankfurt • Berlin
Brussels • Vienna • Oxford • Warsaw

Xavier Kalck

George Oppen's Poetics of the Commonplace

PETER LANG
New York • Bern • Frankfurt • Berlin
Brussels • Vienna • Oxford • Warsaw

Library of Congress Cataloging-in-Publication Data

Names: Kalck, Xavier, author.
Title: George Oppen's poetics of the commonplace / Xavier Kalck.
Description: New York: Peter Lang, 2017.
Includes bibliographical references and index.
Identifiers: LCCN 2017029268 | ISBN 978-1-4331-4305-2 (hardcover: alk. paper)
ISBN 978-1-4331-4306-9 (ebook pdf) | ISBN 978-1-4331-4307-6 (epub)
ISBN 978-1-4331-4308-3 (mobi)
Subjects: LCSH: Oppen, George—Criticism and interpretation
Classification: LCC PS3529.P54 Z74 2017 | DDC 811/.52—dc23
LC record available at https://lccn.loc.gov/2017029268
DOI 10.3726/b11599

Bibliographic information published by **Die Deutsche Nationalbibliothek.**
Die Deutsche Nationalbibliothek lists this publication in the "Deutsche Nationalbibliografie"; detailed bibliographic data are available on the Internet at http://dnb.d-nb.de/.

Cover photo: Plaque in commemoration of the Paris Commune at Père-Lachaise Cemetery referenced in Oppen's poem "Eros," NCP 120.
(Photo by Xavier Kalck)

The paper in this book meets the guidelines for permanence and durability of the Committee on Production Guidelines for Book Longevity of the Council of Library Resources.

29 Broadway, 18th floor, New York, NY 10006
www.peterlang.com

Printed in Germany

Table of Contents

Preface

Monographs devoted to a single author are often structured around a roughly linear chronology which follows the production of the work and its reception—a life's work and the work's life—leaving the reader with little by way of justification beyond the relevance of said author, whether it was meant to be demonstrated, questioned, or whether relevance must quite simply be assumed. Multiauthor monographs may seem to present something a little different, yet they too will often prove equally linear, if in a slightly subtler way, by imposing the linearity of a conceptual framework on a reluctant variety of texts and contexts. This book hopes to offer an alternative; however, even if successful, its outline may come across as somewhat unsettling. Although this is a single author monograph, which focuses on the reception of the work of George Oppen, it is not essentially concerned with historiography. This book is an empirical investigation into what literary criticism can hope to achieve and into the fabric, and fabrications, of literary knowledge—how it is made, assembled, and why it sometimes tells a lie. I have therefore chosen to present this exploration as such, with its occasional digressions and repetitions, instead of packaging my findings into more readily digestible precepts. If my reader is kind and patient enough, I firmly believe this explicitly experimental method will prove most adequate for a study devoted to issues of methodology. For methodology is not only a crucial aspect of this book, it is the very subject of this book. What "the commonplace" means for Oppen's poetics and how this translates into a common awareness of a shared history is a question that cannot be answered by literary critics unless the commonplaces that make up the critical consensus are also discussed. I will go as far as to say that this analogy is inherent in Oppen's own practice and in the poetic goals he set for himself, that require critics to engage with his work from the communal perspective of a common language, which puts great pressure on the truthfulness of one's own critical discourse. I insist on the matter because I must address the perhaps unusually critical slant of this piece of literary criticism, which could lead some to believe that my remarks are at times directed ad hominem. They are not. When I question specific positions and specific critical beliefs, I aim at clarifying these positions and beliefs as objectively as possible for the sake of methodological progress, and not in the name of a competing school, coterie, theory, or out of personal preference. I can only hope that my carefully detailed close readings of the secondary sources, which make up a large part of my primary sources, will testify to the integrity of my endeavor.

Acknowledgments

I am immensely grateful to Michael Heller for his time and kind notes, and to Hélène Aji and Denis Lagae-Devoldère for their precious advice. Warm thanks are due to Rachel Blau DuPlessis, who encouraged me to revise and improve the initial manuscript. This book would not be without the support of Elisabeth Angel-Perez, head of the VALE research center at Paris-Sorbonne University, and the help of the Paris-Sorbonne University commission for research.

Copyright Credits

Abbreviations

ON	DuPlessis, Rachel Blau and Quartermain, Peter, eds. 1999. *The Objectivist Nexus: Essays in Cultural Poetics*. Tuscaloosa: Alabama University Press.
MP	Hatlen, Burton, ed. 1981. *George Oppen: Man and Poet*. Orono: National Poetry Foundation.
FM	Nicholls, Peter. 2007. *George Oppen and the Fate of Modernism*. Oxford: Oxford University Press.
NCP	Oppen, George. 2002. *New Collected Poems*. Edited by Michael Davidson. New York: New Directions.
CP	Oppen, George. 1975. *Collected Poems*. New York: New Directions.
SP	Oppen, George. 2007. *Selected Prose, Daybooks, And Papers*. Edited by Stephen Cope. Berkeley: University of California Press.
SL	Oppen, George. 1990. *Selected Letters of George Oppen*. Edited by Rachel Blau DuPlessis. Durham, NC: Duke University Press.
ML	Oppen, Mary. *Meaning a Life*. Santa Barbara: Black Sparrow Press, 1979.
TP	Shoemaker, Steve, ed. *Thinking Poetics. Essays on George Oppen*. Tuscaloosa: University of Alabama Press, 2009.

Introduction

In the Land of Uz

> It seems to me I know some essential things that Williams, Pound, Stevens never knew.
>
> —SL 181

Are you interested in commonplaces? If so, you know that some commonplaces are trivial trite truisms, every-day stock-phrases, barely one step away for full-blown prejudice, while others are generally accepted statements, notable examples of widely shared opinions about which a community has reached a consensus. Once, they might be written down in what used to be called a book of common places, or a commonplace book. For commonness, like ordinariness, or plainness, evokes all at once the quality of being undistinguished and democratic. What one calls common may be vulgar, coarse, second-rate, it may also be elementary, familiar, something we all share—sometimes it is both. In the last decade of the nineteenth century, that ambiguity was celebrated by Walt Whitman:

> The commonplace I sing;
> How cheap is health! how cheap nobility!
> Abstinence, no falsehood, no gluttony, lust;
> The open air I sing, freedom, toleration,
> (take here the mainest lesson—less from books—less from the schools,)

> The common day and night—the common earth and waters,
> Your farm—your work, trade, occupation,
> The democratic wisdom underneath, like solid ground for all.
> (Whitman 1982, 651)[1]

Labelled "democratic wisdom" and providing "solid ground for all," Whitman's commonplace seems a direct illustration of American groundlessness made into a resource of its own (Fredman 2009, 5). In Williams' *Paterson*, anthropomorphized natural landmarks are not only likely sources for a common language but precious filters, rich with form:

> (What common language to unravel?
> . . combed into straight lines
> from that rafter of a rock's
> lip.) (Williams 1963, 15)

Today, the word commons points to shared public resources as well as to the resourcefulness of sharing, of thinking and of acting collectively. The appeal of that notion seems ever greater, from health and environmental issues to intellectual property battles and the evolution of academic publishing through Creative Commons licenses. In *Governing the Commons: The Evolution of Institutions for Collective Action* (1990) or in *Understanding Knowledge as a Commons: From Theory to Practice* (2007), economist and Nobel Prize recipient Elinor Ostrom has revived the idea of singing the commonplace in a way that makes Whitman's poem surprisingly prophetic. However, the commonplace, like its not-so-distant cousin, common sense, has never stopped being a hotly disputed concept. From Aristotle's "koinê sumpheron" to the Latin "utilitas communis," "sensus communis," and its great many echoes through the centuries in "res publica," "res communis," and the various contexts for the word "communism," speaking of the commonplace or of common sense requires many precautions.

Looking at "The Commonalities of *Common Sense*," Robert A. Ferguson attributes Thomas Paine's success with the notion in part to his rhetoric—the powers of a "plain" style being any pamphleteer's dream—and in part to the inherent plasticity of populism in an open society—from democratic ideals all the way to demagoguery. As Sophia Rosenfeld writes,

> For the first 200 years that followed the publication of his *Common Sense*, Paine had served as the patron saint of radicals and revolutionaries everywhere, from the French and German republicans who called for a return of his spirit in 1848 to New York intellectuals who launched a socialist magazine at the height of the Depression under the banner, once again, of revolutionary common sense. (Rosenfeld 2011, 255)

Contrary to what one might have expected, Paine was then successfully "appropriated as a sage of the right," after "a self-proclaimed conservative, Reagan, during his presidency, frequently mined the pages of the original 1776 *Common Sense* for pithy, patriotic quotes" (Rosenfeld 2011, 255), in a fashion that has been eagerly emulated since by a vast array of conservatives. In other words, it seems that common sense, like the commonplace, cannot escape its basic ambivalence: because it is superlatively common, it can indeed belong to anyone. Consequently, common sense, like the commonplace, moves from common knowledge to common prejudice, and has done so since Plato's separation of *doxa* from *epistêmê*. Kant later duplicated Plato's division when he chose to isolate aesthetic judgment (which, to achieve universality, relies on a common sense intersubjective agreement that a given work exemplifies the concept of beauty) from moral judgment pertaining to ethical or political matters (it must rely on a formal imperative, since moral conduct is decided outside intersubjective relations, transcended by the moral imperative), for fear that popular bias would contaminate the new epistemic horizons that were opening up. Yet, one year after Kant's birth, Vico's *New Science* had argued in favor of common sense as the very basis for a history of human nature. Vico went as far as to suggest that Homer's poetic work was the product of the vulgar common sense of his time, and not the pure invention of a single genius. Closer to us, Gadamer, after Vico, held that common sense—sense as it is produced by a community—was not necessarily foreign to, or an enemy of, universal reason and the objective truths of science. In *Truth and Method*, he attempts to unearth "the political prehistory of this aestheticized concept" (Rosenfeld 2011, 245). With a different outlook, Hannah Arendt also sought to apply Kant's aesthetic judgement to a political context. For some now "saw in that quintessentially Enlightenment category, common sense, or *sensus communis*, a way to revive democracy with a community oriented, participatory, and ultimately humanist face" (Rosenfeld 2011, 245). Arendt's take on Kant's third *Critique,* in which she differs substantially from Gadamer, consists in an attempt at transposing Kant's interpretation of common sense as that which allows aesthetic judgments to be intersubjective (and not merely a matter of idiosyncratic tastes). Arendt's focus is therefore on the communicability of aesthetic judgments as an instance of intersubjective relations that, paradoxically, she wishes to consider outside the realm of aesthetics. What draws Arendt to Kant's work is its "claim to a nonobjective mode of judgment that nonetheless rises above interest and particularity," one "that will allow for both plurality and impartiality" (Norris 1996, 184). As Norris comments, after others, Arendt's position is formalist to a dangerous degree, since "[w]hat Arendt has done, in short, is to transform a transcendental principle into an empirical one" (Norris 1996, 188), without providing the substitutive empirical foundations that would have solidly grounded this transformation on her side of the argument.

Whereas similarly dangerously formalist positions would be held within the literary avant-gardes of the late twentieth century, in December 1972 a young poet named Michael Heller wrote a letter to a senior poet named George Oppen, who picked up on a particularly significant sentence from that letter and wrote back: "'the commonplace is at the moment lost' Well, I'm glad I read that. One can make a life out of that sentence" (SL 252). Oppen's answer raises two important questions, which seem to point in two separate, perhaps incompatible, directions. One is the reason, one wonders, for that loss: what caused it, and how does one know it has been lost? The other is just as critical, although more implicit. Oppen writes that he is "glad" he read that sentence, which one "can make a life out of." A formidable reversal is taking place here: one can gain from this expression of loss, hereby converted into a life-lasting resource. Literature has certainly often benefited from the special alchemy that allows all kinds of losses and tragedies to be transubstantiated, once written down, into remarkable achievements. One need only think of such canonical rhyming couplets as, "Yet do thy worst, old Time, despite thy wrong, / My love shall in my verse ever live young" (Shakespeare 19), which proclaim the sonnet's metaphorical victory over mortality.

Yet in this particular instance, it is the expression of tragedy, not its skillful rearranging for the purposes of poetic transposition, which Oppen praises in Heller's letter to him. The sentence does not alleviate any of the symptoms suggested, nor does it offer any solution to the matter. To understand why this is the case, one ought to consider that Oppen had had that sentence in mind when writing "The Book of Job And A Draft Of A Poem To Praise The Paths Of The Living" (NCP 240), which features a rewritten version of the sentence, as a note in Oppen's *Selected Letters* makes clear (SL 410–11). One way to summarize Oppen's long poem would be to say that it expands on a line from an earlier poem—"The lyric valuables. From disaster" (NCP 50)—and attempts once more to draw those "lyric valuables" from such a terrible source. From Oppen's poem to the actual book of Job, the loss of the commonplace can actually be traced back to the story of Job. As the book goes, there was a man in the land of Uz, whose name was Job, who was so beside himself with grief that when his three friends came to him, after they had heard of his horrible predicament, it took seven days and seven nights before any spoke. The first to speak was Job,

> Then Eliphaz the Temanite answered and said,
> If we assay to commune with thee, wilt thou be grieved? but who can withhold himself from speaking? (Job 4: 1–2)

The King James version translates "commune," others often choose a variation on "communicate." In any case, in a text so thoroughly devoted to making sense of an event through talking, and eventually by being confronted with God's speech, the oratory precaution seems significant in so far as it foregrounds the act of addressing one's fellow man. The words of Gadamer come to mind, when he writes that, "[t]o reach an understanding in a dialogue is not merely a matter of putting oneself forward and successfully asserting one's own point of view, but being transformed into a communion in which we do not remain what we were" (Gadamer 2004, 371). Finding a common ground, agreeing on a common sense, supposes one accepts this attempt to "commune," and its potentially transformative powers. Hopefully, I am not here trying to force an allegory of reading into Eliphaz's introduction. What I hope to do is to provide a wider and more dynamic context to Oppen's statements such as "Life depends on the meaning of the commonplace" (DuPlessis 2015, xvi) than has often been provided beyond a factual and general acknowledgement of one's own time and place. I am asking whether Oppen's turn to Job suggests that the "loss of the commonplace" resulting from disaster may also be apprehended as a crisis in terms of communion, or common sense, that is, as a sign of dialogical loss. Job's confrontation with God resonates in Oppen's poems through the poet's search for a statement which would spark an answer from the whirlwind, for Oppen was interested in Job rather than his comforters, about whom "Oppen notes that 'to Job's comforters nothing will answer and nothing speaks'" (FM 164). The importance of intersubjective dialogue is nonetheless crucial because of Job's solitary situation, which the relationship between poet and reader, or poem and readership, implicitly remodels into a new kind of dialogue. That is why the book of Job stands as the epitome, or the test, of the limits of common sense, or of the limited sense one can make of one's common circumstances, since like Job's comforters, one cannot withhold from speaking either.

To explain what I mean, consider the following letter Oppen wrote to George Johnston in 1969, which remarkably summarizes his poetic endeavor:

> I stopped writing   perhaps you know   for some twenty odd years.   To begin with, the catastrophe of human lives in the 'thirties   which seemed to me to put poetry and the purposes of poetry in question ----- I wrote of that in a poem called Pro Nobis. But, later, that we had a daughter. And still hesitate over a line, thinking of my daughter reading it   tho she is twenty-seven and in no way weak.   Of course a father should be invulnerable   But of course she would know by now that he is not -- Of course it is true I mean to put these things in the public record   And in the public music.   We know, we both know, there is, at least, no other possible safety for us.   For any of us. For the children either (SL 186)

The catastrophe located here in the thirties, but also, implicitly, in the subsequent war decade, and in the mounting threats of those post-war years, does more than underscore or contextualize the testamentary value of one's words as an acknowledgement, not of strength, but of vulnerability in the face of history. As these lines suggest, the purpose of poetry is to put things both "in the public *record*" and "in the public *music*." There lies the possibility of a new commonplace—and hence a "possible safety for us." The notion of a public record and a public music needs to be taken literally: the poem is aimed at the commonplace, rather than it aims at standing and speaking prophetically in its place. In comparison, Whitman, who depended on "polyvocality and the multitudinous self" (Frank 2007, 419), needed to assimilate the representational powers of words to political representation to bring about the music of his own public record. Oppen's precise account of precariousness, on the other hand, seems to hold no promise of empowerment through poetic mastery. In Oppen's own words, speaking of his friend and fellow-poet Charles Reznikoff,

> [...] the difficulty being that poets and poet-students are the audience of poetry   They read and praise work they can learn from, have learned from There is nothing to be learned from Reznikoff
>
> consummate art, consummate craftsmanship And a man walking the streets of New York, his head—his Jewish head—full of history [...] (SL 217)

It may seem odd for Oppen both to praise a poet's craftsmanship and declare that nothing may be learned from him.[2] As he clarifies, he meant "one cannot learn Fashion, the Night Town of poetry from Rezi [...] but one learns that poetry can matter, and can matter very much" (SL 218). Unlike poets or authors whose work, it is said, will always exceed or supplant their reader's insufficient efforts to comprehend their complexity, will forever foil the decipherer's attempts at cracking their magnitude (chiefly sustained by the charade of those very attempts), Oppen's writing undermines its own artfulness. Another way of looking at it would be to say that Oppen's simplicity and poverty are militant choices, aimed at disempowering the reader. What matters then, but that one learns poetry matters? Some have taken issue with that line of questioning, believing it to be too limiting, if not a self-serving ploy. Yet reflexivity does not exist in a vacuum in Oppen. Even there, speaking of Reznikoff, its purpose is to frame and prepare for one's vision of that "man walking the streets of New York, his head—his Jewish head—full of history." Elsewhere, Oppen proposes a vision of himself, along the same lines, as "one of those who from nothing but man's way of / thought and one of his dialects and what has happened / to me / Have made poetry" (NCP 167). But outside of biographical vindication—one's life legitimating one's writing—how does one proceed? This book was written to answer that question.

My two main objectives here are as follows: to call attention to new ways of reading George Oppen's poetry, and to call into question previous interpretations of his poems. To do so, I focus on three major issues surrounding Oppen's work: matters of song, the role of perception, and the question of context. The first three chapters identify Oppen's poems as remarkably readable compositions, which are only elusive if one chooses not to listen to their specific formal characteristics. The first objective of this book is therefore the exemplification of a new methodology, based on new readings of Oppen's poems. Bearing in mind that dysfunction often really shows function, I plead for a critical shift toward prosody as interpretive pragmatics. Chapter 1 introduces Oppen's idea of the poem as a structure of meaning, by looking at his assessment of other poets' work, then by applying these critical statements to Oppen's own poetry. In it, I show that Oppen is quick to dismiss a poem when it dispenses with common experience, and that his practical sense of a common language becomes a prerequisite in terms of composition. Oppen's statements on poetics, which have a distinct moral or ethical aura to them, are thus put to the test as analytical tools. Chapter 2 explores the evolution of Oppen's poetry over the years, and the debates surrounding Oppen's changing syntax and prosody, with a view to challenge the assumption that the poems' grammar and rhythm can only be understood, and indeed valued, for what they undo rather than what they actually do. To demonstrate this, I confront several prosodic theories and provide a specific case study of Oppen's poem "Song, The Winds of Downhill," in which I asks how one may build a song from the common—though shattered—resources of language. In Chapter 3, I consider other perspectives on past or alien types of rhetoric or rhythm. Focusing on biblical texts, which have always been a productive, if disputed, model and resource for poets, I suggest that literary scholarship may learn from crossing disciplinary boundaries to explore new rhythmic possibilities. Adapting a different and new methodology, I propose several close readings of Oppen's late poems and show that they can be read as very articulate compositions, that they do add up to song, and to a common song indeed.

After having seen how Oppen's syntax composes the poem's peculiar song, it becomes possible to understand how the poem rearranges the perceptions which allow it, and which it produces. Critics, however, have often set aside perception and looked for representations instead—political representations, representations of the mind, anything but particulars. In the next three chapters, I discuss the general role of perception in Oppen's empiricist project as the faculty thanks to which the loss of the commonplace becomes visible, and through which it may be recovered. Beginning on a different scale, Chapter 4 deals with the image, and the disputes around the status of images in Oppen's poetry as abstractions or as concrete visual data. I argue that the image cannot be differentiated from the statement where it is found, and which it supports, to the point that one should really speak of the image as a statement—often presented as a quotation—and thus suggest that to oppose perception and conception in Oppen is misguided. Starting with a detailed analysis of Oppen's image of the girder, from a poem by Charles Reznikoff, I offer a journey into Oppen's personal use of the category of the real, which in the end refers not to the spectacle of things, matter, or objects, but to history as evidence of time. Chapter 5 studies Oppen's image-statements in history, measured against the political readings of Oppen's work. But when reference and relevance are thought to be one and the same, when political value gets conflated with poetical economy, and one tries to pigeonhole Oppen accordingly, when the need to find Oppen at fault or to make him a role model takes precedence over the patient historicizing of the poems, then Oppen's own conflicted relationship with poetry as a useful art becomes obscured. Moreover, even when poetic representations are no longer questioned for their political representativeness, his empiricism causes Oppen's perceptions to be still found lacking on another level. Chapter 6 defends Oppen's realism and empiricism against a variety of interpretations which, either from a materialistic, existentialist or from a generally formalist point of view, downplay the role of experience in Oppen's poetry. Arguing for the importance, always, of perception over inception, I retrace the logic of Oppen's critical views on poetry in his essay "The Mind's Own Place," and shed some light on Oppen's very practical Marxism.

In the last three chapters, I ask why and how critical readings of Oppen have developed philosophy or theory-based rationales that explain Oppen's poems outside their original contexts. However, I do not do so to prepare the groundwork for my own substitutive and competitive grand notions. Rather, this study is based on the belief that criticism of prior critical writing, if it may seem grating at times, merits special attention in and of itself. This serves a clear methodological purpose: to critique the partial and misconstrued philosophical readings of Oppen's poetry. A particular point will be made again and again: that the selecting of philosophical nuggets to bolster or create a philosophical framework for reading Oppen is at best a suspect activity and, more often, neither true to the context, history, and scope of the philosophical source nor to Oppen's own relationship to those philosophical texts. Chapter 7 is concerned with readings of Oppen that rely on Martin Heidegger to explicate his poems as though they were pages from Heidegger himself. Specific case studies provide opportunities for a larger discussion of the uses and limitations of genetic criticism as well as the characteristics of Oppen's habit of quoting and misquoting. I insist on the importance of historical contexts far above and beyond that of cotexts, and argue against disembodied readings of Oppen's images, and poems. The chapter ends with a comparative look at Paul Celan's relationship with Heidegger, and proves how pervasive this philosophical illusion really is. Chapter 8 broadens the philosophical spectrum to include the field of ethics, although there have been fewer attempts at reading Oppen through the work of Emmanuel Levinas, and Levinas himself will regularly only be alluded to when serving as a form of intellectual warranty for ethics-based criticism. But much may be learned from studying the critical habit of systematic sampling and its dangerous disregard for prosodic or conceptual integrity, that turn Levinas' texts, as well as Oppen's, into mere pretexts. This chapter further questions moralizing rationalizations and the role of literary criticism's moral figures, such as Adorno, in alleviating one's sense of crisis when coming to terms with the inhibiting weight of history. Choosing Oppen the historian against Oppen the philosopher, Chapter 9 studies Oppen's so-called simplicity, questions his interest in the primitive, and explores the systematic contextualization of experience that takes place in spite of, or alongside, his phenomenology of astonishment. I especially look at Rilke's possible influence on Oppen, and turn to the subject of childhood, or children, in Oppen's poetry, not as symbolic figures of privileged perceptions, as might be expected of a poet known for his concern over forms of disclosure, but as instances of historicization, which open a path towards the recovery of the commonplace.

Notes

1. Interestingly enough, a recent essay on the commons written by a French philosopher and a French sociologist opened with a quotation from this same poem by Whitman (Dardot and Laval 2015, 15).
2. For an introduction to the connections between Oppen and Reznikoff, see Ballan, Joseph. 2017. "Poetry of Secular Memorialization: Charles Reznikoff's 'Kaddish' and George Oppen's 'In Memoriam Charles Reznikoff'." *Studies in American Jewish Literature*, 36/1: 71–83.

References

Dardot, Pierre and Laval, Christian. 2015. *Commun: Essai sur la révolution au XXIème siècle*. Paris: La Découverte.

DuPlessis, Rachel Blau, ed. 2015. *The Oppens Remembered: Poetry, Politics, and Friendship*. Albuquerque: University of New Mexico Press.

Ferguson, Robert A. 2000. "The Commonalities of Common Sense." *The William and Mary Quarterly* 57/3: 465–504.

Fredman, Stephen. 2009. *The Grounding of American Poetry: Charles Olson and the Emersonian Tradition*. Cambridge: Cambridge University Press.

Frank, Jason. 2007. "Aesthetic Democracy: Walt Whitman and the Poetry of the People." *The Review of Politics*. 29/3: 402–430.

Gadamer, Hans-Georg. 2004. *Truth and Method*. Translated by Joel Weinsheimer and Donald G. Marshall. London: Continuum International Publishing.

Hesse, Charlotte. 1990. *Governing the Commons: The Evolution of Institutions for Collective Action*. Cambridge: Cambridge University Press.

Hesse, Charlotte and Ostrom, Elinor. *Understanding Knowledge as a Commons: From Theory to Practice*. Cambridge, MA: The MIT Press, 2007.

Norris, Andrew. 1996. "Arendt, Kant, and the Politics of Common Sense." *Polity* 29/2: 165–191.

Rosenfeld, Sophia. 2011. *Common Sense: A Political History*. Cambridge, MA: Harvard University Press.

Shakespeare, William. 2007. *Shakespeare's Sonnets*. Edited by Katherine Duncan Jones. London: Thomson Learning.

Vico, Giambattista. 1999. *New Science*. Translated by David Marsh. London: Penguin Books.

Whitman, Walt. 1982. *Poetry and Prose*. New York: The Library of America.

Williams, William Carlos. 1963. *Paterson*. New York: New Directions.

CHAPTER ONE

Structures of Meaning

In 1977, Oppen wrote to Diane Meyer,

> I no longer have time, time, time to force the meaning, the statement on the reader Time to argue. I must trust him, her, to know where we are. To TRUST himself, herself: to TRUST me: to say yes. To say yes, we know, we are also here. (SL 339)

Oppen's words, which apply here to his very late poems, reflect strangely on his earlier poetry. The idea that Oppen would authoritatively "force the meaning" on the reader in his poetry from the 1930s or early 1960s seems quite inadequate, until one considers that Oppen is most likely referring to the indisputable forcefulness with which each poem presents itself to the reader as a statement. This feature, which involves directing the reader towards the statement that is the poem, does fade away with Oppen's poetry from the 1970s. However, if Oppen's later books have been received as less accessible, his aim seems to have been, on the contrary, to be more direct then than ever before, with a view to restoring "trust" in a common awareness.

Bearing this in mind, one might recall the early criticism of Oppen's work and be surprised again. As Oren Izenberg remarks, such early criticism "denied the poet's vision by focusing on the way that the particulate materiality of his poems rendered them incomprehensible, characterizing their maker as a kind of idiot-boy stutterer," although later "this critique has been revived as praise" (Izenberg 2006, 805). To illustrate his point, Izenberg offers this quotation from Peter Nicholls about Oppen's poem "The Occurrences" (NCP 212): "I am not sure I completely understand this poem, but nor am I sure I am meant to. The syntax seems broken, precarious, though to describe it as fragmented would misleadingly assume a reconstitutable logic of propositions" (ON 250). Yet this should not lead one to dismiss the poem's syntax, and meaning, as impossible to understand, or as only partially understandable, as if Oppen's poems meant to keep the reader at a distance, when he explicitly argued otherwise in his letters. Arguably, "fragmented" would be a misnomer for the reason Nicholls mentions. But "incompletely meaningful," "forever ambiguous," or "that resists interpretation" sound like equally inappropriate phrases—both because the trick of indeterminacy is merely an old strategy to ensure the text's inexhaustible appeal will be forever renewed, and because Oppen never advocated difficulty for its own sake. It is rather one's own understanding, which needs to adapt and open itself to other avenues besides a "reconstitutable logic of propositions." Looking for other avenues to explore, it seems the shortest way to the heart of Oppen's poetry is his frequent debunking of false language, which often takes the form of repeated warnings against the use of "unearned" words, because "[e]verything which is not earned is corrupt" (SL 143). These statements are often quoted when trying to sum up Oppen's poetics, and accepted in the abstract as easily recognizable words of poetic wisdom. This chapter puts them to the test. Oppen writes:

> [...] the words will NOT make the poem: the poem must make, remake, restore the words They must be earned, at the very least   They won't earn a poem for you (SL 225)

If the poem makes the words and restores their meaning, rather than vice-versa, then one must find out how. Oppen's emphasis on the poem's own agency is enough to call attention to his compositions as highly purposeful structures, however difficult it may be to grapple with them. For a practical illustration of Oppen's *ars poetica*, here is what Oppen had to say, presumably in 1963–64, about a poem by Octavio Paz:

> The poem is opaque. He is stating facts which refer back to the things I already know, which never exist in the poem. "Wounds"—because, yes, a word makes a mark, a wound, it impresses itself. "Effulgent" because it illuminates, yes. Those are things I know about words. But there is no place in that poem for the wound, there is no scene in which the effulgence takes place. It is just something I too understand. So that he is saying only "me too," which is the ve~~ry hea~~rt ˆ*sign*ˆ of Provincial poetry.

> he knows, or thinks he knows, from Rimbaud that such things can be done, but the poem does not earn the right to do it. The words are not really opposited, therefore the whole weight falls on the word But, so that it ~~becomes~~ merely a grammatical contraption … *in which nothing actually happens.* (SP 58)

The poem has yet to be located with some certainty. "Effulgence" translates "fulgor" in "Ootacamund," in Charles Tomlinson's 1979 Penguin edition of Paz's *Selected Poems*, and Oppen knew Charles Tomlinson well enough to dedicate a collaborative poem to him (NCP 158), but there is no "wound" in the poem, nor for that matter in Eliot Weinberger's translation in his later collected edition for New Directions. Closer to Oppen and to Oppen's years in Mexico, Muriel Rukeyser's 1963 translation of Paz's *Sunstone* for New Directions may have been perused by Oppen. In it, "wound" and "splendor"—for "fulgor" again, a likely transliterative candidate for "effulgence" in some other translation—appear on the same page (Paz 1963, 23). Because it is unclear which of Paz's poems Oppen was writing about, I limit myself to his own remarks on Paz, however dismissive they may seem, especially out of context. Oppen insists on the poem's sense of place—here its lack of one in which meaning would "happen." To avoid what Oppen elsewhere calls the "me too" of "the generalized meaning" (SP 68) of words, the poem must share in that outside where meaning happens. From this perspective, the poem's integrity depends on a balance between its own formal achievement and what has happened that is being fleshed out in the poem. In the same vein, Oppen states:

> […] it is impossible for a man to become an artist by having an idea, by making an invention. Art can come only from a very dangerous thing to do. To search for the roots of one's own existence and one's own sensibility. And to try to body that forth, to cause it to appear in clarity—(SP 124)

One cannot shy away from those words and their implications. They are the necessary background that justifies Oppen's judgments. Another example would be those he elusively calls the "French Moderns" in his notebooks from the early to mid-1960s:

> […] merely abominable poetry, to state it briefly
>
> they believe they can throw words into the poem […] and they believe the words will fill the poem with meaning […]
>
> It is the proper purpose, or the first purpose of the poem to restore the meaning of words. (SP 68)

Naming one French poet, Oppen expands on his position:

> Rene Char etc
> I do not think that a poem can be filled with meaning by being filled, like a bag or a jug, with words. On the contrary is the poem, the structure of meaning which restores the words to clarity. The word is the burden, the words are the burden, of the line which it must bear^~~lift~~^ up into meaning (SP 69)

In these notes, Oppen is addressing what he considers to be mistaken readings of Williams' definition of the poem, "the 'machine of words' which resolves everything --- until one steps out the door" (SL 145). Outside the door lies what the poem must confront if meaning is to happen in it. Oppen puts this concern very plainly when addressing some of his contemporaries. To give a sense of Oppen's unflinching resolution, here is one more scathing dismissal:

> (of the poets surely of the Black Mountain do you notice this characteristic: that nothing ever happened to them)
>
> I am bound by some things that happened That they happened -- yes, it is a kind of stupidity, I register this as a kind of stupidity, I feel it is so But in the non-happening is -- there is a quality of simple snobbery (SL 252)

Prosodic completion testifies to the direction of a process within the poem and well as without, towards the poem. One of the paradoxes in Oppen's poetry, and in his critical statements, is that one may be surprised at first to find out that the poem—a "structure of meaning"—depends on nondescript "things that happened" for its own meaning to "happen." If that is the case, then the word "structure" sounds somewhat odd. One would expect a structure to be productive in its own right, rather than to be an echo chamber for that which happened—whatever that might exactly be in the end—even if what Oppen seems to be saying is that the poem's meaning relies on the active structure of the lines as a process rather than as a finished piece of architecture.

All these passages seem to ask for the impossible: to rely on the poem's composition as an almost separately meaningful entity instead of the evocative power of words, and to require that what happens in the poem somehow be bound by what one has found "out the door." It is as though Oppen insisted on maintaining a double distance: a distance between the words and their arrangement on the page, combined with an almost greater distance, in the poet's eyes, from the page itself, in contrast with the outside world. Rather than a contradiction, I would venture that both distances are expressions of the same critical self-awareness. It is the same equilibrium that Oppen seeks for the poet in the world and for the words on the page, which is grounded in the basic assumption that each of these two relationships is dependent on the other. This works not so much as a hidden allegory in the poems' composition, but as a practical concern. Sharing his knowledge of "some things that happened" is Oppen's first step in trying to set up a renewed sense of the commonplace.

On the other hand, when meaning is imposed on the poem, all prosodic patterns become secondary to whatever "grammatical contraption," as with Paz's poem, secures the semantic delivery. In Paz, it is the word "but," and it is a very similar syntactical device which Oppen questions when reading the work of T. S Eliot. Writing to his sister June, Oppen quotes the following from Eliot's "Burnt Norton," in *Four Quartets*, omitting the last line:

> We move above the moving tree
> In light upon the figured leaf
> And hear upon the sodden floor
> Below, the boarhound and the boar
> Pursue their pattern as before (Eliot 1963, 191)

Drawing a parallel between Eliot's dogmatic use of his poetry in the *Choruses from 'The Rock'* and his own refusal "to write communist verse," Oppen concludes with this pronouncement: "Have to write one's perceptions, not argue one's beliefs" (SL 22). He then adds:

> (By the way; the above quote from Eliot : I stopped it abruptly just before the last line which is
>
> But reconciled among the stars.
>
> You see: poetry does criticize itself. A false statement makes bad verse. Even an Eliot can't smooth it. It's this which makes possible some kind of rational criticism, which saves one from pure whim, pure 'taste'
>
> (Read that passage -- it's interesting. Dazzlingly beautiful, and startling how hopeless the 'but' is -- (SL 21)

The fact that Oppen singles out syntax as the place in which to exercise "rational criticism" underlines how decisive one's understanding of the inner workings of poetic syntax really is. Eliot's conjunction is "hopeless" not because it introduces argument instead of prolonging the perception—Oppen certainly never refrained from inserting pithy comments into his poems—but because it completely surrenders the perception to the argument, as though all of it had been nothing but ornamental preparation for the concluding line.

If this is indeed "rational criticism," then the reasoning should apply to a variety of objects. Consider, therefore, Oppen's own "Waking Who Knows":

> the great open
>
> doors of the tall
>
> buildings and the grid
>
> of the streets the seed
>
> is a place the stone
> is a place mind
>
> will burn the world down alone
> and transparent
>
> will burn the world down tho the starlight is
> part of ourselves (NCP 273)

Oppen's final "tho the starlight is / part of ourselves," bears a certain resemblance to Eliot's "But reconciled among the stars." Yet in Eliot the statement is coordinated via the conjunction alone: it finds its place within a larger preexisting system. It is part of a whole, which it does not create. In Oppen, the lines ease the reader into the realization to come through incantatory repetition. Crucially, the disclosure is carried first and foremost by the prosody, which rests on the subtle syntactic ambiguity surrounding the absent subject in the last lines. The world will burn down, though we are part of it, and should stop it from happening. This suggests we will burn the world down, though that burning power (the starlight understood as the sun's light) is also what keeps us alive. Or the starlight will burn the world down (which the sun will do eventually) and destroy us, though being but stardust to begin with, we would continue to share in a common physical universe. Every time, these combined levels of interpretation are essentially produced by prosodic and syntactic means.

The two poet's cosmogonies could not be further apart, but to a certain extent, it may be argued that Oppen seeks to acknowledge a reconciliation of his own in this poem, despite overwhelming differences with Eliot's "But reconciled among the stars." Eliot's reconciliation relies on mythical assumptions: the boar's pattern begging for its own constellation among the stars hides a reference to the Erymanthian boar, whose capture was Hercules' fourth labor. Reconciliation, it would seem, is a matter of mythical, astrological divination. Its hermeneutics reveals signs, which were already present in the firmament. What one, as a reader, has come to share is the realization of a preexisting order, a harmonious restoration of relations, if not a cleansing and a reconsecration. The interpretation seals the perception hierarchically from above.

However, Oppen's lines are not utterly disconnected from past cosmological thinking. They call to mind Parmenides' fragment 15, with its homonymic wordplay around the phrase "allotrion phôs," which points to the light from outside—that of the moon, which borrows its light from the sun—but also includes a pun on Homer's expression, "allotrios phôs"—the stranger, the man from outside. Oppen translates the fragment as follows: "Astray over earth / Bright in darkness / Its light also a wandering foreigner" (SL 396). He later rewrites these lines in "Neighbors," this time as "the voice of the poem a wandering / foreigner more strange / and brilliant / than the moon's light the true / native opening" (NCP 284). Oppen's appropriation of that fragment, and of that light, is based on a recognition of light's native strangeness, which recalls the conclusion of "Waking Who Knows." Oppen's "bright light of shipwreck" (NCP 167), from *Of Being Numerous*, might also very well be a variation on the same starlight.

In contrast to Eliot, the form of Oppen's poem does not offer a structure which the reader could synthesize as specular knowledge: the knowledge involved in the title is inseparable from the how the poem unravels. One enters the poem through the "doors of the tall // buildings" but the previous line break suspended "the great open" in such a way that these "doors" paradoxically limit one's perception, now locked on an observer's contemplation of the building's imposing stature from outside, or on the prospect of an exit into "the grid // of the streets." These redirections are built into the poem's cadence, which inserts syntactical disruptions between epithet and noun or between the first and second nouns in a noun phrase. These prosodic splits prepare for the two-line cluster beginning "is a place," which repeats the generic word, "place," in an effort to suggest a possible sense of grounding, which the structure of the line will not allow to be predicated on a recognizable connection. Instead, alliterations on sibilants and variations on dentals and plosives make the series in "place," "place," "street," "seed" and "stone" into one rhythmically salient knot illustrating what "is," "is." Within this structure, going from "street" to "seed" and then to "stone," Oppen's derivation seems irredeemably circular and barren, even including the growth, as it were, of a "tall / building" out of a seed of stone. But Oppen does not understand "seed" and "stone" as being diametrically opposed. In the earlier "Sara In Her Father's Arms" from *The Materials*, Oppen speaks of Sara's "little seed eyes" (NCP 51). Elsewhere in Oppen's poetry, one's eyes grow from seeing stone, from drawing "Blood From the Stone" (NCP 52), from confronting eroded mineral realities, such as "the rounded rocks of childhood" (NCP 55). The city streets (potentially also their obscenely seed-strewn pavement) contain the seed of stone out of which grows the mind's sense of place. Through this chiasmus, the occurrence of the word "mind" does not cause the poem to drift away from perception. In fact, the odd compound, "place mind," reads with "place" as the verb: one needs to place one's mind, to assign a position to it. Otherwise, one's mind imposing its "will" on what "is" may result in the world burning down—a prospect reminiscent of the last stanza from "Time of the Missile," which "Waking Who Knows" rewrites to a large extent:

> Place of the mind
> And eye. Which can destroy us,
> Re-arrange itself, assert
> Its own stone chain reaction. (NCP 70)

As in *Seascape: Needle's Eye*, where one reads, "We have been ignited / Blazing" (NCP 215), which seems to be a sign of a "force of clarity, it is / Of what is not autonomous in us" (NCP 193), in "Waking Who Knows," the light of atomic destruction shines on the transparent surface of the-world-as-ourselves. The atomic fire that threatens to consume the earth is associated with the sun, and through the solar system, to the cosmos of which humanity is a part. In that, Oppen does attempt a reconciliation of his own, between terror and acceptance, which is illustrated in the questioning "who" from the title, answered by the last word of the text—"ourselves." Oppen's indictment of Eliot's "false statement" therefore does not revolve around a simple opposition between the beliefs of one poet and the beliefs of another. Neither does it depend on a clear-cut distinction between perception versus beliefs. What Oppen considers "false" in Eliot's statement is not that it is a statement, nor that it is not a statement he would make, but that it is falsely stated through an authoritative form of utterance. Arguing the poem's belief means arguing it out of the reader's perception of the poem's prosody, which must always answer and instantiate the perception.

In this respect, Parmenides' remark may well be the model for the divided constructions of Oppen's prosody. Like the moon's light, which is the light of the moon and not its own, the poem's images are both native and foreign: words estrange the reader from the text into the position of an outside onlooker, while the things seen inherently pull the reader in as part of the same world. Prosody comes into play to articulate this astronomical problem. For this configuration could, under different circumstances, translate as a failure to see or speak. It is not the case here because, since the starlight is part of ourselves, the division between a native and a foreign light takes on atomistic proportions: the same atoms make up the stars, their light, and ourselves. Thus Oppen's prosody shines a light of its own on Parmenides' Homeric pun. Oppen's lines rely on an ambiguous syntactical distribution across line-breaks to allow for a dramatic increase in what William Empson already drew attention to, in *Seven Types of Ambiguity*, which is the role of selection within one's awareness of a simultaneity of meanings (Prickett 1986, 164). Unlike optical illusions, when a picture shows two different things yet cannot show both these things at once, but only separately, as one switches from one illusion to the next (Gombrich 1960, 5), Oppen's prosodic units resolve the inevitable delay in optical illusions between one image and the next, as the pace of the line rhythmically combines simultaneous meanings. Lines may not always be coterminous with grammatical or semantic boundaries, the various meanings that coalesce around line-breaks are always coextensive with each other. It is the absence of such condensation, of that simultaneous handling of ambivalence, combined with the breaking down of rhythmic coherence, which Oppen resents in Eliot's use of the conjunction *but* in "But reconciled among the stars." As an after-the-facts statement, it comments too late on a sequence, which it cannot sufficiently justify, when it should have been built into the sequence to the point that the sequence itself should have been the statement.

Regrettably, Oppen's syntax and prosody have been relegated in favor of other, more visible—in every sense of the word—aspects of his work. Charles Bernstein's pique at Oppen for using "clarity as a tactic" (TP 199), in his article, "Hinge, Picture," is a remarkable example. Bernstein wishes that Oppen's poems did not achieve "resolution through scenic motifs, statement, or parable," for Oppen's poems "might, given his compositional techniques, outstrip such controlling impulses" (TP 199). Bernstein ends his article with stanzas "generated using an acrostic procedure (G-E-O-R-G-E O-P-P-E-N) to select lines, in page sequence, from *Collected Poems*" (TP 199). Here is the second one:

> Outside, and so beautiful
> Populace, sea-borne and violent, finding
> Passing, the curl at cutwater,
> Ends its metaphysic
> Nature! because we find the others (TP 200)

This is meant to exemplify Oppen's "use of the line break as hinge," which "taps into a horizontally moving synaptic/syntactic energy at the point of line transition" (TP 199). In the process, this text means to offer a liberated version of Oppen's method—as if Oppen had at last outstripped "such controlling impulses" such as the criterion of clarity, not to mention, in his later work, his "allowing an almost symbolic or allegorical vocabulary ("sea," "children") to take hold." (TP 199). Aside from the fact that both sea and children are important recurrent signifiers in Oppen's work from the start, what is one to make of this acrostic procedure, "borrowed [...] from Jackson Mc Low" (TP 199)? The fact that, by all accounts, this technique would have been anathema to Oppen should cause one to dismiss it immediately. However, it may be a useful opportunity to differentiate between form and constraint to conclude this preliminary investigation into Oppen's sense of structure. Oppen had this to say on the title of his first book, *Discrete Series*:

> That's a phrase in mathematics. A pure mathematical series would be one in which each term is derived from the preceding term by a rule. A discrete series is a series of terms each of which is empirically derived, each of which is empirically true. [...] I was attempting to construct a meaning by empirical statements, by imagist statements. (Dembo, 1972 174)

The difference Oppen makes here between a mathematical and an empirical series is key to his emphatic distinction between form and constraint, between constructivist effort and systematic pattern. Using Oppen's terms, it appears that Bernstein's acrostic follows the prerequisites of a mathematical, nonempirical series. Significantly enough, this is the topic of Oppen's last correspondence included in the *Selected Letters*. Responding to French poet Claude Royet-Journoud, who "had asked Oppen to send a one-line poem for an anthology he was editing with Emmanuel Hocquard" (SL 424), Oppen wrote in September 1981:

> I am truly sorry to refuse anything that you ask of me, but I cannot bring myself to write poetic "exercises."   We come back to that old saying: a poem is a poem is a poem.   (and never an exercise)
> it is tied to the world, and the stones of the villages.
> Again sorry to refuse to do anything you ask of me,
>
> Best wishes,
> George (SL 353)

Oppen's awareness of the issue is apparent in his resorting to an ironic repetition when protesting that "a poem is a poem is a poem." Whereas one might think at first that Gertrude Stein whom Oppen seems to be alluding to would side with Royet-Journoud in this matter, Oppen's phrase illustrates what he finds lacking in such exercises, and points to the specific completion he seeks to achieve in his own poetry. Oppen is expressing a distrust towards procedures that lead to the "verbal labyrinth" of "Poetry as Word-System," to put it in Marjorie Perloff's words (Perloff 1981 108). Instead, Oppen resorts to his typical trope of mixing scenic precision with almost generic abstracts in wishing to anchor the poem in "the world, and the stones of the villages." Going back to Bernstein's acrostic, the case I wish to make is that instead of presenting us with a way out of outmoded or limiting symbols, allegories, "scenic motifs, statement, or parable," representational trinkets or hermeneutic knick-knack, Bernstein's procedure merely displaces meaning away from the experience of the poem into a questionable experiment. The point, Bernstein tells his readers, lies in the following "structural allegory [...]: the autonomy of the root, the individual, allowing for the music of the social, the numerous" (ON 199). However, it seems that the individual, George Oppen, is rather literalized in the process, being reduced to the letters making up his name, while "the music of the social, the numerous" is nowhere to be found, unless the alphabet as a system of signs is meant as an allegory of social systems. There are many instances of poets signing their names into their poems, by way of their initials, puns and other types of double entendre, from Shakespeare's *Sonnet 135* to Zukofsky's "z-sited path are but us" (Zukofsky 563). Yet such a practice is not to be found in Oppen. Even his frequent use of the word "open," though it certainly merits attention, never qualifies as a veritable signature. Stranger still is the idea of the beginning of the line as "root." Bernstein acknowledges that Oppen's habit of opening a line with a preposition constitutes "the typical Oppen hinge" (ON 199), but first speaks of the line break as the hinge. But what is so specific about Oppen is that this hinging never take places in any systemic fashion, much less in any linear way. In Oppen, not only does the reader face a suspensive hinge from line one, but each line is itself balanced on dual hinges left and right—hinges at both ends, so to speak. So that when Bernstein says that "[i]n some of the later work, [Oppen] abandons any singularity in his lineation" (ON 199), it would be much more accurate to explain how these bifold hinges have either eaten away at the core of the line, or how they are no longer needed to weigh down the line. In any case, the logic of the acrostic is so perfectly foreign to Oppen's composition that it blocks any possibility of a hinge here, which again could never be so explicit in Oppen. In other words, making the posts apparent paradoxically knocks the door down. The reader is forced to operate the acrostic as if one had to hit the release lever to get the typewriter carriage back in its place with every new line, and the structure of meaning that is the poem is lost.

References

Dembo, L. S., and Pondrom, Cyrena N., eds. 1972. *The Contemporary Writer: Interviews with Sixteen Novelists and Poets*. Madison: The University of Wisconsin Press.

Eliot, T. S. 1963. *Collected Poems 1909–1962*. London: Faber and Faber.

Empson, William. 1947. *Seven Types of Ambiguity*. New York: New Directions.

Gombrich, E. H. 1960. *Art and Illusion*. London: Phaidon Press.

Izenberg, Oren. 2006. "Oppen's Silence, Crusoe's Silence, and the Silence of Other Minds." *Modernism/Modernity* 13/1: 787–811.

Paz, Octavio. 1991. *The Collected Poems 1957–1987*. Edited by Eliot Weinberger. New York: New Directions.

———. 1979. *Selected Poems.* Edited by Charles Tomlinson. Harmondsworth: Penguin.

———. 1963. *Selected Poems.* Translated by Muriel Rukeyser. Bloomington: Indiana University Press.

———. 1963. *Sun Stone.* Translated by Muriel Rukeyser. New York: New Directions.

———. 1991. *Sunstone / Piedra De Sol.* Translated by Eliot Weinberger. New York: New Directions.

Perloff, Marjorie. 1981. *The Poetics of Indeterminacy: From Rimbaud to Cage.* Princeton: Princeton University Press.

Prickett, Stephen. 1986. *Words and The Word: Language, Poetics and Biblical Interpretation.* Cambridge: Cambridge University Press.

Zukofsky, Louis. 1993. "A." Baltimore: Johns Hopkins University Press.

CHAPTER TWO

Rhythmic Obligations

Oppen's own structures of meaning have been said to be much less "graspable" than he had hoped. It is not always easy to recognize either "the *thing*" meant to be grasped in the poem, or indeed the poem itself—"form," "music," "every note"—as a "graspable" object, to use Oppen's own words in a letter to Jane Cooper:

> [...] to use silence, not to be caught up in a cadence, obliged to a cadence ? Which would leave form, music, as that which makes the poem graspable, the music itself, and every note, for the sake also of the *thing* grasped But above all, and most amply, the silences: the breaking of rhythmic obligations. (SL 199)

Fundamentally, the reader's difficulties stem from this necessary "breaking of rhythmic obligations." But before going into what this entails exactly and how he breaks them, it should be noted that Oppen's cadences ought not to be considered from the perspective of a homogenous prosodic practice. Because his body of work spans several decades, important evolutions come into play. Indeed, looking at the critical response to these evolutions gives one ample opportunity to understand Oppen's processes. Unfortunately, matters of allegiance, belonging, and the general partisan wars that plague so many discussions of the modernist heritage have greatly complicated any attempt to offer a general view of the issue. Ranging from the 1930s to the late 1970s, Oppen's work has not escaped the "frightfully efficient," though equally frightfully inhibiting, "taxonomic engine" (Izenberg 2006, 792) that drives literary criticism. If the discrepancy between Oppen's prosody before and after the sixties—that is, before and after *Of Being Numerous* (1968)—is generally acknowledged, what conclusions should be drawn from that observation is open to debate.

Some critics find fault with Oppen's later poetry, viewing it almost as antithetical to his early work. As Eleanor Berry points out, Norman Finkelstein seems to be saying as much when describing Oppen's trajectory as going from objects to the mind (MP 430). Yet Finkelstein is cautious to underline how this "process has come full circle," with "the objects of experience […] subsumed into the subjective consciousness, even as consciousness, at the beginning, seems lost among objects" (MP 430). Berry's "Language Made Fluid: the Grammetrics of George Oppen's Recent Poetry" (1984), which provides an articulate picture of the debates surrounding Oppen's late prosody, concludes with the same "thematic shift" as Finkelstein, saying that if "the poetry of the four earlier books was concerned with naming and praising things of the world, the more recent poetry is concerned with language, music, song, the poem" (Berry 1984, 315), as rocks are replaced by the sea as the poems' motif. But Berry eventually mitigates her statement by adding that this is a matter of "intensification" (Berry 1984, 316) rather than one of contradiction or change. This would seem to contradict Berry's initial observation that critics will often address Oppen's fragmented syntax and line breaks as a single coherent object, oblivious to its evolutions (Berry 1984, 305). If this evolution is but a matter of intensification, then the coherence of the whole can be preserved.

Even when critics describe a radical change in Oppen's prosody, their observations remain strangely applicable to both sides of the argument. For instance, Blau DuPlessis, when discussing the deep changes in Oppen's prosody after the sixties and studying the "simultaneous hovering-over and forward-pulsing […] on the scale of the smallest unit" (MP 143) together with the other "syntactic ways that contradiction is organized and sustained" (MP 146) in Oppen's late poetry, concludes that this endows the poems with "the inner dynamic of gnomic fragments" (MP 146), whose unresolvedness she contrasts with Pound's poetics of fragments. On the other hand, when in 1981 Marjorie Perloff speaks of Oppen's elliptical clusters, she chooses to quote essentially from Oppen's work before *Of Being Numerous*, not afterward, as Berry herself remarks. Yet Blau DuPlessis's wording here, based on the study of Oppen's later work, does seem quite in tune with Perloff's broad summary of the typical features in Oppen's verse: "[e]llipsis, riddle, radical condensation, abstraction, equivocal syntax, and the fragmentation of semantic units" (MP 229). If there is a distinction between "gnomic fragments" and "elliptical clusters," it does not seem to be a crucial one. Oppen's method may differ over time, yet one is tempted to conclude to a relative homogeneity in the effects it produces. Moreover, Oppen's halting prosody being one of the better-known features of his poetry, it is very easy to take the poems' actual processes for granted, and let one's perception of Oppen's prosody be guided by preexisting general assumptions.

When prosody does become a pressing issue, the issue is more often one of periodizing than of prosodic study. Initially, Oppen's early prosody is used to differentiate him from his early post-Imagist contemporaries, in the case of *Discrete Series* (1934). At the other end, some Language poets have found Oppen's work with syntax instrumental in constructing lineage and in foregrounding their own agenda. Nonetheless, the classification of Oppen's work, with *Discrete Series*, *The Materials* (1962), *This in Which* (1965) and *Of Being Numerous* on one side, and *Seascape: Needle's Eye* (1972), *Myth of the Blaze* (1972–75), and *Primitive* (1978) on the other roughly holds. What I would suggest is that it is as much a simplification to regard Oppen's work prior to *Seascape* as a solid whole where "language is nominative and deictic" (Berry 1984, 311) and his last three books as the fluid objectification of language patterned into processes (Berry 1984, 322), as it is not to address the differences between the various stages in Oppen's prosody at all. In the end, the move from "objects" to "processes" tells one more about the critical rhetoric of the last decades of the twentieth century than about the progression in Oppen's work. Having noted that after a certain point, lineation is no longer cogent with syntactical boundaries, one wonders where to go. Focusing solely on that change, one risks turning the work against itself, as it were, pitting the earlier against the later work, or vice-versa.

On a larger scale, the problem testifies to how compelling some tensions remain, within modernism, between supposedly more legible Imagism-based monads and reputedly resistant epic-oriented longer poems. Opposing Oppen's *Discrete Series* to his *Myth of the Blaze* does not tell anyone a lot about Oppen's work, but rather replays the well-known antagonistic preference games that oppose Williams', Pound's, Zukofsky's or even Olson's shorter productions with their longer work. Needless to say these categories are only used here for convenience. "Length" is not exactly a precise concept in poetics, and requires careful defining to become productive. No matter whether some of these poets continued writing one-page poems after they had completed their magnum opus, the short-early-easy vs. long-late-difficult division remains, under various guises, pregnant with implications.

For example, to say that in Oppen's late poetry, "it is not the unity of individual poems that strike me, but the distance the language moves between the beginning of a piece and its end" (Berry 1984, 321) could perfectly well apply to and even be said to originate from the sequences in *Discrete Series*, as well as the later books.

The question depends on one's definition of one's unit of choice: poem, poem sequence, or book of poems. These are sometimes impossible to disentangle. As for what happens in longer, apparently less coherent texts, Berry decides against indeterminacy:

> The critically placed syntactical element does not always hover between two possible roles; in many cases, it is seen, after a second reading, as unambiguously in a single role, syntactical interpretation having been initially impeded—and thus forced into consciousness—by the absence of punctuation and the placement of the line-division. (Berry 1984, 319)

Moving from certainty to ambiguity, from restrained ambiguity to full-blown ambiguity, one finally arrives at disambiguation. Does this mean that the hovering, as it were, simply takes longer after *Seascape*? These observations are accurate to the point that they offer a general view of the matter at hand, but they are difficult to sustain in poem by poem, line by line analysis. For instance, Berry sees a tipping point in "the fourteen-part poem 'Route' in *Of Being Numerous*" (Berry 1984, 313). After that poem, Berry finds that Oppen abandons the line as a palpable unit (Berry 1984, 313). "Route" is relevant in that evolution as a transition poem because in it Berry finds "divisions of the text into rhetorical units longer than lines but nonetheless operating as lines" (Berry 1984, 313). Although Berry states that Oppen returns to the line unit in his poetry of the seventies—an apparent contradiction—she remarks that he returns to "the line as a unit" after it has been irremediably "undermined" (Berry 1984, 313). For Oppen is now "throwing lineation out of phase with the syntactical divisions of the text and eschewing punctuation" (Berry 1984, 313). To use Berry's words, "Route" was the moment of the "swelling" of the lines, a problem that Oppen resolved through "perforation," Berry's term for Oppen's habit of punctuating his poems with blanks or unexpected spacing. Berry's phrase to describe "Route" as a poem made up of "rhetorical-rhythmical units" (Berry 1984, 313) may not be quite sufficiently explicit, Oppen's "aim to bring to consciousness syntactical interpretation" (Berry 1984, 313) is undeniable. More debatable is Berry's conclusion that Oppen's efforts at raising the reader's syntactical awareness rests on a "possibility for polyvalence" (Berry 1984, 313). This seems to hint at a general unmooring of Oppen's *Materials* into a drifting *Seascape*. I would argue that the narrative that takes one from stability to polyvalence is too convenient.

In her example, Berry discusses Oppen's "Song, the Winds of Downhill"—"the first poem in which Oppen abandons line-initial capitalization" (Berry 1984, 314). Berry speaks of its "loosely strung syntactical elements" (Berry 1984, 314), its systematic enjambment causing "non-stop flow" (Berry 1984, 314). But the idea of a flow seems too one-sided: if line breaks trigger a kind of flowing, they may also produce other effects, such as a type of pulse, a halting or a stuttering. In addition, one wonders whether intralinear spacing should be placed on the same level as line breaks, and whether they operate as factors of continuity of discontinuity. Oppen's poem does rely on his own brand of what could be called hypallactic line breaks, his "horizontal spacing" (Berry 1984, 315), which causes the reader to remain suspended as each line break withholds and delays attribution and indeed predication to the point of misdistribution—hence my use of hypallage extended to a prosodic figure. However, Berry's prosodic analysis soon rests its case. Syntax has become a means of "rhythmical divisions" (Berry 1984, 314) and the word rhythm, much like the word music when used for impressionistic effect, often ends prosodic discussion rather than stimulates it.

While Bernstein argues that Oppen's technique is impaired by a "commitment to clarity" (TP 198), Berry finds it empowered by a commitment to fluidity—which in Oppen is very much connected to clarity. Indeed, speaking of a thematic *and* prosodic change (Berry 1984, 315) causes Berry to account for thematic features using prosodic ones, or vice versa. Taken out of this precise context, remarks about a poem's noticeably fluid dynamics, when that poem's general thematic drive is the sea, could be taken as an instance of overused mimeticism, with the text patterned after its own topic. On the other hand, the sea and sailing make up recurring topics and patterns in Oppen's poetry. The reason for the increasing presence of these motifs may be found in the following analogy, from a 1975 letter written by an older Oppen: "And of course I feel sometimes too armored with all those poems *written* - - - - - written, I would like to be adrift again - - I am afraid, I mean, that I might lose the sea" (SL 301). However, going back to the poem at hand, one might ask whether it is in fact so loosely strung, and whether its rhythm really offers just a continuous flow, fraught with Heraclitean drama, or not.

Speaking of rhythm can be a way around using words like "punctuation" or "syntax," without addressing what the word rhythm implies. Even then, "rhythmical divisions" look very much like punctuation and syntax thinly disguised. Lineation may have been less strained by Oppen before *Of Being Numerous*, but its immediate correlatives—meaning, legibility and overall coherence—have been repeatedly put to the test prior to *Seascape*. *Discrete Series*, if taken as a serial work indeed, stretches the individual boundaries of its multiple single poems to a considerable extent. As for the cogency of *The Materials* and *This in Which* combined, it never escapes the reader that unity is not achieved in spite of disjunctions, puzzling arrangements or ellipsis, but through those very techniques. In other words, one must ask what does change with "perforation," and why Oppen chose spacing instead of, or as, punctuation. Berry suggests that "[o]ne answer would seem to be that there are no conventions for punctuation of his new syntax of loosely connected fragments (Berry 1984, 314). Still, it is questionable whether loose connections can achieve prosodic form in those terms.

All in all, what this preliminary discussion of Oppen's "Song, the Winds of Downhill" shows is that it is relatively easy to agree on Oppen's foregrounding the decisive role of syntax, but much more difficult to build on that foregrounded syntax beyond standard considerations about disjunction or indeterminacy. Prosodic description is even impaired by the very logic of indeterminacy, and its tendency toward an exclusively negative emphasis—praising what the poem does *not* do, what it will not indulge in and what it calls into question, rather than what the poem actually *does*. One then falls back on the disjunctive aspect of the lines, which does not amounts to much of a descriptive tool, but will be occasionally found hovering above the poems like an evasive formal theme. Meanwhile in Oppen, syntax carries the burden of the poem's proof in such a way that meaning becomes a prosodic constraint, so that studying Oppen's prosody is a prerequisite for the poem's reader, not an extra layer of analysis to be added to one's predetermined reading. When critical concepts replace prosodic problems instead of solving them, registering the presence of parataxis becomes an equally paratactic critical activity, forever adjacent, forever disconnected.

On the basic assumption that someone's disorder is someone else's rhetorical system, I would like to focus on Oppen's prosody with the belief that therein lies not only access to Oppen's late poetry, which is notoriously troubling in that respect, but access to much of Oppen's work and more so, to Oppen's significance as a poet. Addressing the debates surrounding Oppen's prosodic evolution and style, in terms of syntax, lineation and spacing, against the background of the many difficulties inherent in prosodic analysis concerned with non-metrical poetry, I will pay particular attention to attempts at providing new rhythmic tools outside the isochronic syllabic-accentual tradition—the intonational approach and phrasing specifically—and propose a meticulous and contradictory scanning of Oppen's poem "Song, The Winds of Downhill," complete with a rhythmic study taking into account Oppen's four recorded readings of that poem.

When reading the poem for the first time, one wonders whether this poem can ever be scanned in any meaningful fashion. Syllabic-accentual metrics would seem to be of little use, since free verse will not take metrical scansion as such. Attempting to scan the poem may nonetheless prove instructive, in what it will reveal: that one lacks the tools to properly account for the poem's rhythm. Using the rhythmic markers presented in Thomas Carper and Derek Attridge's *Meter and Meaning: An Introduction to Rhythm in Poetry* (2003), which refines the system developed by Attridge in *The Rhythms of English Poetry* (1982), here is a possible metrical scanning of the poem using a limited version of Derek Attridge's beat-offbeat system[1]:

'out of poverty
O o B -o-

to begin
-o- B

again' impoverished
o b o B ~o~

of tone of pose that common
o B o B o B o

wealth
B

of parlance Who
o B o B

so poor the words
o B o B

would with and take on substantial
O O O O b o B -o-

meaning handholds footholds
B o B o B o

to dig in one's heels sliding
o B -o- B B o

hands and heels beyond the residential
B o B o b ~o~ B -o-

lots the plots it is a poem
B o B o O o B

which may be sung
o O o B

may well be sung (NCP 220)
o b o B

I have chosen what I hope is not an intrusive scansion. After all, scansion is never either strictly descriptive or strictly performative, as though interpretation could ever be securely segregated from a priori verse structure or linguistic competence (Novell-Smith 2013). Still, one seems to learn no valuable lesson from this exercise. Various levels of emphasis are revealed by what, in another context, one would call trochees, spondees, or anapests, but this remark itself goes a long way to show how fixed metrical forms are inescapably at the back of any dual rhythmic system based on equivalences. Worse, the poem's hollowed out lineation gets virtually erased and the poem's structure realigned into the semblance of a metrical flow, which my choice of reading a triple offbeat on emphasized syllables line 8 is powerless to stop. One might think that the attempt was set to fail from the start, because Attridge's symbols are simply not meant for free verse. Attridge warns that it "may seem perverse to apply metrical analysis to verse that is avowedly nonmetrical" (Attridge 1995, 172), yet he proceeds to do just that on the grounds that poetry can never be free of "the fundamental rhythmic forms we have discussed" (Attridge 1995, 172), claiming that in fact, if free verse will amend it may "approach the movements of regular meter" (Attridge 1995, 176) when properly scanned, though by "not wholly engaging with meter, such poems cannot avail themselves to its full capacity for expressive and memorable shapings of sound" (Attridge 1995, 176). Both offhand and definitive, Attridge's dismissal will only concede that free verse "may gain a heightened ability to capture the movements of thought, speech, and feeling that run through our daily lives" (Attridge 1995, 176). To be fair, Attridge does proceed to summarize prosodic work on phrasing as an alternative to the limitations inherent in applying metrical solutions to nonmetrical texts. But his survey of phrasing in *Poetic Rhythm: An Introduction* concludes that phrasing, even more than metrical scansion, is in the ear of the beholder, and that it is not particularly concerned with free verse. Furthermore, by refusing to combine structural relations with what Attridge calls the movement of language in the poem—one a matter of meaning, the other one of rhythm—he will not take that key step that binds rhythm and semantics together.

The underlying assumption seems to be that rhythm and semantics do not need to come together, because in order to be meaningful a system of prosody requires the type of symmetrical recurrences that precisely cannot be found in free verse. Prosodic theories have indeed had a more or less stubborn tendency to divorce semantic and rhythmic levels of analysis—not using rhythm to account for meaning, but dealing with the analysis of rhythm as an autonomously meaningful activity. In fact, no marker is available to account for the way in which non-metrical poetry uses line-breaks and spacing as an alternative, if the word is not too reductive, to the syllabic-accentual system of emphasis that is meter. It might have been tempting, for this purpose, to adapt markers for implied offbeat (ô)—"an offbeat which occurs where there is no word or part of a word that occupies the space between two beats (and where no punctuation or other obvious break creates a distinct pause)" (Attridge and Carter 2003, 35)—or for virtual offbeat, which signals a distinct pause in the line's progress with [o], and to use these to apprehend syntactical continuities and disruptions in Oppen's poem. But resorting to such markers would imply that one allows the compositional syntactic specificity of nonmetrical verse to be conceived of with the tools of meter still.

Since free verse cannot be scanned metrically, critics have argued that phrasal scansion is the answer. The question then soon arises as to what it should be based on. Phrasal scansion needs syntactical shapes to be tuned to intonational patterns. Yet as with the scanning of a metrical line, which requires word-stress to fit a fixed stress pattern, or vice versa, how these two levels are balanced remains highly delicate. Some have begun to answer these difficult questions. Alan Holder's plea for a "pitch-focused analysis" (Holder 1995, 233) that will address what eludes "stress-based scansion" (Holder 1995, 233) rests on his claim that "[*p*]*itch* analysis reveals the essential structure of the whole of the line, the skeleton of its gestalt, a gestalt for which no a priori model need be invoked" (Holder 1995, 233). Letting go of meter seems always prompted by a commendable wish to achieve truly scientific description, free from preconceived models, yet this promise of pragmatic progress tends to be realized only through the discovery of a new supermodel. It is legitimately doubtful whether finding the skeleton for the line's intonational Ur-gestalt will ever truly reveal the poem's rhythm. In a work so dedicated to eradicating meter, it is not a little surprising that meter's most heinous crime—disembodying speech—gets repeated as the cure for that offense. One may be quite convinced by Holder's liberating arguments, for instance his defense, after Elisabeth O. Selkirk, of the metrical grid versus the metrical tree as a proper representation for the English sentence, in the sense that metrical grids are less prone to rely on preexisting units than trees, and therefore better suited to phrasing (Holder 1995, 154). The representation of pitch accent scansion remains troublesome nonetheless. Here is Holder's reading of the first line of Pound's classic haiku:

ri fa crowd;
The appa tion of these ces in the (Holder 220)

Holder's choice of disarticulating the words twists the line's skeleton into odd postures, even though attempting to present a readable scansion of any poem makes typographical arrangement a recurring problem. Despite an apparently broader outlook, Holder's pitch-patterns seem to duplicate the dichotomy that he rejects so strongly in Attridge and others between stressed and unstressed syllables (Holder 1995, 66), between regular and irregular, normal and deviant. More productive is Holder's suggestion that one should consider the line-ending "as an intonational terminal" (Holder 1995, 226), and study of how "line-boundary/intonation-terminal may cut into a syntactic or sense unit" (Holder 1995, 227). Yet again, Holder's "pitch-pattern arrangement" of the first line of Sylvia Plath's "Ariel" ends up creating line boundaries in the form of intonational terminals, making syntactic or sense unit difficult to parse:

> Sta
>   dark
>   sis
>   in
>   ness
> (Holder 1995, 229)

One is looking at a geometrical-acoustic representation which may have its merits phonologically, yet does not convince prosodically, unless one accepts the breaking up of lineation to the point of morphological reengineering as a necessary step in prosodic interpretation. David Crystal's piece, "Intonation and Metrical Theory," which Holder presents as what inspired his own findings, concludes with the project of moving "away from the atomistic approach of the syllable and stress phoneme" so one may "talk of a text as being *organized* as poetry" (Crystal 1971, 33). If pitch leads to an even more atomistic approach, then one is indeed a long way from developing an "account of the whole range of non-segmental phonological contrastivity" (Crystal 1971, 33). Intonational rather than metrical scansion, if it will merely substitute one segmental approach for another—supported by a debatable opposition between the artifice of meter and so-called natural speech—would leave the key question raised by Crystal unanswered, which was that of "the interrelation of the phonological patterns noted with syntax" (Crystal 1971, 33).

Leaving aside pitch movement, one can easily demonstrate the importance of intonation group boundary. Intonation per se, as a suprasegmental level of analysis, constitutes a highly practical segmenting means of studying texts, as with J. C. Wells' "three Ts," in his *English Intonation, An Introduction* (2006): tonality, tonicity, and tone, with tonality dealing in parsing or syntactical "chunking" (Wells 2006, 7), tonicity as a matter of locating accent or "nucleus placement" (Wells 2006, 9), and tone as pitch movement, fall, rise and fall-rise. The end of Oppen's "the Tongues," for instance, poses a simple syntactical problem regarding the possessive "his," which may be addressed most directly through the placement of intonational group boundary:

> that force   the words
> out of that whirlwind his
> and not his strange
> words surround him (NCP 275)

One's reading depends on how one lets the two possessive pronouns suggest syntactical relations. The line break after the first "his" underlines the dispossession evoked in the next line, while it stands out as a postposed modifier of "that whirlwind," suggesting it is God's ("His"), as though capitalization were an intonational feature. The second "his" raises even more questions: the words that surround him may be "his / and not his strange / words," or the whirlwind may be "his / and not his" while "strange / words surround him." To a certain extent, these meanings are meant to coexist. Yet the beat of these four lines suggests a definite rhythmic parsing. When the space between "that force" and "the words" is understood as a key intonational feature, one then reads what would look like:

that force   the words
out of that whirlwind   his and not his
strange words   surround him

The poem's remarkable achievement lies in the last line break. The dispossession takes place over the break: the emphasis on "words" underlines a strangeness which otherwise might not be apparent. A poet might very well be surrounded with words, but it is "strange" that "*words* surround him." The impetus on "words" in the last line repeats the outward push from "*out* of that whirlwind," from "that *force*." The reason why Oppen does not choose the symmetrical lineation I have adopted is obvious: it loses the whirlwind. Restoring the poem's own motion, one may now read, using | as the mark for intonation group boundary:

that force | the words |
out of that whirlwind | his
and not his | strange
words | surround him (NCP 275)

Because the binary separations I have underlined are in fact distributed across the line breaks, the whirlwind is set in motion in a way that equally dispossesses the reader of words that are his and not his own, since they have been made strange to regular intonation. Including pitch movement is tempting, yet I would immediately wish to propose several. Using simply the two markers \ for fall and / for rise, setting aside other intonational declensions, the poem could read:

that \force | the \words |
/out of that \whirlwind | /his
and not /his | strange
\words | \surround him (NCP 275)

It could also be argued that the first line here should receive more of a hammering kind of emphasis, or that "not" and the final "words" deserve more prominence. In many ways, Berry's remarks about Holder's intonational approach ring true: "linguistic stress [...] may be promoted or demoted by metrical set or even by mere lineation"; "aural aspects" should be studied along visual ones; "the intonational integrity of the line" is not a given, and depends on "intonational phrase boundaries within lines and the continuation of intonational phrases over line-divisions" (Berry 1997, 879). Thus, it is never just a question of promoting parsing over scanning, but how to combine the two. For when intonational readings outsource their parsing to linguistic stress, they simply repeat the shift away from meter, as T. S. Eliot described it when he said that "[e]very revolution in poetry is apt to be, and sometimes to announce itself as, a return to common speech," encouraging the belief that "[t]he music of poetry, then, must be latent in the common speech of its time" (Eliot 1975, 111–112). Eliot's chronological view of today's poetic diction as yesterday's common speech may seem anachronistic when one is dealing with systematized views of intonation, yet in this debate one must be wary of the illusion of using common speech as the final standard. What basis might exist upon which to decide how intonation should lead the way into the poem remains unclear.

Intonational and syntactic sequences connect, if only because intonational analysis relies on a preparatory sequencing that is syntactical in nature. The question is no longer whether voice and grammar or sound and structure are interrelated, but how those connections may be worked out into manageable prosodic series. Far from an attempt to resuscitate Olson's breath-group, which would require "donning a kind of prosodic breatholator" (Holder 1995, 203), I now propose to test Holder's "position that what I have called phrases, which, as I have designated them, are both syntactic and sense units, coincide with the intonational units of a given poetic text" (Holder 1995, 209). In so doing, I hope to show that differentiating between syntactic and intonational levels of analysis still relies on the premise that tone and text may be dealt with, even hypothetically, as separate entities, as though one might have an idea without a sentence, or read a poem and then parse it.

While I do not seek to fetishize a poet's own voice, it so happens there are four separate recordings of Oppen reading "Song, The Winds of Downhill," from the beginning to the end of the seventies. The fact that these are several distinct occurrences should help mitigate the methodological narrowness of my using only the poet's voice, and serve as a reminder that one's choice need not be between eternal fixed forms or a singular performance. These recordings prove a remarkable resource in showing the limits of the search for the intonational ground upon which the poem stands.

I propose to scan the poem again, essentially in terms of intonational groups, using only the marker |. Nonetheless, I must make two preliminary remarks. First, that marker indicates pauses that occur in cases of irregular intralinear spacing as well as for line breaks. This sometimes signals what a comma would sound like, sometimes what a period would sound like. For comfort, it has not seemed useful to differentiate. However, one should be aware that most often, it signals an actual pause, when one distinctly hears the poet take a breath before he resumes his reading. At times, breathing is inaudible, which would have made for an ambiguous sub-marker, had the nuance been included. Most of these longer pauses occur at line breaks, some with irregular intra-linear spacing, none in regular intra-linear spacing, when | does not signal inhaling.

Secondly, one should consequently not pay attention to spacing or line breaks as they appear on the page. It should be assumed that the words are read continuously from one | to the next. This is certainly the most surprising element when listening to Oppen read this poem or indeed others. Outside of these pauses, which may be highly disruptive, the words cohere with no less speed than anyone would use when asking "how do you do?" This aspect requires careful consideration, since marking intonational boundaries would otherwise amount to adding more holes to the road, instead of giving directions. The examples are given in chronological order, the undated one last, preceded by the information given on the PennSound platform, and with additional contextual remarks whenever necessary.

First, here is Oppen reading at San Francisco State University on May 3, 1972, then broadcast by KPFA (Berkeley) on June 2, 1972:

'out of poverty |
to begin |

again'   impoverished |

of tone of pose that common
wealth |

of parlance   Who |
so poor the words

would | *with* | *and*   take on substantial |

meaning | handholds | footholds |

to dig in one's heels   sliding

hands and heels | beyond the residential
lots | the plots   it is a poem

which may be sung |
may well be sung |

As one might expect, the most substantial pauses concentrate on line endings or intra-linear spaces. Exception are noted mostly when the syntactical unit seems thus expressly preserved, as in "so poor the words" followed by those words, or in cases of verb modification or noun-epithet relationships, such as "sliding hands and heels," "common wealth," or "residential lots." Yet one cannot draw a final conclusion: the pauses between "begin" and "again," or "impoverished" and "of tone," in the early lines of the text, break up the expected speech pattern in a way that does not allow for easy recovery. Moreover, as the next examples show, Oppen never maintained the same reading twice.

Here is a second reading, at the University of East Anglia, Norwich, England, July 5, 1973. On the recording, it has just been put to Oppen that there is something essentially American about his poetry, which might make it quite foreign to his English audience, if one could not already easily hear the idiom on the page. Oppen answers that he first read Pope without any awareness of iambics, then proceeds to read "Song, The Winds of Downhill" as an example of the permanence of rhythmic structures within a poem, in spite of accentual differences, saying that although "we think that an enunciation can be wrong, that an accent can be wrong" we need "to place words so that they must be understood even if precisely the sound is not the same, their impact, their musical impact remains the same." Oppen's insistence on the prevailing rhythm of his lines, over possibly significant dichotomies in terms of pronunciation, including intonational shifts, testifies not only to his confidence in his prosody, but to the paramount nature of syntax-as-cadence for Oppen, who reads:

'out of poverty
to begin |

again'   impoverished

of tone of pose that common |
wealth

of parlance   Who |
so poor the words

would *with* | *and* take on substantial

meaning handholds | footholds

to dig in one's heels sliding |

hands and heels beyond the residential
lots | the plots | it is a poem |

which may be sung |
may well be sung |

The breaks here between "common" and "wealth," between "sliding" and "hands and heels," along with the linking of "impoverished of tone" show how my previous comments on the first reading are immediately called into question by this new reading. What can be learned, and will be confirmed in the following example, is that some prosodic halts seem more pivotal than others, in that they can be found at the same place in different readings. So far, "to begin," "Who," "substantial," "lots," and the rhyming couplet in "sung" are all followed by a marked pause.

Here is a third reading, referenced "From Selected Readings, a 1979 recording." It is a strikingly much faster reading. I should add that instead of the word "parlance," line six, Oppen reads "knowledge." Given the date of the recording, seven years after the publication of the poem in *Seascape*, it is most likely a slip of the tongue, however meaningful, rather than an indication of his reading an earlier or later version of the poem.

'out of poverty
to begin |

again' impoverished
of tone of pose that common |
wealth

of knowledge Who |
so poor the words

would *with* *and* take on substantial |

meaning handholds | footholds

to dig in one's heels sliding |

hands and heels beyond the residential
lots | the plots | it is a poem |

which may be sung |
may well be sung |

As noted about the second reading, pauses after "to begin," "Who," "substantial," "lots," and the two "sung," seem structurally necessary, to which one would add the pause after "poem" in the second reading, this third one, and the fourth. Here is the fourth and final reading, referenced "Poems Formerly (and Incorrectly) Attributed to the Poetry Center at the San Francisco State University (Location and Date Unknown)":

'out of poverty |
to begin |

again'   impoverished |

of tone of pose that common |
wealth |

of parlance   Who |
so poor the words |

would | *with* | *and*   take on substantial |

meaning handholds | footholds |

to dig in one's heels   sliding

hands and heels | beyond the residential
lots | the plots | it is a poem |

which may be sung |
may well be sung |

As a summary of the variations between these four readings, I indicate below after each marker how many times each pause occurs in all readings combined:

'out of poverty |2
to begin |4

again'   impoverished |2

of tone of pose that common |3
wealth |2

of parlance   Who |4
so poor the words |1

would |2 *with* |3 *and*   take on substantial |3

meaning |1 handholds |4 footholds |2

to dig in one's heels   sliding |2

hands and heels |2 beyond the residential
lots |4 the plots |3 it is a poem |3

which may be sung |4
may well be sung |4

Pauses lines two, six, nine, and twelve, along with the two final pauses in the rhyming couplet remain unchanged through all four readings, which makes it six out of twenty. Within the rest of the poem, key disjunctions keep syntactical distribution highly ambivalent when one would hope for directions. Such a difficult line as "of parlance Who" is remarkable: instead of a pause due to the space after "parlance," the line continues as though an expected relative clause were coming, leaving the reader or the audience with the abrupt unpunctuated question "Who." On the whole, the procedure fails to offer a sufficiently reliable pattern, not only because these intonational signs restrict the poem's cadence to a single performance every time, when the poet himself greatly varies his readings, but because they effectively write off Oppen's spacing and line breaks. Moreover, if parsing is the condition of intonational analysis, this poem instantiates parsing into a kind of song. The poem explicitly focuses on intonational suspension and projection—in other words, the possibility of song—by questioning the difference between function words and content words, thus endowing syntax with special semantic value, and beyond syntax, intonation. No elucidation is therefore possible that would imply bringing an end to the hesitant parsing. The poem must, quite literally, "begin again" upon each reading. Being "impoverished // of tone" means exactly that one must relinquish the comforts of tone down to one's basic syntactic certainties. This is not a case of metrical or musical harmonies rendered useless by the prosaic rhythms of common speech, but a case of the intonational harmonies of common speech being called into question by the poem's rhythm. One wonders how to move beyond parsing, then, if in this instance the poem defeats the very possibility of it taking place.

Richard Cureton's *Rhythmic Phrasing in English Verse* (1992), to which Holder's work is largely indebted, has the ambition to move toward yet another level of architectural concerns—what Cureton calls rhythmic hierarchies, thus bridging the gap between "versification (i.e., conventionalized language patterns used in particular poetic traditions) and linguistic prosody (i.e., a particular subset of grammatical structures that includes a syllable structure, the phonological hierarchy, and stress patterning)" (Cureton 1996, 34). What is fascinating about Oppen's poem is that while it does not fit any traditional prosodic scheme, linguistic prosody would fall short of accounting for its rhythm because it relies on such unconventional language patterns. Although I cannot remotely do justice to Cureton's rhythmic apparatus, I will provide a quick overview of his "temporal poetics" (Cureton 2000, 362), following his own succinct account when preparing for his analysis of Yeats' "The Sorrow of Love," in which he addresses Jakobson's notion of poetic function separated from non-poetic linguistic forms (Jakobson 1987). The first key association Cureton makes is between meter, which "scans beating," and grouping, which "scans the voice" (Cureton 2000, 374), as these "different rhythmic components organize different types of perceived prominence and segmentation" so that "[w]hen combined, beating and grouping form a phrased measure" (Cureton 2000, 374), which may then be subdivided into prosodic hierarchies, ranging from intonational unit, phonological phrase, clitic[2] phrase, to syllable:

> Clitic phrases group unstressed and weakly stressed syllables around one primary stress. Phonological phrases group vocally related clitic phrases, usually phrases in a modifier-modified relation in the syntax. Intonational units group phonological phrases; they represent one tonal melody, stretched across one unit of discourse information. (Cureton 2000, 375)

The argument that meter, as beating, is inseparable from grouping might seem odd, for Cureton begins *Rhythmic Phrasing* with an in-depth analysis of the dangers of conflating meter and phrasing (Cureton 1992, 36). Yet what Cureton accuses Attridge of doing in amalgamating meter and phrasing is to subordinate phrasing to meter, and in fact to traditional accentual-syllabic meter, until phrasing is but a shadow of meter cast upon larger segments than the usual syllable count. Cureton's cognitive treatment of rhythmic experience, on the other hand, not only redefines meter as beating, but subsumes it into the broader concept of grouping. However, as Berry again notes, Cureton's concept of grouping does not differentiate essentially between metrical and non-metrical verse (Berry 1997, 876). Consider nonetheless the following summary of Cureton's definition of rhythm, which I must quote at some length:

> Rhythm is *componential*. There are four general components of rhythm that provide the basis of our temporal experience. As rhythmic components, let's call these (1) *meter*, (2) *grouping*, (3) *prolongation*, and (4) *theme*. As times/temporalities, let's call these (1) *cyclical*, (2) *centroidal*, (3) *linear*, and (4) *relative*. […]
>
> Structurally, these four rhythms reflect the forms of time they create. *Meter*, which creates cyclical time, is strongly repetitive (although not entirely so, by any means). […] *Grouping*, which creates centroidal time, is repeatedly centering. It divides a temporal stream into small groups of events, each of which has one and only one prominence, a kind of rhythmic core. […] *Prolongation*, which creates linear time, relates present events to distant departures/arrivals, either by anticipating an imagined future or extending an experienced past. *Theme*, which creates relative time, links varied, usually peripheral, events to some imagined, but usually absent, center, creating a network of loose family resemblances. (Cureton 2002 93)

Without going into all of the details of Cureton's distinctions, one should note that he convincingly argues against the "poetic schizophrenia" that forever divides texts into a myriad of competing levels of interpretation, each suited for different materials—"visual, rhythmic, versificational, grammatical, semantic, pragmatic, intertextual, and so on" (Cureton 2002, 91). In the end, however, Cureton's logic is a temporal one, and its scope thus proves limited as well. Meter as repetition and grouping as cluster formation may both be quickly enough adopted for immediate practical use, but prolongation and theme, with their essentially temporal, that is musical, connotations, are not without some problems. Contrary to Holder or Attridge, I do not believe that the fundamental issue with Cureton's system are its roots in music. As Cureton explains, he does not

> attempt to develop a linguistic theory by way of music theory […] but a theory of rhythm. And like Lerdahl and Jackendoff's theory of musical rhythm, it is essentially a cognitive theory, whose basic principles are tied only loosely, if at all, to a theory of language. While language is the input to this rhythmic theory, its basic principles and the basic representations it elaborates refer only minimally to language per se. (Cureton 1992, 46)

The case may nonetheless be made that a minimally or non-language-based theory of rhythm is of doubtful use when considering purely linguistic realities. To speak of "a cognitive theory of rhythm developed to explain our rhythmic response to music in order to establish a theory of our rhythmic response to language" (Cureton 1992, 46) is to make the specific choice of not developing a cognitive theory of rhythm derived from "our rhythmic response to language," without any musical detour. Another way of saying this would be to ask how Cureton plans to refrain from making rhythm something nonsemantic, by disconnecting rhythm for its poetic material. Cureton's answer consists in redefining the terms of the debate. In "Meter and Metrical Reading in Temporal Poetics" (2012) he provides a vast overview of his system. Explaining his "temporal paradigm," "both within language and elsewhere," he lists an impressive array of "evolutionary products": "the family, orality, polytheism, the classical virtues, myth, metaphor, alliteration, syllables, words, past tense, 3rd person, etc." (Cureton 2012, 112–113). The four divisions Cureton applies then to what he details as "the poetic paradigm" range from the "psychological and neurological," the "historical and cultural," the "literary and rhetorical," the "prosodic and syntactic," the "semantic and thematic" (Cureton 2012, 114–115), offering such extended "contexts of use (physical, biological, socio-historical, cultural, etc.)" (Cureton 2012, 237) that one registers the totalizing effort, but would be hard put to find a practical use for it. When Cureton provides detailed readings, as in his "Analysis of William Carlos Williams, 'To a Solitary Disciple'," the anatomy of the patterning may be as thorough as humanly possible, the exercise is one of internal reading exclusively: not Williams' text but its textures—to use Cureton's own word in his article—are microscopically analyzed. The issue is not even so much of one scale, but rather the fact that rhythmic investigation is not required to any significant degree in reading Williams' poem to begin with. The poem may grow richer after critical scrutiny, it reads well enough on its own. In matters of prosody, much depends on the level of necessity for rhythmic clarification. If nothing decisive hangs in the balance—if the poem still essentially reads the same on quite a basic level—one's interest may remain, as it were, purely academic. Such is not the case with Oppen's poem under discussion, or many of Oppen's poems in fact, which demand rhythmical and syntactical decisions be made from the start for any reading to be achieved at all.

Berry's remarks about Oppen's loosely composed poem remind one of the type of deprecating comments made about texts whose structure, for lack of proper understanding, is deemed disorderly, chaotic, or are considered to be devoid of structure at all. Sometimes the dismissal is made in praise: what the poem lacks, it does so proudly, negatively, differently—it resists. Defenders of paratactic texts—whatever their other names, "innovative," "avant-garde," "radical," and there will be others—will on occasion translate bafflement into manifesto. Yet the terms of the debate remain unchanged: the poem may flaunt what it fails to do, it is still being read through the same prism it denounces.

Notes

1. For readers unfamiliar with this system:

   B: emphasized beat (emphasized syllable).
   b: unemphasized beat (unemphasized syllable).

O: emphasized offbeat (emphasized syllable).
o: unemphasized offbeat (unemphasized syllable).
-o-: double offbeat (two unemphasized syllables).
~o~: triple offbeat (three unemphasized syllables).

For a stimulating take on the use of prosody in the context of contemporary poetics, see Lacy Rumsey, 'The Obstinate reader: Prynne, prosody and degrees of engagement'. *Thinking Verse* I (2011), 44–66.

2. Clitic designates an unemphatic word pronounced as part of the preceding or following word, hence deprived of an accent of its own. Clitic phrase designates the accented compound.

References

Attridge, Derek and Carper, Thomas. 2003. *Meter and Meaning: An Introduction to Rhythm in Poetry*. New York: Routledge.

Attridge, Derek. 1995. *Poetic Rhythm: An Introduction*. Cambridge: Cambridge University Press.

———. 1982. *The Rhythms of English Poetry*. London: Longman.

Berry, Eleanor. 1984. "Language Made Fluid: The Grammetrics of George Oppen's Recent Poetry." *Contemporary Literature* 25/3: 305–22.

Berry, Eleanor. 1997. "The Free Verse Spectrum." *College English* 59/8: 873–897.

———. 2004. "Working Prosodies: Finding What Will Suffice." *The Antioch Review* 62/1: 104–112.

Crystal, David. 1971. "Intonation and Metrical Theory." *Transactions of the Philological Society* 1–33.

Cureton, Richard D. 2013. "Analysis of William Carlos Williams, 'To a Solitary Disciple.'" *Thinking Verse* III: 51–107.

———. 2012. "Meter and Metrical Reading in Temporal Poetics." *Thinking Verse* II: 112–237.

———. 2000. "Jakobson Revisited: Poetics, Subjectivity, and Temporality." *Journal of English Linguistics* 28/4: 354–392.

———. 1992. *Rhythmic Phrasing in English Verse*. London: Longman.

———. 2002. "Schizophrenic Poetics: A Proposed Cure." *Journal of English Linguistics* 30/1: 91–110.

———. 2004. "Temporal Poetics: Rhythmic Process as Truth." *The Antioch Review* 62/1: 113–121.

Eliot, T. S. 1975. *Selected Prose*. New York: Farrar, Straus and Giroux.

Holder, Alan. 1995. *Rethinking Meter. A New Approach to the Verse Line*. Lewisburg: Brucknell University Press.

Izenberg, Oren. 2006. "Oppen's Silence, Crusoe's Silence, and the Silence of Other Minds." *Modernism/Modernity* 13/1: 787–811.

Jakobson, Roman. 1966. "Grammatical Parallelism and Its Russian Facet," *Language*, 42/2: 399–429.

Nowell Smith, David. 2013. "Editor's Introduction: Scansion." *Thinking Verse III* 1/14. http://www.thinkingverse.com/issue03.html

Rumsey, Lacy. 2011. 'The Obstinate reader: Prynne, prosody and degrees of engagement'. *Thinking Verse* I, 44–66.

Selkirk, Elisabeth O. 1984. *Phonology and Syntax: The Relation Between Sound and Structure*. Cambridge: M.I.T. Press.

Wells, J. C. 2006. *English Intonation: An Introduction*. Cambridge: Cambridge University Press.

CHAPTER THREE

That Common Wealth of Parlance

To make sense of "Song, The Winds of Downhill" without recourse to inadequate prosodic descriptions, one might bear in mind the following disclaimer from Oppen:

> I think I don't care at all about design, pattern across the paper, the canvas, or the poem's surface […] I'm not sure I ever visualize anything but depth. … Or a point, a detail so sharply defined that I'm shaken by the implication of space
>
> like describing a wave in the middle of the sea (SL 220–1)

The absence of immediately recognizable patterns has had many diving for depths indeed. However, forms need not be fixed to exist. Far more than the need to include a volta in a sonnet, form as the imprint of a cognitive outlook is precisely, to keep using Oppen's word, the type of construct that gives one access to depth beyond the text's surface. The image used by Oppen in this letter is illuminating: in terms of surface, "a wave in the middle of the sea" could hardly be deemed a recognizable pattern, far less a reproducible one. Oppen refuses to disconnect the sea's surface from its weight, its depth, and its energy. The wave cannot be singled out as ornament, but as the "implication" of the spatial forces that produce it, which roots one's visual perception in time, through tidal repetitions. Oppen's lack of interest in design explains his preference for disclosure: while a design comes together and freezes, however internally dynamic it might be, disclosure requires a cadence that will repeat, flux-like, as the peak of a wave that comes and goes upon each reading. Armand Schwerner remarkably caught what Oppen was doing when he wrote the following, from "prologue in six parts," in which he mentions Oppen by name a few lines down:

> What he might establish
> came only from the destructions of the wind
> artless in its gyrations (Schwerner 1999 66)

Oppen's purposeful artlessness, combined with the evocation of "the destructions of the wind" as the only guideline to decipher the poem's composition, can discourage the reader from looking any further. And if one does look, one must be careful not to present a model for interpretation so much as a step by step exploration—an exercise, that is, in the pragmatics of reading. The effort is not intended to fit the poem into some preconceived grid, but to bring about another methodological outlook. The type of syntactic attention this will require will seem odd to quite a few readers, yet when looking at other and past types of textuality, one soon realizes that there is no such thing as reading, but a varied history of specifically oriented modes of reading—not reading but traditions of reading. *Scriptura continua*, for instance, required a set of skills in ancient readers of unseparated text, which to the grammatical sensitivity of today's Western readers would seem irrelevant for its arduous eye-voice gymnastics. A cognitive process so entrenched as silent reading is nonetheless only a few centuries old. Because unseparated texts made oral reading an aid to decoding, the growth of silent reading in the European Middle Ages was directly related to the practice of spacing words, as paleographer Paul Saenger has shown. Similarly, Oppen's prosody makes demands on the reader's silent parsing of the poem that challenge one's silent reading of the poem on the page. This one historical example suggests that beyond calling into question one's habits or assumptions as a reader of poetry, what Oppen does reaches into the very heart of one's sense of literacy.

When Oppen's *New Collected Poems* came out in 2002, Jeremy Harding's review in the *London Review of Books* used in its title a remark Oppen had made, reported as follows by friend and fellow poet Carl Rakosi: "I don't know if you have anything to say but let's take out all the adjectives and we'll find out." If I may draw the following parallel, I would say that because Oppen would so bare his poems, one must accept the truth about one's own skills as a reader to be laid bare. This book is in many ways but an attempt to thus meet the poet half-way and "take out" one's critical "adjectives" as well: to learn to shed one's critical illusions down to one's most basic readerly skills. In other words, one cannot argue for interpretive pragmatics and not first present, in sufficient details, what that process would look like—in this case, a prolonged practical case study in prosody.

Looking for examples of how scholars have dealt with texts whose structures have eluded them, because they seemed irredeemably disjunctive, asyntactic, or in any way evasively arranged, one may learn a lot from Brian McHale's analysis of John Ashbery's "The Skaters." Although McHale's focus is on the form of the long-poem, he calls attention to a common critical bias when studying challengingly composed poems:

> Critics, who in this respect (if no other) may be regarded as representative readers, tend to proceed by selecting 'key' lines or passages, treating these as interpretative centers or 'nodes' around which to organize the heterogeneous materials of the poem. (McHale 2000, 566)

Recreating these "nodes" becomes a way of injecting salience back into the poem, now that rhythmic prominence, no longer easily assignable, has stopped pointing the reader in the right direction. Naturally, fixed-form poems can be enigmatic as well, but the hermeneutic sleight of hand that McHale insists is taking place deserves careful consideration. In the absence of rhetorical and rhythmic tools capable of accounting for the scattered free verse poem, one is tempted to do just what McHale describes and pursue ready-made interpretive nodes. Going back to "Song, The Winds of Downhill," it seems obvious that one can pick up on the themes of poverty and renewal and then extract adequately gnomic bits of wisdom ready to be turned into catchphrases. My own choice of "that common // wealth // of parlance" as title and topic certainly makes me guilty of that same very bad habit. The problem with that habit is twofold. Instead of accounting for the text as a whole, one decomposes it even more, and what lies around these meaningful clusters tends to be treated as non-meaningful. As McHale further remarks:

> Other materials come to be subordinated in various ways (explicitly or, more often, implicitly) to these "key" passages, for instance as exempla or illustrations, or as figurative or allegorical restatements—that is, as metonymically or metaphorically related to the "nodal" material. Alternatively, material lying outside the "nodes" is simply passed over in silence, so that the poem is reduced, in effect, to a skeletal structure of points that yield most readily to a particular interpretative orientation, the rest having disappeared, like the soft tissue in an X-ray image. (McHale 2000, 566)

In the case of "Song, The Winds of Downhill," my selection of "that common // wealth // of parlance" as an emblematic statement is then highly objectionable. Oppen's poem does not make rash claims, nor does it issue statements to be obeyed, or its cadence would be fraudulent. The poem must somehow manifest what it is saying, and be an instance of parlance as a form of common wealth—but how does one go about proving it demonstratively? More importantly, how does one argue that, without resorting to the types of devices I have just called into question?

Looking at past examples of such disputes and trying to establish a precedent, it seems that acknowledging there is a type of rhetoric in rhythm outside any metrical mindset has often meant invoking the tradition of biblical verse, especially in times of prosodic unrest. Understanding rhythm as rhetoric, locating rhetoric within rhythm, is already what Blake does, in the name of the presumed formal qualities of the Bible:

> One important precedent for Blake was biblical verse, which relies on syntactic and semantic parallelism—that is to say, the lines are determined by their internal structure as meaningful units, not by a metrical scheme. (Attridge 1995, 169)

Attridge immediately goes on to say that "Blake, however, frequently used run-on lines to counter the somewhat static and cumulative effects of a meter based on parallelism" (Attridge 1995, 169). Blake's poetry may be metrical, Attridge's phrase "a meter based on parallelism," right after having commented on Blake's choice to use "syntactic and semantic parallelism" and *not* metrical schemes, suggests that parallelism is in the end nothing but a type, albeit an exotic one, of metrical poetry. That may very well be the case, yet the many attempts to use the Bible as literary credentials, and especially for the purposes of prosodic renewal, should be put into context. Before Blake's "rejection of rhyme and meter" (Cushman 1993, 27), Milton's note on the verse of *Paradise Lost* included in the fourth issue of the first edition, in 1668, attacks "the modern bondage of rhyming" (Milton 2005, 2). In "The Reason of Church Government" as well as in *Paradise Lost* or *Paradise Regain'd*, Milton refers to the Psalms as a higher form of poetry, especially superior to ancient Greek poetry (Kugel 1981, 225–226). Blake would distance himself from Milton in his address to the public in *Jerusalem*, calling Milton and Shakespeare's blank verse "as much a bondage as rhyme itself" (Blake 1979, 313), praising instead his own choice of producing "a variety in every line, both of cadences & number of syllables" (Blake 1979, 313). However, both used the Bible as a yardstick with which to measure their intended prosodic revolutions. The Bible has undoubtedly often served as an instrument of legitimation on a technical level—playing the Hebrew Bible against Latin or Greek templates—as well as in terms of authorship—sanctioning the secular poet's divine inspiration or talent—and each of these poets' positions require more careful examination than could be provided here. As Stephen Cushman notices, Walt Whitman's free verse looked to the Bible "for authority and inspiration" (Cushman 1993, 27) in similar fashion. In his recent study, *On Biblical Poetry* (2015), F. W. Dobbs-Allsopp also explores the connection between free verse and biblical poetic templates by looking at Whitman's prosody. A *Technician of the Sacred* in his own right, to put it in Jerome Rothenberg's words, Whitman's search for "primeval times" (Whitman 1982, 1139) and his hope of unifying "the oldest and newest Asiatic utterance and character," "this America of ours" and the Bible, derive from his belief that "[e]ven to our nineteenth century here are the fountain heads of song" (Whitman 1982, 1142–1143). Greater formal freedom, greater authenticity, greater universality, the list of the reasons why one would turn to the Bible as poetry could go on. Yet as Kugel has pointed out, one often does not know what that "as" implies (Kugel 1981b, 217):

> The whole history of attempts to find the 'meter' of the Psalms, or indeed to assign to them any organizing structure at all, are essentially a projection of our own literary expectations of poetry onto those parts of the Bible we label poetry. (Kugel 1981b, 226)

Notwithstanding the fact that Whitman was aware the Hebrew Bible did not rely on features such as rhyme or meter, as he puts it in "The Bible as Poetry," and despite his use of the Bible as counter-model, Whitman "never connects his own rejection of rhyme and meter directly with Hebrew poetry" (Cushman 1993, 27). Since "[t]here is no word for "poetry" in biblical Hebrew" (Kugel 1981, 69), one could conclude Whitman was right, and bring this discussion to a close. Surely, the hermeneutics of twentieth century American poetry and the study of biblical texts make strange bedfellows. But consider, first, the fact that twentieth century American poets have been highly involved in the exploration of expressly different types of textuality, both non-Western and pre-modern, as well as in methodologies for handling textual documents borrowed from explicitly non-literary scientific perspectives—history, anthropology, philology, archeology, among others. Secondly, bear in mind that when faced with an apparently loosely composed, if not almost patternless poetical text, one finds oneself in a situation not unlike that of any modern Western reader confronted with ancient biblical texts. Elusive linearity and pervasive parataxis are common characteristics in both instances, in terms of a reader's initial puzzlement. Curiosity alone would be motivation enough to go and compare each other's methods and techniques when tackling such a fundamental and recurrent feature. Armand Schwerner's *Tablets* are a case in point. Still, Oppen's reaction to Schwerner's archeological poetics showed he did not share Schwerner's humor in decomposing language, nor did he seem to have felt very concerned with ethnopoetics. As he wrote to Jerome Rothenberg in 1968, "I suspect we've become for good and all a loose set of Adams and Eves and incapable of Shamanism" (SL 180). The popular "Longinian assumption that the Pentateuch's sublimity makes it 'poetic' without it having to conform to the conventional structures of verse" (Prickett 1986, 41) unites the language of creation and the creations of language in a common *poiesis*—a term whose etymological backing hides many of its historically constructed assumptions—and many poets since have turned to biblical verse as a wealth of common parlance, both on a practical level in terms of shared textual history, and figuratively, as being prototypically "poetic" in the sense that words partake of the world's creation and celebration—but not Oppen.

Despite Oppen's clear secularism, some attempts have been made to read his poetry against the background of Jewish textuality (Kimmelman 2009) and Jewish thought. Mysticism will often, ever so surreptitiously, come in to validate formalist doctrines that have little bearing on Rabbinic practice. Namely, opposing Christian and Jewish approaches based on 2 Corinthian 3: 6, "the letter killeth, but the spirit giveth life," results in the absurd contradiction that splits both sides into allegorists and literalists (Jeffrey 1996, xvi). The polemical divide is all the more irrelevant since a supposed Jewish fascination for the materiality of linguistic signs would precisely be considered idolatrous by that hermeneutic tradition. As for modernist or post-modernist open-endedness, David Stern has shown for instance that "multiple interpretation in midrash bears little connection to the notion of indeterminacy," although he also stresses that "indeterminacy may still remain a significant category for understanding our own reading of midrashic discourse" (Stern 1988, 135). His own *Midrash and Theory: Ancient Jewish Exegesis and Contemporary Literary Studies* (1998), or Geoffrey H. Hartman's and Sanford Budick's *Midrash and Literature* (1986), contain many incentives not to rush to simplistic conclusions on these matters. What I am about to suggest is thus quite different from a concealed theological or philo-Semitic reading of Oppen. My only concern here is with biblical verse as a prosodic model. Mine is a practical and technical hypothesis, in which I suggest that prosodic research can learn from the historical study of compositional techniques.

As I have been insisting so far, there may be such a thing as syntactic, semantic, and rhythmical recurrence or form without meter, and not as a new meter. Although he was not without predecessors (Meynet 1998), Robert Lowth's groundbreaking *Lectures on the Sacred Poetry of the Hebrews*, delivered in 1741 as his Oxford Poetry Lectures, then published in Latin in 1753 and English in 1787 (Prickett 1986, 41), began in the exact opposite direction. Lowth's aim was to "integrate the Bible into the same world of aesthetic standards occupied by the Greek and Roman classics" (Kugel 1981, 274), without using Greek and Roman standards to understand what he viewed as a distinctively different biblical style. Indeed, Lowth's influence on the English and German Romantics revolved chiefly around "a confused and often inchoate, but amazingly dynamic, group of ideas centering around the notion of the 'poetic'" (Prickett 1986, 242). Lowth investigated the structure of Hebrew biblical texts and specifically the notion of *parallelismus membrorum*, or parallelism of the members—a correspondence from segment to segment that induces balance—to show that although the meter of Hebrew poetry had been lost, as Lowth assumed it had been, "evidence of its presence" (Kugel 1981, 74) was noticeable in the periods and verses "*delineated by parallelism*" (Kugel 1981, 74). Today, Lowth is known for his "discovery" of parallelism, yet one should bear in mind that to Lowth, it was the "substitute meter" (Kugel 1981, 74) which he could then derive from this pattern that concerned him the most, not necessarily the chiastic structures he studied themselves.

However decisive parallelism could have been in freeing poetry from the very need for meter, it only confirmed how central the role of meter remained, particularly when securing regularity within a system whose defining feature was its sublime chaos (Kugel 1981, 279). Apparent disorder could not be considered on its own terms, but as a sign of poetic license checked by the ghost of isochrony, lying deep in its bosom, secretly ensuring that the method to this madness was not too unfamiliar. On the other hand, parallelism would grow to embody the most distinctively poetic feature of language. After a quotation from Gerard Manley Hopkins on the inescapability of the "principle of parallelism" dating back to "Hebrew poetry," Roman Jakobson begins his assessment of "grammatical parallelism" using "the suggestive etymology of the terms PROSE and VERSE—the former, *oratio prosa* < *prorsa* < *proversa* 'speech turned straightforward,' and the latter, *versus*, 'return.' Hence we must consistently draw all inferences from the obvious fact that on every level of language the essence of poetic artifice consists in recurrent returns" (Jakobson 1966, 399). The metrical assumptions in the phrase "recurrent returns" as well as, avowedly, in Lowth's notion of parallelism, reveal a common metrical bias. Fortunately, the idea of parallelism—originally a metrically derived literary notion—has since grown into a proper rhetorical investigative tool for biblical exegesis.

Putting it ever so succinctly, one may say that classical Greek and Latin models of rhetorical analysis have, over the past three centuries, gradually been refined so that one can more accurately explore the texts of the Bible, as well as the Qur'an and other antique Middle-Eastern texts—Ugaritic, Akkadian, and Pharaonic. Under the general heading of Semitic rhetoric—Semitic in the large linguistic meaning of the word—this method of composition has been more and more widely acknowledged, because of its relevance in dealing with major sacred texts, and since it was "systematized and theorized by Roland Meynet" (Cuypers 2010, 8), thus providing a compelling array of techniques. As Michel Cuypers remarks, Semitic rhetoric differs from Greek concerns for continuity and "progressive development" in that it relies on "the principle of symmetry" (Cuypers 2010, 8). Summarizing Meynet's findings, he writes:

> The symmetry, in Semitic rhetoric, can take three forms or "figures of composition": "parallelism", when related textual units reappear in the same order (ABC//A'B'C'); the "mirror composition" (or chiasmus or inverted parallelism), when related units reappear in inverted order (ABC//C'B'A'); "concentric composition" (or "ring composition"), when a center connects the opposite sides of an inverted parallelism (ABC/X/C'B'A'). (Cuypers 2010, 9)

As Meynet cautions in the introduction to his *Treatise on Biblical Rhetoric* (2012), Semitic rhetoric should not drift away into stylistics, nor become a pretext for anachronistic readings of Greek and Latin forms back into biblical texts. Neither is it a purely genetic approach to the scriptures as historical documents. Biblical rhetoric is the study of the rules that govern the formation of biblical texts. The essential characteristics of biblical rhetoric, Meynet demonstrates, are that "*it is more concrete than abstract, it uses parataxis more than syntax, it is more involutive than linear*" (Meynet 1988, 173)—syntax here referring to subordination, against coordination or juxtaposition. Because I cannot do justice to the level of scrutiny and the wealth of observations upon which Meynet builds his study, I will simply focus on one of the most illuminating features he discusses, that of concentric constructions. Sometimes referred to as "ring composition"—as in Mary Douglas' useful anthropological survey *Thinking in Circles: An Essay on Ring Composition* (2007)—it is a revealing example of what biblical rhetoric might teach the literary critic, in that previously inscrutable parables or enigmas, once understood through this prism, become eminently readable. Such a project allows one to reach another level of analysis, beyond the blind sampling of gnomic elements when faced with enigmatic constructs. Meynet observes:

> [...] rhetorical analysis resides in finding procedures which will enable the cutting up, in a more scientific or at least more objective manner, of the text in its diverse units and to determine the function of each of those units in the whole. These procedures give exegesis the means to sharpen the capital notion of context: for example the context of a pericope is not necessarily the pericope, or pericopes, which precedes or follows it, but the whole of the units which constitute the superior units to the envisaged pericope [...] (Meynet 1998, 181).

Only when context is the chief concern, does the search for these "focal points" avoid rehearsing the quest for statements or pericopes—sections or subsections of a religious text—which promise immediate interpretive command from privileged vantage points, to the detriment of textual cohesiveness. Cohesiveness, rhetorically speaking, pertains to argumentation, not in a linear "Graeco-Roman fashion," leading up to "a conclusion which is the point of resolution of the discourse," but "organized most of the time in an involutive manner around a centre which is the focal point, the keystone, through which the rest finds cohesion" (Meynet 1998, 175). Surprisingly enough, McHale's comments about Ashbery's poem seem echoed here:

> By isolating small units, the formalist school has been greatly helpful; but by keeping those separate, it has done little to promote the understanding of the wholes made up by those units. It has not taught us to "read things correspondingly." So that our exegesis still suffers from a sort of psychosis, the most obvious symptom of which is the scattering of the body of the text. (Meynet and Bovati 1995, 97)

Meynet's argument, that the *Proverbs* were composed, rather than, as it had long been believed, only compiled, begins with the wish that commentaries would "venture beyond the study of the pericope" (Bovati and Meynet 1995, 97), that is beyond the interpretive clusters discussed earlier. Consider the following example, which helps one visualize the process:

> [...] in both cases we have concentric constructions, since they are focused on one single element. In the following example:
>
> *I will praise you* among the peoples, Adonai,
> *I will proclaim you* among the nations – Ps 57:10
>
> One might say that the vocative "Adonai," with which the first member ends, is omitted in the second [...]. At all events, it occupies the centre of the construction and the segment could therefore be rewritten as follows:
>
> —*I will praise you* among the peoples,
> ADONAI,
> —*I will proclaim you* among the nations (Meynet 2012 164)

As another example, here is a passage from Amos 2:4, in which I have drawn attention to the segments used in Meynet's analysis, in a slightly different translation than the King James, as follows:

> Thus saith the Lord; For three transgressions of Judah, and for four, I will not turn away the punishment thereof; *because they have despised* the law **of the Lord**, and *have not kept* his commandments, and their lies caused them to err, after the which their fathers have walked.

Meynet offers this reading of a "more pronounced" concentric composition, "according to the plan ab | x | b'a'":

:: Because *they-have-rejected*
—the Law
of YHWH
—and-his-decree
:: *they-have-not-kept* (Meynet 2012, 165)

What is striking in Meynet's presentation of the architecture of these texts is that what has so often been rewritten, in translation, as prose, suddenly appears on the page as would-be poetry due to the specific kind of spacing used to illustrate the construction. Although Meynet's spacing does not have a rhythmical purpose, and Meynet speaks of rhetoric in a manner which sets rhythmic elements aside, as nonsemantic, the geometric resources of Semitic rhetoric in this respect point to a form of cognitive rhythm. Semitic rhetoric—parallelism, mirror composition and especially concentric construction—shows that paratactic, non-linear texts need not be subsumed under linear categories before they can make sense. The method itself is by no means an overreaching one: symmetries are often only partial, and forcing a systemic model onto poetic texts in the name of Semitic rhetoric could not be further from my very practical goals. However, when one adapts these findings to the study of poetry, they do suggest that the structures of a-syntactical texts are worthy of dedicated interpretive procedures.

Before applying some of the rhetorical techniques analyzed by biblical scholars to Oppen's "Song, The Winds of Downhill" (NCP 220), I should clarify that I will not use the same wealth of descriptive instruments—and differentiate between member, segment, piece, part, passage, sequence, or section—when partitioning the text. This might invite distrust, since these tools guarantee much of the methodological accuracy in the approach in question. I chose not to for two reasons: one, these terms were devised to differentiate among the details of an otherwise continuous, sometimes opaque, homogenous compact text, while Oppen's late poems are both already scattered to great extremes, and recognizably delineated as poems. Hence the second reason: since lineation no longer answers for linearity, the problem becomes one of understanding how meaningful the text's composition may be through decisive reconnecting. I have therefore considered it sufficiently convincing to present the reader with an architectural representation of the poem's rhetorical framework, which would certainly have to be further refined. I must also point out that I will sometimes combine structures, which Meynet studies as separate, such as concentric or specular constructions.

To illustrate how productive such a nonlinear approach may be, I propose to read "Song, The Winds of Downhill" as an AB/A'B'/A"B" construction, in which each pair is composed as a paradox:

A	B
'out of poverty to begin again' impoverished of tone of pose	/ that common wealth of parlance Who
A'	**B'**
so poor the words *would with and*	/ take on substantial meaning handholds footholds' to dig in one's heels
A"	**B"**
/ sliding hands and heels beyond the residential lots the plots	/ it is a poem which may be sung may well be sung

Schematically, the structure reveals the following progression. The first two sets of pairs seem quite similar: A and A' point to poverty, destitution, want; B and B' evoke wealth, substance, hold. Each antithetical attribute is translated into its opposite. In the last pair, A" revolves around loss—digging in fails and ends in uprootedness. B" brings pride and consolation—the achievement is asserted, yet its uncertainties are acknowledged. Every time, the transition from A to B takes place through a kind of inline enjambment, as though the line broke off before the line break, and is marked here with the symbol /. Reading the poem this way certainly dismisses any potential looseness attached to what previously might have been seen as an evasive composition.

Should one care to move further into the detail of the poem, one might also suggest a reading, which would combine the three levels of rhetorical analysis already laid out: parallelism, mirroring, and concentric construction. In doing so, I use the notion of parallelism again, yet in a slightly altered sense, restricting it to the level of the sentence, although it may be quite improper to speak of sentences in this poem—statements rather. I do so after Kugel's analyses of biblical paradoxes, to show how apparently unrelated statements complement each other. Among Kugel's revealing examples, here is the following from Ecclesiastes 7: 1: "Better a good name than good oil / and the day of death than the day of birth" (Kugel 1981, 10). As Kugel observes, "reputation" versus "material possession" sounds like a reasonable alternative, yet the second half baffles the mind, as birth would immediately seem preferable to death. The conceit rests upon implicit associations: good oil, like a newborn, belong to the realm of tangible, physical and perishable or precarious realities (connections including the use of oil on babies, and their initial namelessness), while someone's name precisely does not die but retains its value as reputation, upon one's death (Kugel 1981, 10). Parallelism then describes, in this sense, previously unacknowledged related units. As for mirror composition and concentric composition, the mapping out of the poem I propose uses these notions unchanged, although together.

Understanding the poem "Songs, The Winds of Downhill" as a concentric construction, I propose to consider the lines "that common / wealth // of parlance Who" as the central statement in the poem around which all else revolves, according to an AB | X | B'A' model, where X marks that central statement, in small capitals below. AA' and BB' respectively illustrate parallelisms and mirror compositions. From A to B, and from A' to B', these facing words build up powerful parallels. From A to B', and from B to A', these diagonally opposed clusters are each inverted pictures of themselves. The final parallel is incomplete, as A" receives no obvious complementation. Such instances are not uncommon in biblical rhetoric, and the discussion will show how this occurrence fits the general dynamic.

A   B
'out of poverty   take on substantial
to begin
          meaning   handholds   footholds
again'   impoverished
          to dig in one's heels
of tone of pose
          that common
wealth
of parlance   Who
A'   B'
so poor the words   it is a poem
would   with   and   which may be sung
          may well be sung
A"
sliding   ———
hands and heels beyond the residential   ———
lots   the plots   ———

The central notion in the poem seems to be that poverty is where the poem's song originates, outside of any tone or pose and counting on usually discarded function words. Offering new modalities, new relations, new combinations—a direct commentary on the three words "would," "with," "and"—the subjunctive of "will" indicates prospection, while the preposition "with" and the conjunction "and" may suggest the need to organize and come together. Yet the linguistic-social allegory proves dissatisfactory, for it reduces the poem to that: a transparent symbolic representation, complete with autobiographical hints in the mention of new beginnings. More is at stake, if one looks at the tension in the poem between poverty and wealth, and its apparent resolution in a paradoxical "wealth" which qualifies the proposed poverty as, desirably, as shared resource.

The center of the poem, as I read it, is "that common / wealth // of parlance Who." "Parlance" as idiom contrasts the "wealth" of a language's many specific uses and users with language as "wealth," as symbolic indicator of wealth within a class society, and that contrast is doubled by the two meanings of "common," shared alike as well as undistinguished. Poverty then figures prominently within that statement of one's common wealth. I have kept the pronoun "Who" in the line because without it, the dynamic of the entire poem would, I believe, be lost. "Who" comes in to break into the statement being made and both restricts its scope and takes up the advice it contains. The pronoun interrogates this assumed commonality, in search of a particular instance. Using "Who" and not "which" repeats the specificity of "parlance": language as it is actually spoken by people who will speak to each other, not as an abstract reality—linguistic community, or linguistic competence. "Who" also suggests the answer "me," the poet, as an eminent representative of the linguistic community, although the next line in the poem, "so poor the words," challenges poetic authority.

This reflects on the modulations of the song promised in the end. Its inflections will be decisively dis-posed in a-tonal fashion. In fact, "out of poverty" is phonemically where the song initiates: the poem's harmonies are entirely made up of a distribution of dentals and plosives (voiceless and voiced) around various realizations of the vowel "o": *o*u*t* - *po*ver*ty* - *to b*egin - im*po*verishe*d* - *to*ne - *po*se - comm*o*n - *p*arlance - Wh*o* - s*o* - *poo*r - wor*d*s - wo*uld* - wi*th* - an*d* - *t*ake - *o*n - su*b*-s*t*antial - han*d*hol*d*s - foo*t*hol*d*s - *d*ig - *o*ne's - sli*d*ing - han*d*s -an*d* - *b*eyon*d* - resi-*d*ential - l*o*ts - the *plot*s - i*t* - *po*em - *b*e - *b*e. Now going step by step, the first set of parallelisms combine origin and result into a single mirror effect:

A	B
'out of poverty	take on substantial
to begin	
	meaning handholds
footholds	
again' impoverished	
	to dig in one's heels
of tone of pose	

Because of poverty, meaning is again possible—a meaning which itself is "poor" because it is basic, fragile even, in its recurrent beginning. "Handholds" and "footholds" take up the structure "out of poverty," and explicit the extraction that takes place: poverty becomes a lever for meaning, in the form of one's hold or grasp. The same connection may be established between repeated impoverishment and securing one's position, with a further clarification: while poverty might be assimilated with notions of loss, digging in evokes a resilience that may counter deprivation as well as be revealed by it—underlined in the phonemic proximity between "to begin" and "to dig in." In the process, handholds and footholds bring the poem to ground level. Implicit images of callous hands and feet may not necessarily spring to mind, yet the insistence on rhyming extremities (uttermost parts of the body and extreme limits) is noticeable. The hands and feet motif extends into the list of three poor words immediately afterwards in the poem, as the very supports of the body of the text. If read continuously, the sequence "*would with and*" might even be said to transliterate as "*would withstand.*" The second set of parallelisms prolongs the first:

A'	B'
so poor the words	it is a poem
would with and	which may be sung may well be sung

While poverty was first directly recompensed, here the focus is rather on the effects of the deprivation, with a view to contrast what is deemed absent with what still stands, coloring the lack with a sense of pride regained. The words at one's disposal may be so poor that what they would do or say, what with, and in the hope of adding what, cannot be put into words, which explains the blanks between them. The conditionality expressed in "would" points to desires that are out of reach, echoing the poor conditions at hand: "with"—blank—"and"—blank. On the other hand, if one accepts the inverted image as one of enriching poverty, of a restoration through dispossession, then these three words are perfectly self-sufficient. Linguistically, they figure the handholds and footholds of speech, the very nimble, wrist or ankle-like articulations of meaning. The alliterative assonance in "poor" and "poem" helps compose the poem's conclusion, contained in the crucially placed "well" in the last line. The word refers back to "wealth" and engages the notion again, through the prism of craftsmanship, against other songs the poem's title may suggest: Shelley's "Ode to the West Wind," the "Western Wind" poem Oppen loved so, or Charles Simic's poem in *White* (1972) which begins with the lines Oppen quotes in this poem (NCP 396). Well, in this case, contrasts with how "poor" the song's choices might seem to some. Regarding the last element, this final slipping away may very well be intended, in circular fashion, to send the reader back to the beginning of the poem:

A"

sliding ————

hands and heels beyond the residential ————

lots the plots ————

As if it were a form of self-comment, or embedded illustration of the poem's discourse, these lines invite the poem to begin again "out of poverty," both through poverty and as a way out of it. The newly found "handholds" and "footholds" are not endowed with permanence: without the comforts of "tone" or "pose," one is "sliding" or falling "beyond" any sense of belonging, any sense of residence. Yet that whirling sensation, far from contradicting the previous digging in, stimulates it. Reeling, one must look again for the handholds and footholds, which hold the promise of substance. This is where the chiastic structure becomes so important:

A	**B'**
'out of poverty	it is a poem
to begin	
again' impoverished	which may be sung
	may well be sung
of tone of pose	

Here comes the "Who" question again: the poem asks who will sing that song, who will recognize this as song (as the presence of the word song in the title already suggests). In the end, this may be how poor the poem is: not unfinished, but reduced to such extremes that it does not appear to the reader as a set composition, and only as the possibility of one. As I have attempted to show, this supposes another type of composition altogether. As with the previous parallel disposition, the connection from A' to B may be understood as conclusion or commentary:

A'	**B**
so poor the words	take on substantial
would *with* *and*	meaning handholds footholds
	to dig in one's heels

These poor words are where meaning is located, where and how one may get hold of substantial meaning. In this configuration, I would insist on the overall chiasmus: poverty / poem (with the implicit paronomasia in poverty-poetry), and now meaning / words. At the center of the chiasmus, "that common / wealth // of parlance" brings cohesion to the whole, while giving urgency to the statement in the interrogative "Who" at the line's edge, as an address to whoever, "sliding beyond" in the incomplete last member A", might find a way "out of poverty / again" into that "common / wealth."

One example alone being insufficiently representative, one must look further into Oppen's late poetry to illustrate similar rhetorical traits. In Oppen's "Confession" for instance, many recurrent threads, images and terms, make for a relatively easier text to map out:

> 'neither childhood
> nor future
>
> are growing less' guilts   guilts
> pour in
>
> to memory things leak I am an old ship
> and leaky   oceans
>
> in the bilges ordinary
>
> oceans in the bilges I come to know it is so guilts
> guilts
>
> failures in the creaking
> timbers but to have touched
> foundations keelson the cellars
> as all this becomes strange
>
> enough
> I come to know it is home a groping
>
> down a going
> down middle-voice the burgeoning
>
> desolate   magic   the dark
> grain
>
> of sand and eternity (NCP 258)

The first three lines are a quotation from some of the last words in the ninth of Rilke's *Duino Elegies*: "Weder Kindheit noch Zukunft / werden weniger" (Rilke

2009, 306) which might translate literally as "Neither childhood nor future / will lessen," grow less or diminish. Oppen is presumably using the Leishman and Spender classic translation from the thirties, put out by Hogarth Press, which uses the form "are growing" when others have since preferred variations. The quotation is especially interesting in that Oppen stops before the last line in the elegy: "Überzähliges Dasein / entspringt mir im Herzens," again literally "Supernumerous existence springs up in my heart." Instead of picking up on these words, which strongly remind one of Oppen's title poem, "Of Being Numerous," he breaks off and introduces the theme of guilt. The interruption itself might suggest a reading of "less" as the conjunction "lest," as though the lines were "lest guilts guilts / pour in // to memory," as if no future growth were possible without, or for fear that one would forget that guilt. Such a reading is confirmed as the promising association of "childhood" and "future" in the first lines of the poem repeats itself in the series of antitheses at the end, "the burgeoning // desolate," "the dark / grain," culminating in that last word "eternity"—eternal life as much as the end of life. The final "sand and eternity" rewrites Blake's lines from "Auguries of Innocence" with dust-like sand as an image of eternity—uncannily close to the title of Paul Celan's first collection *Sand from the Urns* (1948)—in connection with Oppen's sense of childhood taking place by the sea (SL 238, 251). Grain of sand or burgeoning seed in the dark, the "magic" growth is sustained despite the desolation and the guilt so pervasive in that poem. On the other hand, the growth requires that one go through and experience the guilt, for Rilke's "spring up" has become Oppen's "going down." The repeated pairing of the word "guilts," immediately followed by the image of a leaky "old ship" or "creaking / timbers" prepares for the downward motion in the poem, shipwrecked or ship-wracked with guilt.

A more ambiguous parallel connects the two passages that evoke the drowning of the ship. The word "bilges" and the phrase "foundations keelson the cellars" answer each other across the opposition between "ordinary // oceans" and "all this is strange / enough." Heller notes that Oppen's confession is "tonally so closely connected with aging and death that it is almost an overhearing similar to those extreme moments of near death during the war when scraps of remembered poetry would come to him" (Heller 2012, 73). It opens with scraps from Rilke and as an assertion of the poet's own voice, it is built around Oppen's skillful ocean-readiness against the engulfing strangeness that surrounds him, which almost causes the reader to add an exclamation mark after "enough." As for the final quasi-rhyming statements, "I come to know it is so" and "I come to know it is home," the implication seems to be that the time when death approaches and near death moments combine in the poem's sense of estrangement, as Heller noticed. All these elements may be singled out, and their connections suggested, in the following arrangement of the poem, in which each parallel is separated by a series of dashes, and the central statement is in small capitals. Because the similarities are so striking, I have refrained from drawing unnecessary extra attention to them using additional emphasis such as specific fonts:

'neither childhood
nor future

are growing less'

the burgeoning

desolate magic the dark
grain

of sand and eternity

---

guilts
guilts
pour in

to memory things leak I am an old ship
and leaky

guilts

guilts

failures in the creaking
timbers

---

a groping

down a going
down middle-voice

---

oceans
in the bilges ordinary

oceans in the bilges
strange

but to have touched

foundations keelson the cellars
as all this becomes

enough

I come to know it is so

I come to know it is home

My next example is Oppen's "Disasters" from *Primitive* (NCP 267–269). Since I shall quote extensively from the poem when sketching its rhetorical outline, and because the poem takes up three pages in the *New Collected*, I shall not reproduce the poem below. I have chosen this poem for its intricate structure and because of its many embedded references or sources, which, although they have received previous comment, have tended to be dealt with separately. To repeat the observation put forth by Berry: "Oppen's grammetrical form enables the poems to deconstruct their own statements; the resistance offered by the form to a reader's attempts to reduce them to single meanings is the nature of its difficulty" (Berry 1984, 319). This poem's apparent disconnections seem to make it an ideal candidate for indeterminacy. But this tangled poem reassembles into a coherent structure, if the reader will follow the cues given in the four statements in italic: "*it is dreary / to descend // and be a stranger*"; "*we wanted to know // if we were any good // out there*"; "*the five // bright elements*"; "*O // O I see my love I see her go // over the ice alone.*" The gradual estrangement of age, youth's desire to test its own value, the world's sharp dazzling outlines, tragic loss: all these fragments do seem to beg for integration within some form of narrative, some delineated, if not linear, progression. Yet based on these elements alone, the effort would dangerously discard the poem's already existing progression, which is built on three, not four, key moments. The first two pivotal pronouncements seem closely interrelated within one single movement, until the explicit line, "the song / changes." The poem subsequently demonstrates relative unity until the question "can they [...] dance?" The last movement then returns to the initial "disorder," this time colored with biblical allusions. The connection between the final "desert" and the introductory "Disasters // of wars" has already been noted, and argues for the poem's overall cohesion.

Shirley Kaufman's account of the poem's composition provides useful information in this respect. She reads lines 7 to 9, that describe a descent, as a reference to the Oppens' trip to Israel, when they "descended from the airplane in Israel in September 1975," and Oppen's "sister" and "love" going "over the ice alone" as pointing to Abba Kovner's *My Little Sister*. Kaufman writes: "In Kovner's poem the sister, a child placed in a Dominican Convent during a winter storm, to save her life while the Jewish community outside the convent is destroyed, becomes an allegorical figure in the end, the sister of all Jews" (Kaufman 1985, 152). Oppen's "my lost / sister" may also be said to relate to his older sister Elisabeth, who had died upon the Oppens' permanent return to the United States in 1960—a death which Oppen is reported to have assumed was a suicide (SL xviii). As for the "young / brother," whom Oppen did not have, it may pertain to his young brothers in arms lost during the war. The "caves of the hidden / people" have been identified, possibly, with "the caves in the Judean desert where the Essenes lived the monastic life during the decline of the Hasmonean kingdom, and where the Dead Sea Scrolls were discovered. (We walked with Mary and George through these excavations on a plateau rising above the Dead Sea)" (Kaufman 1985, 154), though Kaufman also believes these could be an echo of Oppen's war memories of the foxhole. John Taggart also traces these lines back to Kovner's poem (Taggart 1998, 65). The few lines in italic have otherwise all been sourced. Cynthia Anderson, in her presentation of the drafts of "Disasters" in *Ironwood*, points to the "five elements" as originating in *The Religion of the Manichees* (Anderson 1985, 146–7). She also reminds us that the lines "*we wanted to know / if we were any good / out there*" are a rewriting from Sherwood Anderson's "Song of the Soul of Chicago" (Anderson 1985, 146). Taggart provides a possible source for the lines "*it is dreary / to descend // and be a stranger*" which he finds in Hawthorne's *The House of the Seven Gables*, pointing to a poet's need for a loved one. Nicholls, on his part, insists on the "disjunctions" in "Disasters" and other poems of that period ("The Poem" and "The Tongues"), that "destroy the familiar bond between the poet and his words, making them seem to come from outside" (FM 190). Yet what one should make of this puzzle of sources remains to be seen.

Trying to connect all these different threads, one might focus on this increased estrangement and say that the poem thus combines the sense of foreignness that Oppen, as an American Jew, experienced during his trip to Israel, with his aging as a form of descent into a foreign land, contrasted with a backward glance at his life's journey. Upon closer examination, strangeness and rootedness may even be said to go hand in hand, as the poem's time-frame points in several directions at once, superimposing the poet's life and the history of the Jewish people, as spatial and temporal planes become entwined. For if the poet is a stranger in 1975 Israel, the biblical and archeological drive of the poem evoke an awareness of shared origins. Still, this brief summary of the poem's dynamics neglects many other important aspects. Therefore, I now proceed with a methodical rhetorical analysis of this long poem, by Oppen's standards, which I present in three movements. As the lines selected will testify, these movements are not consecutive, but interwoven, although not completely disconnected from the poem's linear development. The first would read:

DISASTERS

// of wars o western   the wind has blown the sand about
wind and storm   and we are alone in light
                                        // and wind
                                        and fire and water and air *the five*
                                        // bright elements
                              the sea dawns
in the sunrise verse with its rough
/ beach-light crystal extreme   the people the salt
sands dazzling under the near   and terrible hills whose armies
and not less brutal feet journey   // have marched

The elemental quality of perceptions is a recurrent feature in *Primitive*, and in "Disasters," the role of the wind seems paramount. A rich matrix grows from this "wind," which disseminates into these four clusters, and retains all through the text a great ambivalence since the wind's brightness is half-destructive and half-celebratory. The alliterations in "wars," "western," and "wind" make this wind into the disastrous "storm" of destruction, which opens the poem, and brings it to a close: it desiccates the text's surface until one reaches the final desert, dries up its people, the salt of the earth, into salt fossils, to be trodden by the feet of soldiers. On the other hand, marching armies are contrasted with the "journey" of one's "feet" as part of the same "near / and not less brutal" history, which is figured, as journeys often are in Oppen, in connection to the sea. Here the beach as threshold is both a place of utter desolation and where one will find the "crystals" (also to be paired with the final salt), those see-through minerals that typically suggest "extreme" brightness and dazzling clarity. The poem's second movement mobilizes a greater number of elements:

o western
wind and storm
of politics

I am sick with a poet's
vanity

the gales
of a poet's vanity

the song
changes

legislators

of the unacknowledged

world

we wanted to know
// if we were any good
// out there

the marvel
// of the obvious and the marvel
of the hidden is there
// in fact a distinction

dance
// of the wasp wings dance as
of the mother-tongues can they
// with all their meanings
// dance?

This layout also underlines several parallels at once. Shelley's presence, both through his "Ode to the West Wind" and his *Defense of Poetry*, which Oppen rewrites here, echoes a hidden reference to a twentieth-century *Sturm und Drang* in the "dance // of the wasp wings," which require a detour through Pound's *Cantos*. Michael Kindellan quotes the following from Oppen's daybooks: "Pound's copiousness, for he knew what he thought The fact ruined much (but when the wasp takes him by surprise - -)! whereas for me the writing of the poem is the process of finding out what I mean, discovering what I mean" (Kindellan). Oppen may well have been thinking of Pound's *Canto* 83, when the ant and the wasp come in (Pound 546–7), after the cricket in *Canto* 77. In fact, the notion of "a poet's / vanity" may well be a reference to Pound's *Canto* 80, "Pull down thy vanity, I say pull down. / Learn of the green world what can be thy place / In scalded invention or true artistry, / Pull down thy vanity" (Pound 1991, 535), now thrown back at Pound. The *Pisan Cantos* themselves are an occasion for the poet to reflect upon the winds of war from his seclusion. Oppen may then be asking if Pound succeeded in making all the "mother-tongues" dance in his polyglot song—the wasp in *Canto* 80 is referred to as "Madame La Vespa." Oppen seems to find a common denominator between early the nineteenth century and the 1930s "storm // of politics" in the form of "the gales // of a poet's vanity." But Oppen states that the "song / changes." Rejecting the poet's literary, political or social distinction derived from a belief in some distinction between "the obvious" and "the hidden," Oppen turns to the marvel of the "unacknowledged world."

As with the previous reconstruction, the central statement directs the reader's attention toward an elemental verification: "out there," one will encounter the wind. The conflict in the previous movement between horror and awe gets repeated here as tension between deceit and truthfulness, with deceit as the mask of horror and truthfulness as the path to awe, all under the same homonymic wind: destructive force or revelatory whirlwind, idle talk and natural breath. The last movement, which features two italicized statements, probably requires more scrutiny:

O
// *O I see my love I see her go*
// *over the ice alone* I see

if our story shall end
untold to whom and
// to what are we ancestral

// myself   Sarah   Sarah
[…]   my life

and the caves
of the hidden
people.

in this wind that

// rises like a gift
I see the tent
in the desert

in the disorder

my life
narrows my life
is another I see
him in the desert I watch
him he is clumsy
and alone my young
brother he is my lost
sister her small
voice among the people

it is   dreary
to descend
// and be a stranger   how
shall we descend
// who have become strangers

This distribution means to show how the poem's fall into strangeness rests upon a dual crisis of identity, both a failure to perceive and a failure to be perceived. The incantatory repetitions of "I see" first seem to bring confusion rather than convey a sense of place, combined with growing solitude as child-like siblings and self-image retreat into oblivion. At the other end of the same spectrum, the self fears it will be discontinued as no progeny comes to legitimate it as ancestry. What remains each time is the reference to a "people," which Kaufman proposed was Oppen's allegory of the Jewish people in this poem. The poem's persona may well be said to combine the ancestry to which it turns and the ancestry it wishes were recognized in him. Yet in Oppen's use of the word "people" that identity is far from secure. The poem's "Sarah," assimilated to the poet, possesses a "small / voice among the people," and it is a "hidden / people," so that the poem's previous emphasis on the close relationship between "the hidden" and "the obvious" is now challenged by a "journey / in light" which ends in the shadows of "the caves." Therein lies perhaps the poem's achievement in turning loss into communion. For the loss of the loved one, the sister, one's self, one's neighbor, one's brother, as "my life / narrows" and the "dreary" descent begins, leads to the recovery of oneself in these multiple images, be they images of loss.

Such an interpretation is warranted by the central vision of "the tent / in the desert." It may well refer to Genesis 17–18, when God comes to Abraham and Sarah. It would, given the mention of Sarah, seem an obvious reading. However, this reference occurs within a poem much closer in tone and connotations to the wilderness in Exodus than it is close to Genesis. The time when "my life / narrows" could remind one of Sarah laughing in the tent at God's promise to Abraham that he would have a son, while she is now too old. But Oppen's poem entails no such sense of rejuvenation, rather the fear that ancestry is under threat. If one thinks of the tent in Exodus 33–7, the tent of meeting, then Oppen's poem takes on another color still. That tent is the place where, after Sinai, the revelation continued for Moses. But the tent in Oppen's poem seems devoid of God's presence, and only surrounded by lost children—be they, as in Oppen's "Exodus," the children of Israel. If one reads the poem in a strictly linear way, the storm seems to have left nothing and no one standing, only a few survivors hiding in caves.

At this point, one must remember the wind's "gift / in the disorder," from the beginning of the poem. Knowing the importance of the wind in Oppen's late poetry, especially as the whirlwind from the book of Job, the statement is worth pursuing. If one follows the pattern of the wind through the poem, one will find, in its center, the tent that offers protection from that wind. The poem's many instances of promise and of resilience revolve around that shelter: the wind rising like a gift; the wind blowing the sand about and rushing in the dawn from the sea; the dazzling journey in light and wind, that elemental revelation; the people the wind has dried up into the salt of the earth as well as the crystalline mineral of the real that endures in spite of the wind. In such a reading, the tent is an instance of the marvel of the hidden—only Moses may enter the tent—and the obvious—the Revelation—at once. For rather than a means to comment on Abraham's compromised patriarchy, Oppen's poem constantly reflects the conflicts of prophecy. Once the poet's vanity has been checked, as have been another's dreams of Babel, and one's voice is small—a fragile intimate sisterly and brotherly voice—then all the poem may do is offer its frame to the pervading wind, much like a sail. In studying the poem from this perspective, one realizes how that wind circulates within the text as its very own evasive drive. Not unlike "the air" that is "bare sunlight where must be found / The lyric valuables. From disaster" (NCP 50), as suggested in a previous poem, "From Disaster," the wind in "Disasters" is where to find whatever lyric valuables remain. This is, in the end, the paradox of Oppen's song of the commonplace. Since the poet cannot capitalize on these "valuables, on that "wealth of parlance," it slips through the poem, which must begin out of poverty again and again. In turn, the poem's worth is in the "air," the "wind" that "rise like a gift / in the disorder." Yet, to quote now from "Song, the Winds of Downhill," and as I hope to have demonstrated here, it "may be sung."

The same goes for Oppen's poem "The Book of Job and a Draft of a Poem to Praise the Paths of the Living." Peter Nicholls provides a very thorough analysis of that poem, especially in terms of explaining many of its allusions or references, from the explicit dedication to Mickey Schwerner or the presence of William Carlos Williams, to the role of a painting by Bernard Buffet, a line from Carl Sandburg, or words from Hegel (FM 162–177). Yet as a serial poem, the text's structure and rhetoric as a whole has always been difficult to establish. The poem begins with the direct question, in the first section, "what is the form / to say there is something / to name Goodman Schwerner Chaney" (NCP 240), but does not seem to answer it. The second section conflates name and noun as if one could thus either speak through them, or hear them—the words and the dead: "the words // piled on each other," become "the last words // survivors," and "what shall we say" is answered by the troubling, "sometimes I imagine / they speak" (NCP 242). Section three, under the sign of "Bill" Carlos Williams, deprives one of the resources of the "fancy things" (NCP 242), of art or artfulness. These are no longer a means of contact—a key notion for Williams—for "all that has touched / the man // touches him / again arms and dis- // arms him" (NCP 243). Section four adds another level to this defeat of language: "we suffer" and are at a loss for words, with "the common breath / here at extremity // obsolescent as the breathing / of tribespeople," making Pound's tale of the tribe irrelevant in the absence of any commonplace. Then in section five, while "me," "yourself," "I?" and "this" and "the road" make up a chiasmus-like matrix of dispersion and loss, suddenly "the bell buoy" sounds, "telling // tragedy so wide / spread," "tragedy 'seeking a statement // of an experience of our own'" (NCP 244). This means that the "form / to say" is not to be found in "the words," in "fancy things," in "the common breath," or in the subject, but in what and how "the wind cries" (NCP 244). The sixth and last section explains. Although "we are locked / in ourselves," the paths of the living from the title can be heard, as in the line "tree singing bird note bird rustle we live now" (NCP 245). The focus changes from the need to convey something in words—the need for words to convey meaning—to a kind of listening. One goes from "what shall we say" to "we ring / in the continual bell / the undoubtable bell found music in itself / of itself speaks the word / actual" (NCP 245). The imperative to express becomes a liberating form of attention. Arguably, this might be considered an artificial shift in perspective, for the poet remains in control of the page, if the technical achievement was not so significant. Instead of searching endlessly for the final last word about a "tragedy so wide / spread," as if it could be encompassed and assigned a specific place, one must accept that the "heart breaking / tone row it is not ended / not ended the intervals / blurred ring" (NCP 245–6). With this reversal, wordlessness turns into cadence, while mourning turns to praise, as if both "Job" and "the Living" shared the same endless scale, the unending "tone-row" of "the continual bell." The ringing is produced by the intervals, which means by the composition. Yet contrary to Solomon, who was told exactly how many cubits the temple should be, in any given direction, before "he carved thereon cherubims and palm trees and open flowers: and covered them with gold fitted upon the carved work" (1 Kings 6:35), Oppen counts himself as one of the "wracked monotheists of the weather-side" (NCP 242), and ends his poem on an open "carve // thereon .." (NCP 246). Oppen's phrase, "theologians of the scantlings," suggests as much: the poet as a theologian of the scanty dimensions and measures of the poem as a vessel of its own, built out of a modicum of breadth and breath alike.

References

Anderson, Cynthia. 1985. "Disasters: Versions and Notes." Ironwood 26 13/2: 146–147.

Anderson, Mark M. 1991. "The 'Impossibility of Poetry': Celan and Heidegger in France." *New German Critique* 53: 3–18.

Attridge, Derek. 1995. *Poetic Rhythm: An Introduction*. Cambridge: Cambridge University Press.

Blake, William. 1979. *Blake's Poetry and Designs*. Edited by Mary Lynn Johnson and John E. Grant. New York: W. W. Norton & Company.

Berry, Eleanor. 1984. "Language Made Fluid: The Grammetrics of George Oppen's Recent Poetry." *Contemporary Literature* 25/3: 305–22.

Celan, Paul. 2003. *Die Gedichte. Kommentierte Gesamtausgabe in einem Band*, hrsg. und kommentierte von Barbara Wiedemann. Frankfurt am Main, Suhrkamp.

Cushman, Stephen. 1993. *Fictions of Form in American Poetry*. Princeton, NJ: Princeton University Press.

Cuypers, Michel. 2010. "The Semitic Rhetoric in the Koran and a Pharaonic Paryrus." *US-China Foreign Language* 8/1: 8–13.

Dobbs-Allsopp, F. W. 2015. *On Biblical Poetry*. Oxford: Oxford University Press.

Douglas, Mary. 2007. *Thinking in Circles: An Essay on Ring Composition*. New Haven: Yale University Press.

Hartman, Geoffrey H. and Budick, Sanford, eds. 1986. *Midrash and Literature*. New Haven, CT: Yale University Press.

Heller, Michael. 2012. *Speaking the Estranged. Essays on the Poetry of George Oppen*. Bristol: Shearsman.

Jakobson, Roman. 1966. "Grammatical Parallelism and Its Russian Facet," *Language*, 42/2: 399–429.

Jeffrey, David Lyle. 2013. "Biblical scholarship and literary criticism." In Habib, M. A. R. ed. *The Cambridge History of Literary Criticism Vol. 6, The Nineteenth Century, c. 1830–1914*. Cambridge: Cambridge University Press.

———. 1996. *People of the Book: Christian Identity and Literary Culture*. Grand Rapids, MI: William B. Eerdmans Publishing Company.

Kaufman, Shirley. 1985. "The Obvious and the Hidden: Some Thoughts about 'Disasters'." *Ironwood* 26 13/2: 152–158.

Kimmelman, Burt. 2009. "Tracking the Word: Judaism's Exile and the Writerly Poetics of George Oppen, Armand Schwerner, Michael Heller, and Norman Finkelstein." *Shofar: An Interdisciplinary Journal of Jewish Studies*, 27/3: 30–51.

Kindellan, Michael. "Michael Heller's Speaking the Estranged: Essays on the Work of George Oppen." *All this Strangeness: A Garland for George Oppen*. http://www.bigbridge.org/BB14/OPPEN2.HTM

Kovner, Aba. 1971. *My Little Sister and Selected Poems*. Translated by Shirley Kaufman et al. Harmondsworth: Penguin Books.

Kugel, James L. 1981. *The Idea of Biblical Poetry: Parallelism and Its History*. Baltimore: The Johns Hopkins University Press.

———. 1981. "On the Bible and Literary Criticism." *Prooftexts*, 1/3: 217–236.

Mchale, Brian. 2000. "How (Not) to Read Postmodernist Long Poems: The Case of Ashbery's 'The Skaters.' *Poetics Today*, 21/3: 561–590.

Meynet, Roland et Bovati, Pietro eds. 1995. "*Ouvrir les Écritures*": *Mélanges offerts à Paul Beauchamp*. Paris: Le Cerf.

Meynet, Roland. 2008. *Appelés à la liberté*. Paris: Lethielleux.

———. 1998. *Rhetorical Analysis. An Introduction to Biblical Rhetoric*. Sheffield: Sheffield Academic Press.

———. 2007. *Traité de rhétorique biblique*. Paris: Lethielleux.

———. 2012. *Treatise on Biblical Rhetoric*. Translated by Leo Arnold. Leiden: Koninklijke Brill NY.

———. 2001. *« Tu vois cette femme ? » Parler en paraboles*. Paris: Éd. du Cerf.

Milton, John. 2005. *Paradise Lost*. Edited by Gordon Teskey. New York: W. W. Norton & Co.

Pound, Ezra. 1991. *The Cantos*. New York: New Directions.

Prickett, Stephen. 1986. *Words and The Word: Language, Poetics and Biblical Interpretation*. Cambridge: Cambridge University Press.

Rilke, Rainer Maria. 1960. *Selected Works, II. Poetry*. Translated by J. B. Leishman. London: Hogarth Press.

———. 1977. *Possibility of Being: A Selection of Poems*. Translated by J. B. Leishman. New York: New Directions.

Saenger, Paul. 1997. *Space Between Words: The Origins of Silent Reading*. Stanford, CA: Stanford University Press.

Schwerner, Armand. 1999. *Selected Shorter Poems*. San Diego: Junction Press.

Stern, David. 1988. "Midrash and Indeterminacy." *Critical Inquiry*, 15/1: 132–161.

———. 1996. *Midrash and Theory: Ancient Jewish Exegesis and Contemporary Literary Studies*. Evanston, IL: Northwestern University Press.

Taggart, John. 1998. "Walk Out: Rereading George Oppen." *Chicago Review* 44/2: 29–93.

Whitman, Walt. 1982. *Poetry and Prose*. New York: The Library of America.

CHAPTER FOUR

The Image-Statement

As previous chapters have suggested, to understand prosody as a modality of syntax can decisively improve one's analytical reading of Oppen's poetry, once one has sifted through the many dead ends of metrical analysis. However, many more obstacles need to be overcome before one may hope to gain a clear view of Oppen's achievements, especially due to competing interpretations of Oppen's use of syntax as it relates to vision as much as to cadence. Oppen himself initially seems to have made contradictory remarks in this instance, such as the following:

> I've thought from the beginning that we must make poetry out of the clarity of the human vision—or just let the whole thing go. (SL 38)

> [...] they abandoned the figures of perception for the figures of elocution, of assertion, of syntax (SL 81)

> If one is to move to experience further one needs a syntax, a new syntax A new syntax is a new cadence of disclosure, a new cadence of logic, a new musical cadence A new 'structure of space' (SL 97)

The search for a poetry made "out of the clarity of the human vision" puts great emphasis on perception, while the need for "a new syntax" as an essential condition before one can move further into experience seems to contradict the first remark. However, it is not because, as these three passages suggest, "the figures of perception" and "the figures of [...] syntax" are sometimes opposed by Oppen, that one should jump to the conclusion that what Oppen must have had in mind was no longer human vision, or perception, but forms of revelation and disclosure that turn one's gaze inward. The level of abstraction which syntactical ambiguities will bring to the work, by drawing the reader's attention to the poem's own process of coming into being, may justifiably qualify as a weakening of perception. Like a statement which will be read outside of its full rhetorical context due to its apparent prosodic isolation, a statement's apparently abstract nature, which is really due to syntactic placement, can cause the perception to which it testifies to become secondary to that statement's expected gnomic value.

Moreover, critics have quite logically focused almost exclusively on the level of the line as statement because of Oppen's own insistence on the importance of the statement within the poem, on the poem itself as statement, and indeed on cadence as being fundamentally statement-oriented. The apparent opacity of any given line has convinced critics that these lines should be treated as obstacles to be overcome on the straight road to the poem's meaning, instead of dealing with them as pieces of a puzzle that cannot make sense outside the whole picture. Oppen's syntax, along with his compositional strategies at large, may increase the reader's feeling that the loss of the commonplace irredeemably affects the poem's song. Yet, as we have seen, the poem creates this impression of loss to establish the reality of this peril and to offer an alternative, if one will listen. When studying Oppen's syntax for what it does, rather than what it fails to do, a common song will resonate. But if critics have often failed to acknowledge the need for a rigorous rhetorical and prosodic approach to Oppen's difficult compositions, the reason is not only to be found in the field of prosody. Problems of referentiality, a priori political readings, and various critical slants have made it very difficult to know, or even gain access to, Oppen's sense of perception as a common good. Instead of a shift having taken place at some point, as some have argued, from the object of perception to the conditions of perception, I find this ambivalence to be continuously productive in Oppen.

Essentially, Oppen's images have led critics to narrow the poems down to picturesque "scenic motifs" (TP 199) and, at the same time, to blow them up into a "conceptualization of meaning" (TP 166). Evolved from Blake and Wordsworth, Oppen's "poetic credo" (SL 20), as he put it, exemplifies the problem:

> Behold—not rainbow, which is mist—the full word.
> To see a grain of sand in the world, an hour out of eternity. (SP 127)

As Stephen Cope writes in his notes (SP 259), these are rewritings, namely of the opening lines of Wordsworth's "My heart leaps up when I behold / A rainbow in the sky" (Wordsworth 2004, 417) and of the opening of Blake's "Auguries of Innocence":

> To see a World in a Grain of Sand
> And a Heaven in a Wild Flower:
> Hold Infinity in the palm of your hand
> And Eternity in an hour. (Blake 1979, 209)

The scenery and conceptualizing appear clearly in Wordsworth's and Blake's lines, but not in Oppen's. Dismissing Wordsworth's "rainbow" as an illusionary refraction hiding the actual physical reality of "mist"—which it is, lit up by sunlight—Oppen chooses "the full word" in place of another value-laden and referentially unstable image. Instead of the poem accounting for past perceptions of rainbows or daffodils, thus re-registering one's perception anew, often into an enriched abstraction, Oppen locates conception within a moment of perception that acknowledges its seeing is "fully" dependent on words. Wordsworth's or Blake's lines provide no other sighting but that of a mental vision. Moreover, Blake's lines are inverted: from "a World in a Grain of Sand" to "a grain of sand in the world," one goes from generalization to particularization. As "Eternity in an hour" becomes "an hour out of eternity," a sense of precariousness impairs any aggrandizing of one's situation. It may seem that this is a long way from the idiom-based poetics praised in Oppen's "The Mind's Own Place." But these two lines represent Oppen's position perfectly: when the words from these Romantic or early Romantic lines reappear, they are now bare and verging on the generic, thus overriding the objection as to the poems' supposed excessive use of scenery. On the other hand, they open the poem up to the contrary objection: namely, that the image is not being specific enough, and that it works as a stand-in for a concept. However, no conceptualization of meaning takes place here either. Quoting a more recognizably American modernist line of his—"Street lamps shine on the parked cars" (NCP 179)—from section 26 of "Of Being Numerous," Oppen wrote to John Crawford in 1965, rewriting a slightly altered version of "Rain" from Robert Louis Stevenson's 1905 collection *A Child's Garden of Verses*,

> The rain is raining all around
> It falls on you and me,
> It falls on the umbrella here
> And on the ships at sea

> read on Riverside Drive at the age of 9 from a handbook given to me by my sister Libby. Been trying to say all my life what I recognized then. And I think—by way of a claim to concreteness and having used my own eyes, that the universe is not an abstraction, it cannot be abstracted from anything. (SL 119–120)

Along with the equally rainy lines of the Middle English poem Oppen liked so much as well, "O Western Wind" (SL 147), these lines demonstrate the simplicity and directness of address which Oppen found so precious in Charles Reznikoff's work—namely that very little seems to be said. Oppen's own "Street lamps shine on the parked cars" speaks to this same "claim to concreteness" and use of his own eyes. After Zukofsky's fascination with the dictionary or Frank O'Hara's use of proper names, to quote but two very diverging instances, Oppen's concreteness could seem oddly remote and maybe quite abstract. The implication in "having used my own eyes" is nonetheless that "the universe is not an abstraction"—that no conceptualization can abstract one from it. The context for the line, "Street lamps shine on the parked cars," will show how Oppen maintains a difficult balance between staging percepts and exhibiting concepts, doing neither.

The line appears in the twenty-sixth section in "Of Being Numerous." Before that line, the first part of the section expresses regret that poets are feeling "themselves / The end of a chain," utterly singular and hence incapable of "'Common sense'" (NCP 178). To Oppen, that loss of "the metaphysical sense" (NCP 177) meant disconnection from the facts that make up the social consensus, and the second half of that first part of section 26 names these facts for the "new generation": "the corridors / Of the police" and "the infirmaries" where "Their generation / Wither" (NCP 178). Jailed political activists and wounded soldiers are the two figures conjured up by Oppen, not "to say merely / That poets should not lead their lives / Among poets" (NCP 177). The poet is not pleading for heroic union with the suffering of humanity, but asking how to defend one's single position within a conflicted and numerous world, while the choice between "lead their lives" and "live their lives" underscores Oppen's awareness of the importance and responsibility of personal choice. At the point at which an answer might be anticipated, come the lines "Street lamps shine on the parked cars / Steadily in the clear night" (NCP 179). Then the second half of the section begins, which seems to offer more general considerations. Yet one cannot consider this a form of resolution, for the self-perpetuating "great mineral process" that becomes the explicit topic, however appealingly meditative, remains at a distance, then becomes a threat. The mind's power is said to be "not enough, it is nothing / And does nothing // Against the natural world" (NCP 179). In other words, no conceptualization or abstraction will undo or even mitigate the situation for this generation. The natural world, or "Behemoth, white whale, beast" and in the end the "fatal rock" (NCP 179), sends one back to the facts that have previously been emphasized: "That denial / Of death that paved the cities," the filth of "the pavement" of the "corridors / Of the police," and the place where "the earth is most torn / And the wounds untended and the voices confused" (NCP178). Hard prosaic realities and mythical figures such as Job's Behemoth, Ahab's *Moby Dick* and the "beast" are put on the same level, and equally undermine humanity's future.

As for scenic uplift, the last two stanzas do speak of streets "bright enough, / Fold within fold / Of residence," and of seeing "the pebbles / Of the beach" through water, "flowing / From the ripple, clear / As they have ever been" (NCP 179). Nonetheless, these last two stanzas present only a conjecture, beginning with "O if the streets." The importance of this being a conditional "if" clause cannot be overstated. It is literally the condition upon which the folds may become the ripples, the street the sea and the pavement, the pebbles. One might read these lines as a way out of the network of contradictions in the poem, if only hypothetically, if Oppen's poetry ever pointed toward such escapism. It is the ideal of a see-through vision, down to the clearest singular atomic pebbles in the flow of matter, holding a promise of "residence" that would restore one's sense of "nativeness" (NCP 177) as "The boundaries / Of our distances" recede. I would rather argue that this dizzying conclusion stays out of reach and that what remains for one to hold on to are the two lines, "Street lamps shine on the parked cars / Steadily in the clear night." The assonances in voiceless plosives, the repeated sibilants, and the three echoes in /l/ make it a tighter rhythmical unit than many other lines or two-line clusters in the section. Outside of the last stanza, it is the only other occurrence in the section of Oppen's choice adjective, "clear." Oddly, the line break brings no disruption to the statement's integrity. On the contrary, the position of the adverb "steadily" ensures a certain emphasis on the stability of the picture, as though syntax and perception were perfectly attuned. In fact, the light source and the object are coextensive and aligned in such a way that makes these lines a type of perceptual haven within the section, like perhaps "a grain of sand in the world, an hour out of eternity" (SP 127)—a statement that remains intact. In other words, Oppen's images should not be considered as pictures or concepts, but as statements.

However, one must immediately add that the word "statement" itself is used in various contradicting ways by Oppen. It may refer to the opposite of poetry, as in "the impression of a statement having been put into verse" (SL 104), as he writes to William Bronk. Oppen's promotion of William Bronk's work—the younger poet's 1964 collection of poems entitled *The World, The Worldless*—exemplifies this dialectic of image and statement. Oppen is typically uncomfortable with the idea of a point being "reiterated not in the *image*" but in a "later *statement*" (Clippinger 2006, 108), and thus suggests a cut to Bronk (SL 103). Not only is reiteration also a matter of rhythmic balance—and Oppen's cadences were not Bronk's—but more precisely, image and statement cannot, or should not, be told apart in Oppen. For on the other hand, statements equally point to truthfulness as a form of poetics, thus in section 5 of "Some San Francisco Poems" Oppen praises "a poetry of statement" (NCP 228) and in "The Book of Job", he speaks of "'seeking a statement / of an experience of our own'" (NCP 244). The case has been made that in Oppen meaning is still initiated at the level of the image, but that it has been emptied, or is in the process of being emptied, so that it changes from a perceptive utterance to a conceptual occurrence. But Oppen no longer needs to be protected from short-sighted Imagist readings, and this reading goes too far in the other direction. He was actually well aware of how problematic it was to reconcile image and statement. Oppen wrote in his notebooks: "The words must descend into the depth of the subject matter itself and how can they? They cannot But must Must and Can't are not contradictories" (FM 200). This much needed descent into the subject matter, this desired lexical substantiation, is performed by the image-statement. In the "The Romantic Virtue," an unfinished essay by Oppen that Nicholls includes as an appendix in *The Fate of Modernism*, one finds:

> THE IMAGE THE SPATIAL DIMENSION, THE TEMPORAL DIMENSION: WITHOUT THIS THERE SEEMS NO PROOF, NO RECOGNITION, NO CONVICTION, ARGUMENT, CHATTER
>
> *Absence of the image*, ~~THE~~ ABSENCE OF THE WORLD IN WHICH THE STATEMENT IS TRUE OR NOT — — — — ~~THE POEM MUST CONCEIVE THE WORLD OR IT IS ARGUMENT, CHATTER~~
>
> [...]
> HOW ELSE BUT THE IMAGE CAN THE WORDS DESCEND IN TO THE SUBJECT MATTER ITSELF (FM 201)

The image, according to Oppen, is not so much a visual composition as a sign of the presence of the world "in which the statement is true or not." In other words, the image allows for verification and conviction. Isolating the poem's most statement-like lines from their context leads one to disregard the rest of the poem as landscape, scenery, background, backdrops of visual anecdotes—thus producing images that have been disconnected from what now appear as separate statements.

Before looking at examples from Oppen's work, one should note that Oppen frequently defined his sense of a statement of truth through the work of others, especially Reznikoff's. Writing to Reznikoff about one of his books of poems, Oppen wrote: "The lines 'penniless, penniless' render Eliot simply absurd. The critics would have made these things famous if they were Christian: there is no statement in literature near them" (SL 34). The lines, from Reznikoff's *Inscriptions: 1944–1956*, read:

> Penniless, penniless, I have come with less and still less
> to this place of my need and the lack of this hour. (Reznikoff 1977, 68)

The rhythmic clarity of the lines is certainly compelling. The four-beat repetition of "less" is perfectly balanced in the next line by the fourfold distribution of "place" and "need," then "lack" and "hour." What may have been relevant here for Oppen is Reznikoff's capacity to use reduction as a tool of empowerment, and to be able to do so in the most grammatically economic fashion, going from privative suffix to negative quantifier, as though these diminished means were in fact increasingly sufficient. Reznikoff's poem, it should be noted, is rich with implicit references to the Bible. Taken from Reznikoff's "Hanukkah," the lines in context evoke the lasting courage of the Maccabees in the face of great destruction, and their newly learned humility, in an explicit rewriting of Zecharia (4: 1–6): "Not by might, nor by power, but by my spirit, saith the Lord of hosts." That passage marks a transition in Reznikoff's poem after which he moves from biblical history to an expression of his biblical poetics:

> Speak your learned and witty discourses
> and I will utter my word or two—
> not by might nor by power
> but by Your spirit, Lord. (Reznikoff 1977, 68–69)

Oppen's remark about the lines in his letter—"if they were Christian"—underlines how the refusal of learnedness may also be a means to challenge a specific form of legitimate learnedness. It also goes to show that Oppen's interest in Reznikoff derived both from his powerful images of social destitution, and from a fascination for ascetic commitment rooted in biblical sources. This makes the textual nature of the image here inescapable. Sometimes, the picture is much more readily available, as with another quotation from Reznikoff, the epigram Oppen famously liked to rewrite:

> Among the heaps of brick and plaster lies
> a girder, still itself among the rubbish. (Reznikoff 1976, 121)

In Oppen's 1976 foreword to Reznikoff's *Poems 1937–1975*, the lines become:

> the girder, still itself
> among the rubble. (Reznikoff 1976, 3)

Reznikoff's lines evoke Eliot's "The Burial of the Dead" section of *The Waste Land*, which asks "What are the roots that clutch, what branches grow/ Out of this stony rubbish? Son of man, / You cannot say, or guess, for you know only / A heap of broken images" (Eliot 1963, 63). They also connote the persistence of tradition if one reads them alongside the following lines from Reznikoff's next collection, *In*

Memoriam: 1933, "and from the rubbish heaps that are Jerusalem / rebuild the city; / replant the land" (Reznikoff 1976, 140). In the fifth section of Oppen's "Image of the Engine," the lines "And every crevice of the city leaking / Rubble: concrete, conduit, pipe, a crumbling / Rubble of our roots" (NCP 42) may then also be said to be rich with diasporic undertones. More to the point in the present context is Oppen's editing, and indeed deleting the first line of the epigram, and then breaking its second line into two new ones. If images mean to provide context for the statement being made, that first line of Reznikoff's would seem vital. Instead, Oppen singles out the girder and prolongs his foreword with an explicit allusion to these lines as girders themselves, "still themselves among the rubble" (Reznikoff 1976, 3). The mental representation is made to exceed the spare visual data, but it does not transcend it: the visual data remains the nodal point from which all else unfolds. Yet the connotative value of the image unquestionably outweighs its designated denotative frame.

To try and make sense of these competing directions within Oppen's image-statements, one may start with Oppen's reading of Whitehead. In Daybook IV: II, Oppen quotes Whitehead repeatedly:

> "In these explanations it is presumed that an experiencing subject is one occasion of a sensitive reaction to an actual world" Whitehead, Process and Reality, page 24
>
> I don't know [...] what a non-experienced world would be. [...] I would say with Whitehead that entities actually involve each other by their prehension of each other.
>
> And that science has indeed been proceeding for some time thru a process of division, the division of the object into atoms, etc. The process of division has acquired great prestige, and one is likely to refuse to abstract from the molecule to the bar of steel. And yet there is no question that we experience the bar of steel.
>
> *one is likely to forget that the bar of steel is an abstraction* (SP 205)

The notion of a radical codependence of entities resonates for Oppen as proof that thought is rooted in the subject's experience and that no subject can uproot his or her thinking beyond the co-experience of other subjects. Putting it differently, that "[f]undamental ideas cannot be derived from each other" (SP 181), but through confrontation, through an experience of non-ideational realities. Moreover, the inclusion of the subject's experience within the limits of our "prehension of each other" predetermines the singularity of experience, and makes it part of a collective enterprise. Oppen's quotations are derived from the first chapter, "Speculative Philosophy," in Whitehead's *Process and Reality*. He is specifically rewriting

Whitehead's example of the bar of steel, which speaks directly to Oppen's fascination for Reznikoff's girder:

> There is no justification for checking generalization at any particular stage. Each phase of generalization exhibits its own peculiar simplicities which stand out just at that stage, and at no other stage. *There are simplicities connected with the motion of a bar of steel which are obscured if we refuse to abstract from the individual molecules* [...]. In the same way, there are certain general truths, about the actual things in the common world of activity, which will be obscured when attention is confined to some particular detailed mode of considering them. These general truths, involved in the meaning of every particular notion respecting the actions of things, are the subject-matter for speculative philosophy. (Whitehead 82 *emphasis mine*)

Given the pivotal nature of Reznikoff's "the girder, still itself" within Oppen's poetic worldview, it is remarkable that Whitehead's example of the bar of steel should have so caught the poet's attention. It may well recall Pound's steel dust, which will make up a rose that is not obsolete (Baumann). More crucially, it may seem very odd to think of Oppen being interested in generalizations over particulars. But this would be misreading his as well as Whitehead's take on the issue. The atomistic approach is relevant up to the point when "the process of division" leads one to separate molecule from abstraction. In other words, knowledge of the molecular level should not prevent one from experiencing the bar of steel as an abstraction, once the whole process has been acknowledged. Roughly translated into objectivist terminology, this means that if one looks at historical particulars too closely, one will no longer be able to bring the rays of the object back to its proper focus. Because some feel they have to choose between the molecule and the bar of steel, Oppen's statements have been at times caricatured as either molecular fragments or sententious abstractions. In either case, their palpable and historical reality gets neglected. For instance, in a poignant chapter in *On the Outskirts of Form*, Michael Davidson returns to these emblematic lines: "Reznikoff's 'girder amidst the rubble' is still a girder, yet its meaning has changed. After 9/11, the I-beam and the eyebeam coalesce in a new problematic of perspective that objectivism could hardly have anticipated" (Davidson 2011, 272). However, I would suggest it was not only anticipated, but experienced first hand. Like Williams' "lonely cock atop / iron girders" (Williams 1986, 249), these figuratively towering T-shaped girder structures suffered collapse and ruin in Oppen's own lifetime. His world went from Alfred Stieglitz's photographs such as "The Steerage" (1907) in which a heavy beam cuts across the frame, and from such publicity stunts as the famous 1932 photograph of men on a girder, "Lunch Atop a Skyscraper," to the worldwide circulation of *Time* magazine's pictures of the devastation in Europe and the twisted iron beams at Hiroshima and Nagasaki. As Oppen wrote about his visiting the

French town of Rouen at the war's end: "And I had seen the town rubble: they were bulldozing paths thru the rubble. And of course the rubble was not just stone, you know. There were bodies in it" (SL 50). The switch from "rubbish" to "rubble" already takes Reznikoff's line of 1934 from poverty-stricken Great Depression America to the bombed out cities of Europe in World War II.

What these two examples from Reznikoff have in common is that they seem absolutely self-sufficient. Their relative abstractedness due to lack of context is compensated by that same lack of context which makes them seem all the more solid. However, Oppen insists that meaning is encountered and not created, which is why his poems present the reader with these statements as encounters. This would explain why so many of the statements emphasized in Oppen's poetry are in fact quotations, or meant to be taken as quotations. Often, Oppen's use of quotations marks or italic thus gives the quotations embedded in his work a touch of orality, as though they had been spoken words one had cared to write down. Although for a statement to become exemplary one might imagine it should begin as a particular observation, which through inevitable generalization finds a way to exceed its initial context, Oppen proceeds the other way around. By displaying quotations as signs of preserved or restored meaning, he compensates the expected or implicit generalization in the statement by inserting it, in the context of his own poem, as evidence of a reader's realization. Through the specular effect of insertion, the statement therefore become the image of a statement's impact.

A most vivid instance of this would be the opening of "Myth of the Blaze," where Oppen speaks of "Wyatt's / lyric and Rezi's / running thru my mind" (NCP 247). Oppen spoke of this to Milton Hindus in a letter from 1977 in which he describes being "trapped in a fox-hole" in the last days of the Second World War and "Wyatt's little poem -- 'they flee from me…,' and poem after poem of Rezi's" running through his mind, "and I wept and wept" (SL 338). I am not suggesting that "Rezi's" lyric should only be viewed as an allusion to the girder poem, though "Survival: Infantry" contains the lines "And the smell of explosives / Iron standing in mud" (NCP 81). Regarding the reference made in "Myth of the Blaze" to Wyatt's poem, on a rather literal level, Wyatt's tale of desertion and desire could be said to resonate with the lost soldier's predicament away from home. In fact, in an extended letter to Serge Fauchereau, a critic who was in the process of translating Oppen into French, Oppen provides this illuminating detail about his poem "The Source" from *The Materials*: "the contrast of a woman, beauty of a woman (I was thinking in fact of Wyatt's 'They flee from me that sometime did me seek… -----' For still, still, there might be a beautiful woman in this tenement - -" (SL 328). Therefore, Wyatt's presence in "Myth of the Blaze," by way of Oppen's appropriation of Wyatt's poem in "The Source," suggests lost comfort, lost love, as well as the persistence of comfort in the midst of misery. On the other hand, the poem's formal achievement could be seen as a reminder of Oppen's prewar concern for objectivist perfection, as exemplified in Reznikoff's lines. Wyatt could then be said to serve as an illustration of Oppen's opinion that Reznikoff belongs to the poetic canon as legitimately as the famous sixteenth century poet. The combination of the two poets in Oppen's reminiscent lines, organized around a pattern of loss and resilience, might also imply that the poet would survive the war as the lines had survived in his memory. How these matters combine in Oppen's mind is made clear in a letter to Louis Zukofsky from 1958:

> I found pieces of Rezi's poems and yours going through my head during the whole war. Old men eating food all through Europe: girders still themselves where nothing else was. The sonnet in 'The'—your mother's shoes. (SL 7–8)

The letter largely pre-dates "Myth of the Blaze," and confirms its autobiographical nature. In the poem, however, only Reznikoff and Wyatt are mentioned, not Zukofsky, with whom Oppen had had a serious falling out by the late sixties. Yet one should not forget that Wyatt is featured quite prominently in Zukofsky's 1948 *A Test of Poetry*, including "They Flee from Me" (Zukofsky 1948, 17), and that Oppen shared Zukofsky's interest in sixteenth-century English poetry as a test of the condensation techniques they both appreciated in Pound's work. Moreover, Zukofsky's "mother's shoes" from "*A*"-6, about the passing of the poet's mother, and the "sonnet"—perhaps not from "Poem Beginning 'The'" as Oppen remembers but from "*A*"-7 which contains an explicit image of burial, may well combine and bring about the resurgence in Oppen's mind of childhood memories related to his own mother's death, possibly mixing these with memories of his Zukofskian New York years as a youth. In addition to the "girder" poem, Oppen's phrase about "Old men eating food" recalls the opening pages of Reznikoff's *Poems 1920*:

> Old men and boys search the wet garbage with fingers and slip pieces in bags.
>
> This fat old man has found the hard end of a bread and bites it.
> […]
>
> Showing a torn sleeve, with stiff and shaking fingers the old man
> pulls off a bit of the baked apple, shiny with sugar,
> eating with reverence food, the great comforter. (Reznikoff 1976, 29–30)

What is striking in Oppen's phrasing are the displacements: old men are now "eating food all through Europe" and not in New York, just as the New York girders now stick out after bombings all across Europe. Oppen's late poetry becomes a veritable stage or echo-chamber for these irreducible chunks made up of whatever statement has survived, as though preservation of meaning slowly set in as the only possible restoration of meaning. All these examples point in one direction, which may be best understood if one takes into consideration what Oppen is working against, as much as what he is striving for. As Frank Kermode suggests in *The Romantic Image*, after discussing Joyce's epiphanies as the "equivalent of Pater's 'vision'," (Kermode 2002, 14), "These two beliefs—in the Image as a radiant truth out of space and time, and in the necessary isolation or estrangement of men who can perceive it—are inextricably associated [...]" (Kermode 2002, 14). If nothing else, Oppen's statement-as-an-image is the exact opposite of this definition. The truth-value of Oppen's image lies in it being rooted in time and space, its radiance strictly mediated by its self-consciously ambiguous linguistic nature, while the perceiver is collectivized (specifically or anonymously) to testify for humanity. Oppen was keenly aware of the dangers of the radiant truth shining on the select few. Vincent Sherry provides ample political background on the matter in *Ezra Pound, Wyndham Lewis, and Radical Modernism* (1993), when he writes:

> When Pound endows words with the real presence of images, he is not only overreaching the now customary restraints of language. He is transgressing the ethic of a democratic society built—in his own view, as expressed in "The New Sculpture"—on the infirmity of verbal terms or, more positively, on tolerance for the possibility of multiple meanings in any one word. He has allowed his prize faculty of the eye the kind of power that brings him to a place already recognizable as a position of political extremism, already identifiable as a point on the far right. (Sherry 61)

Compare with Oppen's words about Reznikoff's poem as a statement that may be said to endure like a girder. Oppen speaks of "these poems, these lives, these small precise these overwhelming gentle iron lines and images" (Reznikoff 1977, Foreword). If one considers Oppen's wording carefully, one understands that statements as images are not mimetically inert, nor sublimely silent. They factor in time's disruption as a test of their solidity. Equating "poems" with "lives" in the context of Reznikoff's resilient lines about an equally resilient piece of iron, Oppen is suggesting that the statement in question is not the image of a thing, so much as the dynamic image of one's relation to the world of things, as if the lines' survival shared in the same energy as the girder and took an active part in its permanence. This dynamic combination is apparent in the following discussion of Reznikoff's poetry:

> Those little islands of existence in the city—a streetlamp, an iron fence, a subway station which Rezi saw in the city with so much love are also overawing. They exist at the same time uncompromisingly—and so they seem at the same time to exist uncompromisingly and to be lost. (SP 129)

The image as "island of existence," as with statements one must preserve, is caught in time and suffers loss: it does not always sing the praise of matter. Very paradoxically, the image is said to express loss, to be itself lost, and to stand tall like an existential proof of life. This ambiguity is at the heart of Oppen's strategy, yet it has not received sufficient critical attention. Speaking of images in Oppen has often meant focusing on a reductive sense of wonder before the world, or dealing with Oppen's images as concepts in disguise, as will soon be discussed in greater detail. The reason why Oppen's images as statements, or vice-versa, maintain a great level of ambiguity, as though the image failed and succeeded at the same time, is to be found, I believe, in what the image must avoid. Oppen did not want to accumulate Imagist collectibles, nor did he have patience for the seer's visions. Reznikoff's girder is, in this respect, a case in point. It combines a detailed, quotidian, local inscription, with the stylized sketchiness expected in a modernist two-line piece, complete with a topic that is even mimetically constructivist. Oppen's prolonged fascination with the poem, the shift from "rubbish" to "rubble," down to Whitehead's "bar of steel" argument, all give it special significance. One could even include Oppen's "rust in copper" dream (ML 201–2) here as well: soon before he began writing poetry again after the war, Oppen reportedly had a dream in which, as he later realized, he did not want to "rust" (SL 127). Contrary to copper, the iron girder would rust, yet its poetic preservation saves it from this outcome. In this respect, the apparent abstractedness of the picture leads to the statement of a most personal truth.

What this goes to show is that Oppen's "materials," to use an expressly vague term, are never as one-sided as one might imagine. Neither a song of the world nor a song of the mind, Oppen's poetry is extremely wary of "the pure joy / Of the mineral fact" (NCP 164). In a long letter to Julian Zimet, Oppen states: "My whole life has been a fight against death. Yours hasn't? And death's around us in the dead matter we come out of" (SL 33). He then quotes a poem of his, probably an early version of "The Forms of Love":

> I wrote of our meeting, Mary and I:
> You stepping in
> The old car, sat down close,
> So close I turned and met your eyes.
> Junked long ago—steel,
> Steel and Iron on its rubber tires
> All that night was ours!
>
> That was the first victory in my life over the stone. Or the steel and iron. (SL 33)

The image is ambivalent: a victory over the stone, the steel, and iron—pulsating love and life against inert things—but enabled by a car made of those very materials. Commenting on a poem entitled "Man's Time" (SL 10), which contains elements later to be found in "Birthplace: New Rochelle" and which he connects to "Time of the Missile," Oppen makes a related comment: "—the poem is a poem of the hatred of the 'Stone universe' and of love for ourselves and Linda—and all we have made of the universe by looking at it" (SL 29). Sometimes a balance may be struck and a form of reconciliation be said to take place between "A world of things" and "A generation's mark" (NCP 55). "Birthplace: New Rochelle" glimpses at a possible dialogue: returning to the house of his youth, the poet contrasts the knuckles of his aging hands and the stones' solid resilience under the sun into the image of "the rounded rocks of childhood" (NCP 55). But in "From a Photograph," Oppen writes:

> Her arms around me—child—
> Around my head, hugging with her whole arms,
> Whole arms as if I were a loved and native rock,
> [...] (NCP 68)

From the cold and lethal stone universe to the bedrock of a child's life, the ambiguity is overwhelming. Depending on the light, images of matter, stone, rock, iron, or steel paint very different pictures, which is why one always needs to take the statement being made into account. In "Route," Section 13, the poem's first lines provide a precise sense of the journey of things or the thingness of the word in Oppen:

> Department of Plants and Structures—obsolete, the old name
> In this city, of the public works
>
> Tho we meant to entangle ourselves in the roots of the world
>
> An unexpected and forgotten spoor, all but indestructible
> shards (NCP 200–201)

The "roots of the world" have been corroded into "indestructible / shards," as George and Mary Oppen's commitment, dating back to the thirties, now seems as "obsolete" as the name of the "public works," through an almost homonymic analogy with the word "plant," suggesting a contagious rot. In spite of that public work—working for the public good—"there is no longer shelter in the earth, round helpless belly / Or hope among the pipes and broken works" (NCP 201). But the entanglement endures and may be tracked by its "spoor": "the benevolence of the real," which later in the poem becomes "'Substance itself which is the subject of all out planning,'" then "the incalculable" into which we are "carried." Benevolence may seem a debatable attribute of "the real," especially in this context of urban despair. Yet by acknowledging the real as being benevolent the poem provides the reader with a way to make sense of the "broken works" and "the indestructible / shards," of destruction and survival together. The poem is only a picture of waste and dreariness if substance is expected to provide "shelter" or "hope." When understood as a starting point, however, outside any of the "planning" which would occur in that "Department," then substance is akin to sustenance and subsistence: the structures may not stand anymore, but "we" subsist, and that is, or was, "incalculable" in the sense that it was utterly unpredictable that "we" should survive. As Oppen put it in a letter, "I am trying to write, is maybe the right phrase about the benevolence of the real Sometimes called salvation" (SL 241). As with Reznikoff's previous "islands of existence," the destruction in this section from "Route" enhances the possibility for salvation in the sense of survival and resistance—or as Oppen put it, for victory over the stone.

Such is not always the case. Oppen's "Blood From the Stone" sequence claims the same victory, yet begins with defeat. In its third section, Oppen uses a surprising comparison when revisiting a war memory, and writes:

> There is a simple ego in a lyric,
> A strange one in war.
> To a body anything can happen,
> Like a brick. Too obvious to say.
> But all horror came from it. (NCP 53)

Several images are combined in these lines. Built as a brick lyric, as it were, the poem's statement strikes the reader as solid and impersonal. But the brick and body paronomasia allows for the most gruesome associations to peter out—images of bodies buried under rubble, bodies falling like bricks to the ground, bodies broken or burnt like clay, torn bodies in brick-red horror. The following lines go further in showing the war's disembodiment of the soldiers:

> The need
> To see past every rock, wall, forest
> Among so many, carrying in its frightful danger
> The brick body as in one's hands. (NCP 53)

Fear, danger or death may spring from "every rock," while at the same time, the victim is already brick-like. The poem's concluding lines bring one to the core of the matter, beyond the war years:

> Blood from a stone, life
> From a stone dead dam. Mother
> Nature! because we find the others
> Deserted like ourselves and therefore brothers. Yet

> So we lived
> And chose to live
>
> These were our times. (NCP 54)

The title of the next poem in *The Materials* points in the direction of the "stone, life" of New Rochelle, which one may decompose, beyond the proper noun, as French for "the new rocks," which is also Oppen's birthplace—hence stone and life combined. But Oppen repeats the antithesis here: "stone, life" turns into "stone dead." A "dam" blocks the blood of life from pouring forth. The line-endings frame the near rhymes in "others" and "brothers" within the larger scope of the various cognates "life," "lived," "live." Capitalized at the beginning of the exclamatory nominal clause, the word "Mother" stands out, deprived of a rhyming plural. The line break would seem to make the mother potentially unnatural, or at least to hamper one's vision of (mother) nature as nurturing. It is in others as brothers that one outlives being "deserted." The desertion may indeed be a reference to the presumably self-inflicted death of Oppen's mother when he was a young child. The line begs for many readings, including the accusatory "dam Mother" and the equally troubling anagram, "mad Mother." In the end, the line "Blood from a stone, life" simply represents a child vision of one's blood and lineage finding its source in the headstone under which his mother lies. Oppen writing of "the dead matter we come out of" (SL 33) is, by virtue of Latin paronomasia as well as a Freudian slip, the dead *mater* he came out of. The following lines among the poet's notes, next to a reference to Virgil's account of Queen Dido's suicide in book four of the *Aeneid* (SP 267), confirm this reading:

> We know the circumstances
> Of our origin, more disturbing
> Than the knowledge of death (SP 204)

One might conclude that the "benevolence of the real" comes as a later realization that one has outlived the malevolence of the real. I would rather insist on the fact that dead matter or the stone universe appears, in conflicting fashion, as less disturbing than "the circumstances / Of our origin" and as more acceptable instances of "the knowledge of death." In between these two extremes, as Oppen put it, a form of "salvation" exists. Oppen spoke of his encounter with Mary as a form of salvation: "I swear I knew in three minutes that I was saved" (SL 276). Far from any mysticism, salvation in this instance meant, for a young Oppen, escaping his family and finding work. The real, the world, reality then become words that designate a newly acquired freedom, far from the fallacies of home. There lies the measure of benevolence, which Oppen preserves in spite of so much destruction. I insist on these many ambiguities to show once again that an image makes little sense outside its statement, that is unless it is read as a statement. Unfortunately, Oppen's imagery, and his natural imagery especially, is rarely contextualized as ambiguous. More often than not, it is abstracted into an image of the mind.

In article entitled "Oppen's Heidegger," and in *The Fate of Modernism* (FM 75–76), Peter Nicholls quotes from the end of Oppen's "A Narrative," asking whether the passage "ice-lit / Upper World" (NCP 156) is not a reminder of the "allegory of the cave in Book VII of Plato's Republic" (TP 103). Even if the hint is there—which, after all, it may—the reference alone stops the poem short. The presence of the sea, the mention of breathing and rescuing, given our knowledge of Oppen's use of the figure of Robinson Crusoe, equally makes this "Upper World" the land that emerged from the sea, *terra firma*, which Oppen's "ice-lit" image reminds one is as frail as ice. So why focus solely on a possible reference to Book VII of *The Republic*? If Plato's cave is there, then why not also Kubla Khan's "caves of ice" (Coleridge 2004, 183)? The last section from "A Narrative" opens with the lines "River of our substance," and the case could be made that Oppen is rewriting Coleridge's river-poem. One does find a supposed Plato reference quoted in the opening poem from *Of Being Numerous*:

> There are things
> We live among 'and to see them
> Is to know ourselves'. (NCP 163)

Michael Davidson notes that according to Oppen's papers the lines derive "from Robert S. Brumbaugh, *Plato for the Modern Age* (New York: Cromwell-Collier, 1962)" (NCP 380). Perusing the book, one comes across the following:

> Where Buddha advocates the elimination of desire as the best way of life, Socrates advocates its clarification and direction. There are objective forms which attract us, and *when we see them clearly, we know our real natures* and in some sense actually achieve, through this knowledge, a transcendence of time. (Brumbaugh 1991, 85 *emphasis mine*)

The passage itself is Brumbaugh commenting on the last words in Socrates' speech at the end of *The Banquet*. But quoting this out of context, if it repeats Oppen's quoting habits, would more than rattle any Plato scholar. Reducing *The Banquet* to those lines, in the light of Oppen's rewriting, makes little sense in terms of Plato's reasoning, and even less since "Oppen had chosen, with Heidegger, 'the arduous path of appearance,' a decision with which he deliberately closed the way to any conception of Being as Platonic Essence" (Nicholls 1997, 163). But in that case, why associate Plato with these lines from "A Narrative," beyond Davidson's straightforward scholarly note? The reason is that it allows Nicholls to prepare the reader for a shift toward Heidegger, to explain Oppen's image that "thought leaped" (NCP 156) at the end of "A Narrative." Nicholls quotes from Heidegger's "What is Metaphysics?": "Philosophy is only set in motion by leaping with all its being, as only it can, into the ground-possibilities of being as a whole" (TP 103). Should that "leaping" and Oppen's "thought leaped" be taken as equivalents? No ground appears but the sea in Oppen's poem, so that the words "Miracle // Of place" (NCP 156) are fraught with contradictions. The place, in Oppen's poem, is the sea and his (implicit) boat on that sea—far from any Heideggerian sense of home or place, that "complacent fantasy of tranquil 'dwelling'" (TP 106), which did not appeal to Oppen, as Nicholls also points out. Section 11 itself, from "A Narrative," begins:

River of our substance
Flowing
With the rest. River of the substance
Of the earth's curve, river of the substance
Of the sunrise, river of silt, of erosion, flowing
To no imaginable sea. But the mind rises

Into happiness, rising

Into what is there. (NCP 155)

The rolling, rising "there" layers the lines with a sedimentary /r/ which sounds Oppen's sense of being, echoed in the first person plural "are," the phonemic surging "m-ar[e]-vel of the wave," "its noise seething / In the world" (NCP 156). The dynamic expressed in the leaping therefore alludes to a kind of capsizing, which is key to Oppen's sense of man's condition as shipwrecked, as becomes clear in *Of Being Numerous*, yet it is a desired form of shipwreck at this point. The line goes, "thought leaped on us in that sea," so in that sea and not on it, yet "in that sea we breathe," which evokes a leap of faith indeed, but one that is specific to Oppen's sense of acceptance of one's circumstances and therefore quite far from Heidegger's own circumstances. In Heidegger's "What is Metaphysics?" the leap in question refers to philosophy's giant leap beyond the petty preoccupations of science. The gist of Heidegger's essay, and much of the underlying thread in his reasoning, consists in an attempt to restore metaphysics, and hence philosophy, as the root (and as the horizon) of human knowledge, against scientific knowledge, for "[p]hilosophy can never be measured with the yard-stick of the idea of science"

(Heidegger 1949, 379), a plea which makes the assumption of some homological plunging into Being in Oppen's poem debatable, at least.

Nicholls also reads Oppen's "I thought that even if there were nothing // The possibility of being would exist" (NCP 156) alongside Heidegger's question in that same essay, "Why is there any Being at all—why not far rather Nothing?" (Heidegger 1949 380). But by asking "if," Oppen completely breaks down the premises in Heidegger's essay, which shows no skepticism in choosing Being over Nothing. Speaking of "the *possibility* of being" is equally impossible in Heideggerian terms. Oppen's "Nothing more // But the sense / Of where we are" (NCP 155) hardly seems a valid rephrasing of Heidegger's claim that we "experience in Nothing the vastness of that which gives every being the warrant to be. That is Being itself" (Heidegger 1949, 385). Reduced to a philosophical statement, the image disappears as such, but the statement itself—that the image was meant to support and vouch for—also disappears. This kind of logic applies not only to philosophers, but to poets as well. At the end of his article on Oppen's "poetics of quotation," Nicholls considers *Of Being Numerous*'s opening poem, and especially the last paragraph-stanza in it,

> 'You remember that old town we went to, and we sat in the ruined window, and we tried to imagine that we belonged to those times—It is dead and it is not dead, and you cannot imagine either its life or its death; the earth speaks and the salamander speaks, the Spring comes and only obscures it—' (NCP 163)

Quoting from the notes to the *New Collected*, Nicholls remarks that the long quotation is from Oppen's wife "Mary, verbatim, telling me about Bonnefoy; the next words, beyond what I've quoted, were 'that's what Douve is about'" (SL 129)—the reference being to Yves Bonnefoy's *On the Motion and Immobility of Douve* (1953). As Nicholls points out, the Oppens had access to a translation of the text and may as well have already been reading the original French (Nicholls 2005, 31). Quoting from Bonnefoy's essay on his own poem as well as from Blanchot (whom Oppen did not read), Nicholls speaks of the metaphysics of presence and place at play in Bonnefoy in relation to Oppen. He then focuses on Oppen's phrase, "It is dead and it is not dead." Arguing that, as a quotation, it is itself "dead and not dead" (Nicholls 2005, 32), Nicholls takes this to be a metatextual comment, then looks at it as a way to rework the preceding lines into a reasoning that would be in tune with Bonnefoy's project. This would present "an alternative to the 'sad marvels' recalled in the 'tale of our wickedness' by glimpsing our position as being at the *beginning* of an 'infinite series' as well as at its end" (Nicholls 2005, 32), which would coalesce in the image of Bonnefoy's symbolic salamander as glossed by Bonnefoy in his essay. Adding a detour through Heidegger, Nicholls concedes that there is "nothing to suggest that Oppen knew Bonnefoy's essay (it was first published in *Revue d'esthétique* in 1965), but his own Heideggerian sense of "disclosure" could produce very similar effects" (Nicholls 2005, 33). The paradox of Oppen's "own" *and* "Hedeggerian" sense of disclosure—a revealing phrase if any—finally makes Bonnefoy's presence a purely philosophical one.

Apart from the one poem, "Place of the Salamander," Nicholls does not use the poems in *On the Motion and Immobility of Douve* beyond a few allusions, while Bonnefoy's essay provides much of the interpretive frame. But the fact that the quotation is presented as direct speech from Mary Oppen receives little attention, when "that old town we went to" could easily be read as a direct reference to the time the Oppens spent in France between 1929 and 1932 (ML 117–139), and again in the early 1960s. The second poem in *Of Being Numerous* after the title sequence, "Historic Pun," is an equally direct recollection of their time in France, while the rest of the collection is rife with references to Oppen's time in France during World War II. The last of Bonnefoy's poems in *On the Motion* asks whether "our strength and our glory" can "pierce through the great wall of the dead" (Bonnefoy 1982, 113), and Oppen's *Of Being Numerous*, along with much of his postwar poetry (which is to say much of his poetry) is concerned with breathing life back into the century's "wall of the dead." Nicholls points to the hope of revivification shared by Bonnefoy and Oppen, but seems careful to make this point a philosophical one, when the sensuousness of Bonnefoy's poem and Oppen's concreteness could take one through far more tangible paths. Dealing with the passage as if it were an opaque prophetic truth prevents him from delving into the many ramifications that extend from Bonnefoy's poem into Oppen's, beyond common mentions of stony impenetrability and raw brilliance. Nicholls writes: "In an essay which refers to this passage, Bonnefoy remarks that the salamander 'here present as the softly beating heart of the world, becomes the origin of what is' (*The Act and Place* 120)" (Nicholls 2005, 33). But Bonnefoy is condensing an extremely complex literary heritage in this image. "Douve," which among other things is French for the moat around a castle, is the female addressee in the poem. In this context, the salamander, a reminder of the heraldic blazon for passionate love, is also an emblem in courtly love poetry, and the symbol could even be said to have Romantic undertones, were it not for a deliberately Baudelairian depiction of an "orchestra" of insects devouring Douve's body in the fourteenth poem in the first section (Bonnefoy 1982, 58). The salamander image, which contains a transparent anagram of the Greek for man (*andros*) is said to have a "soft man's head," and Douve is asking "penetrate me" in the same paragraph (Bonnefoy 1982, 96), in the first section of the sequence bearing the title "Salamander." Though explicitly referred to as an allegory in the poem "The Place of the Salamander" (Bonnefoy

1982, 111), its "beating heart eternal" (Bonnefoy 1982, 111) also implies sexual pulsation. Therefore, the fact that those are said to be Mary's words nuances the numerousness of the poet's persona in *Of Being Numerous* and elsewhere—Oppen's dedication of this book and his *Collected Poems* (both New Directions and Fulcrum) is to Mary, "whose words in this book are entangled / inextricably among my own" (NCP 380). The shift in emphasis from Bonnefoy's male speaking I to Oppen's mixed voices completely transforms the role and presence of *On the Motion and Immobility of Douve* in *Of Being Numerous.*

Moreover, if Bonnefoy's "la clarté de nos fenêtres" (Bonnefoy 1982, 111)—literally "the clarity of, or from, our windows"—in "The Place of the Salamander" can be read as a common metaphor for the eyes, Oppen's "*we sat in the ruined window*" connects to his reexamination of the lines from Henry James in his first poem in *Discrete Series*, echoed and examined in section 37 of the poem "Of Being Numerous,"

> '… Approached the window as if to see …'
>
> The boredom which disclosed
> Everything—
>
> I should have written, not the rain
> Of a nineteenth century day, but the motes
> In the air, the dust
> Here still. (NCP 186)

The motif is then repeated in section 3 of "Route,"

> Not to reduce the thing to nothing—
>
> I might at the top of my ability stand at a window
> and say, look out; out there is the world […] (NCP 193)

As "ruined windows," these do not offer protection from the rain or the "weather-swept" (NCP 5) historical world, but let in the air thick with specks of dust and motes, which again point to rubble—"motes, an iron mesh, links // Of consequence" (NCP 187). Those openings contrast with the mind's eye's difficult remembering and imagining of previous times and towns that remain beyond our grasp, though Oppen's tour de force in his long quotation from Mary is that he manages to combine the impossible recollection of past eras and the necessity to be reminded of, and to account for, one's time, now gone by. That may be in the end the purpose of the "Douve" passage: it allows Oppen to reframe his world-view, from his return from his first trip to France around the time of the Depression to his return from France after World War II. Bonnefoy's poem is a window onto his own inaugural window from *Discrete Series*, now recast as the window onto the world of 1968, no longer shared with James' Maud Blessingbourn(e) but with Mary, and "weather-swept" almost to annihilation. The ruin here is pivotal, inasmuch as it testifies to the trajectory of post-Imagist objectivist images which, a product of the constructivist moment, to use Barrett Watten's words, faced active and actual—and not Romantic—ruin. Not ruin as in what remains, but ruin as an active process, the wreckage that happens. In light of Reznikoff's ruined girder rewritten as "rubble" by Oppen, it would seem then that "what is" deserves historical, rather than philosophical, qualification. The reasons for the incompatibility between Oppen's poetry, directed at the completion of statements of truth, and many critical statements made about his poetry, I believe, are to be found in this need to outsource one's interpretation to a preexisting theoretical order, that will restore one's sense of a global meaning and a frame of reference, which the poem at hand so often denies its reader both on a thematic and a formal level.

References

Baumann, Walter. 1967. *Rose in the Steel Dust*. Bern: Francke Verlag.

———. 2000. *Roses from the Steel Dust: Collected Essays on Ezra Pound*. Orono, ME: The National Poetry Foundation.

Blake, William. 1979. *Blake's Poetry and Designs*. Edited by Mary Lynn Johnson and John E. Grant. New York: W. W. Norton & Company.

Bonnefoy, Yves. 1953. *Du mouvement et de l'immobilité de Douve*. In Bonnefoy, Yves. 1982. *Poèmes*. Paris: Gallimard.

———. 1992. *On the Motion and Immobility of Douve*. Translated by Galway Kinnell. Newcastle upon Tyne: Bloodaxe Books.

Brumbaugh, Robert S. 1962. *Plato for the Modern Age*. New York: Cromwell-Collier.

Clippinger, David W. 2006. *The Mind's Landscape. William Bronk and Twentieth-Century American Poetry*. Cranbury, NJ: Rosemont Publishing, Associated University Presses.

Coleridge, Samuel Taylor. 2004. *Coleridge's Poetry and Prose*. Edited by Nicholas Halmi, Paul Magnuson, and Raimonda Modiano. New York: W. W. Norton & Co.

Davidson, Michael. 1997. *Ghostlier Demarcations: Modern Poetry and the Material Word* Berkeley: University of California Press.

———. 2011. *On the Outskirts of Form: Practicing Cultural Poetics*. Middletown, CT: Wesleyan University Press.

Eliot, T. S. 1963. *Collected Poems 1909–1962*. London: Faber and Faber.

Heidegger, Martin. 1949. *Existence and Being*. Edited by Werner Brock. Chicago: Henry Regnery Company.

Kermode, Frank. 2002. *The Romantic Image*. London: Routledge.

Nicholls, Peter. 2005. "George Oppen: The New or the Avant-Guard?" *Journal of Modern Literature* 28/4: 1–12.

Reznikoff, Charles. 1976. *Poems 1918–1936: Volume I of the Complete Poems of Charles Reznikoff*. Santa Barbara, California: Black Sparrow Press.

———. 1977. *Poems 1937–1975: Volume 2 of the Complete Poems of Charles Reznikoff*. Santa Barbara, CA: Black Sparrow Press.

Sherry, Vincent. 1993. *Ezra Pound, Wyndham Lewis, and Radical Modernism*. Oxford: Oxford University Press.

Stevenson, Robert Louis. 1994. *A Child's Garden of Verses*. London: Penguin.

Whitehead, Alfred North. 2011. *Science and the Modern World*. Cambridge: Cambridge University Press.

———. 1978. *Process and Reality*. New York: The Free Press.

Williams, William Carlos. 1986. *The Collected Poems. Volume 1. 1909–1939*. Edited by A. Walton Litz and Christopher MacGowan. New York: New Directions.

Wordsworth, William. 2014. *Poetry and Prose*. Edited by Nicholas Halmi. New York: W. W. Norton.

CHAPTER FIVE

A Dream of Politics[1]

Among the problems regarding how statements exist in a dialectic with images, one issue has consistently interfered with Oppen's emphasis on clarity—the role of politics in shaping the poet's vision. Presenting a political reading of Oppen's poetry has often meant two things. First, it has involved setting up context, topicality, and possibly even content, in the hope of fleshing out the poem's bony frames. As such, this is a useful, if tricky, task. For "political" then seems to mean "historical," if not really "biographical"—a confusion which can pass for a resolution of all conflicts regarding the problem at hand. Secondly, it has implied expressing judgment, either in praise of Oppen's political commitments, or to dismiss Oppen's political commitments and signs thereof in his poetry and among critics of Oppen. Conflict is then limited to rhetorical confrontations, as Terry Eagleton suggests in *The Function of Criticism*, in which the battleground where conflicts exist is the public sphere. I would rather argue, along with Robert Eaglestone, that understanding "criticism as either revolutionary or reactionary" (Eaglestone 1997, 12) offers such a restrictive framework that it discourages from close analysis.

Burton Hatlen has a point when, at the end of his essay on *The Materials*, he describes Oppen as neither adopting "the ostentatiously apolitical stance assumed by Joyce and Stein" nor "the assertively conservative positions of certain well-known members of the avant-garde (Pound, Yeats, Eliot, the Southern Agrarians)" (MP 356)—although many different people are hereby thrown together, and much could be gained by painting a more detailed picture. Still, the resurgence and resilience of Oppen and the objectivists owes a lot to the "cluster of assumptions" about American poetry in the twentieth century, in that they present a precious "indigenous alternative" (MP 357). Hatlen decides to choose between the two options. Declaring that "Oppen's vision of the world remains stubbornly political rather than philosophical" (MP 331), Hatlen stipulates a dichotomy that Oppen never recognized or followed. This is one more instance of taking sides about L. S. Dembo's assertion, "[w]hen Oppen put pen to paper again, it was…as an existentialist, not as a socialist" (Dembo 1988, 137)—choosing between political or existential readings, as though such a choice ever presented itself, when one ought to start questioning the premise behind these fictitious division. In the end, Hatlen believes that Oppen's poetry, "even long after he and Mary left the Communist Party, represents, not a repudiation of or an alternative to the political commitments of Oppen's middle years, but rather an extension of these commitments back into poetry, thus making the third period of Oppen's life a synthesis of the first and second phases" (MP 331–2). However appealing, this type of synthesis will nonetheless almost always prove exaggeratedly bent on reconciling the work with the very tensions it sought to answer, and not dispel.

George Oppen and individually each of the objectivists have served as a starting point in post-war attempts to reclaim something of the modernist heritage, which greatly complicates one's assessment of the facts. In his 1987 essay, "Third-Phase Objectivism," Ron Silliman distinguishes between a first phase—the birth of objectivist poetry in the 1930s—and a second one, the "phase of neglect" which ensued, while the third and last phase consists in "the resurrection of the works of Zukofsky, Oppen, Basil Bunting, Carl Rakosi, Charles Reznikoff, and Lorine Niedecker to public attention virtually overnight in the early 1960s" (TP 163). The word "resurrection" hides the fact that if this coincided with new publications from those poets, these new publications followed a preexisting full-fledged body of works, except for Oppen, who published all but one of his books of poems between 1962 and 1978. Silliman's belief is that the "return of the Objectivists" signaled by Oppen's return to poetry transformed Objectivism "from the aesthetically radical and oppositional poetry of the early thirties to a more conservative (aesthetically, if not politically) phenomenon" (TP 165). Silliman goes on to point out that,

> Oppen's works, from *The Materials* onward, are decisively different from *Discrete Series*, his first-phase volume. This shift is precisely one of stance, and it may well be that a quarter of a century of struggle, with the constraints of daily life, marriage, parenting, with war and exile, with capitalism and its Frankenstein, fascism, render the later position inevitable. However, it is not difficult to demonstrate that it falls outside the original, loosely held program of phase-one Objectivism. (TP 165)

After this strange equation of "fascism" with "fatherhood" or "marriage," which other critics have noted (Wilkinson 2010, 220), Silliman then moves to quote William Carlos Williams' 1934 review of *Discrete Series* and sets it against Oppen's later poetry. It is doubtful, however, whether Williams would have accepted the dichotomy posed by Silliman. As John Seed has argued, Oppen would have agreed with Williams' indictment of poets who "play tiddlywinks with the syllables" (Freeman 1985, 103–104), and as was made clear in the discussion above about Oppen's last selected letter and Bernstein's ill-suited acrostic. The "radical" versus "conservative" worldview has all but prevented critics from presenting accurate accounts of the political and historical embeddedness of Oppen's poetry.

In most remarkable instances, critics have called into question Oppen's emphasis on sight, in the hope of proving it somehow shortsighted. If Michael Davidson's nuanced reading of class consciousness as a poetic perspective in Oppen—the need to "register the incommensurable void between lived conditions and representability" (Davidson 2011, 96)—serves as a reminder of the dangers of ahistorical readings, John Wilkinson's 2010 article on Oppen's poetry, "The Glass Enclosure: Transparency and Glitter in the Poetry of George Oppen," is a case in point. Wilkinson states that Oppen's poems "were always truthful enough to show there is no unmediated seeing" (Wilkinson 2010, 233), but claims that "his poetry constantly belies what he professes" (Wilkinson 2010, 224) because transparency and direct perception never really take place. But the implicit syllogism in Wilkinson's article that equates mediation with distance and then anxiety and then alienation cannot be taken at face value, if only because it is for the most part a device meant to show up contradictions, verging on inconsistencies, that otherwise make up Oppen's (if not any poet's) inevitable—and in his case avowed—struggle with his own poetics. To support his view that Oppen's outspoken concern for clarity is actually belied by his own poems, inasmuch as in those poems seeing is overly mediated and the eye is enclosed in too much glass as well as various other framing devices or supporting surfaces, Wilkinson writes:

> How else to explain, in the work of a poet who scrutinizes every word, that the first poem in each of his first three books, along with the first poem in the first draft of his fourth, presents the act of seeing as from behind a window? (Wilkinson 2010, 224)

But these frames are a repeated instance of Oppen rewriting, as he did in his notes, "the first sonnet in Philip Sidney's *Astrophil and Stella*: 'Fool said my muse to me, look in thy heart and write'" (SP 255 n.14), which reads as follows in Oppen's "Daybook II:III,"

> Fool, look out of the window
> And write. (SP 91)

The framing of his vision through windows and window sills is Oppen's own trademark trope for looking and stepping outside to come into contact with the world. Oppen also wrote, in section 3 from "Route," "I might at the top of my ability stand at a window / and say, look out; out there is the world" (NCP 193). After aestheticizing Oppen to apologize for his "isolation of poetry to protect its integrity" (Wilkinson 2010, 237), Wilkinson does not see that the constant reminders that sight is conditioned on one's own perspective, that these signs of Oppens' "skepticism about the clarity of what can be seen," reveal his "continuing preoccupation with the question of class that he approached from his double consciousness as proletarian and bourgeois subject" (Davidson 2011, 117).

Marjorie Perloff's reasoning, in her 2008 revision of her 1985 essay on Oppen's title poem in *Of Being Numerous*, follows similar lines as Wilkinson's: Oppen's distanced perspective is interpreted as a poet's guilty remoteness. Going even further, Perloff's conclusion takes the politics out of the equation altogether: "What is finally affirmed in this beautiful and difficult long poem is not, I think, any sort of 'populist vision,' much less the possibility of social transformation. Rather, 'Of Being Numerous' is a testimony to the need for—but difficulty of—survival—survival won by the 'curious' ability of *poeisis* itself to make the 'numbers' interlock" (Perloff 2008). This seems a direct echo of Wilkinson (whom she quotes, where in his article he quotes her 1985 article): "Oppen's is an unpeopled world, a strange vision for a lifelong socialist. The animation belongs to stone, sea, sun, and crystal as they respond to the isolated self or the self and his wife. Oppen's sense of humanity was abstract and separate" (Wilkinson 2010, 237). However, the inference is itself rather questionable. To wish to undo simplistic assumptions of political immediacy, either visionary or transformative, may be commendable, but by finding Oppen's world an 'unpeopled' one, Perloff seems to be suggesting that 'the self' is essentially a bourgeois concern, thereby relying on another kind of assumption, this time about what being a "lifelong socialist" might mean. Interestingly, as Alan Filreis points out, one of the tenets of anticommunist literary criticism was precisely the abhorrence of impersonality, as though poetry "had to be about human passion, the emotional sourcework of a deeply coherent self," and must be clearly distinguishable from the "clipped subjectless language used by reporters and political commentators" (Fredman 2005, 175–176). When they accuse Oppen of not being enough of a Communist poet, Wilkinson and Perloff appear to be thinking within this questionable frame.

Perloff's interpretation also serves another objective, which is to preempt Oppen as a language poet *avant la lettre*. At least her conclusion, just above, contains quite the Freudian slip. "Survival," repeated twice: the word resonates with Oppen's work and life and century. It stands as what is silenced about Oppen's silence, when linguistic experiment replaces human experience altogether, for Oppen's survival was not won only through poetic means. As for numbers, Oppen may much more readily have had these lines from Reznikoff in mind: "Of course, we must die. / How else will the world be rid of / the old telephone numbers / we cannot forget? // The numbers / it would be foolish— / utterly useless— / to call" (Reznikoff 1977, 81). Numerousness, in that sense, means "as Rezi proves with the phone book, one *couldn't* live forever" (SL 94). Against supposedly Marxist readings, such as might be found in Burton Hatlen, Eric Mottram or David McAleavey, Perloff rejects the assumption that Oppen's political activities in the twenty-five years when he did not write somehow find their way back into his poetry. Some of her quotations from these three critics are debatable, such as when she singles out Hatlen's statement about "Oppen's infusion of a populist vision into an immanentist poetic mode" (MP 333), failing to add that Hatlen goes on to say that this "does not upon first inspection look very 'political'" (MP 333). Similarly, Mottram's article is much more of a useful and general politically contextual piece than an effort to read Marx into Oppen. The same could be said about McAleavey's piece on "Of Being Numerous." Yet there is in fact "wishful thinking" (Perloff 2008, 5) on Hatlen's part when he introduces his examination of *The Materials* as Oppen's effort to "bridge the gap between poetry and politics, art and 'the people,' language and the things of our world" (MP 335). Nevertheless, Hatlen's analysis of Oppen's "basic poetic strategy," in *The Materials*, "to illuminate for us the significance of human labor by focussing on the materials which are transformed by that labor," as a strategy which "enables Oppen to move beyond a mindless materialism" (MP 337) provides valid access into that book. Regarding the idea that the twenty-five-year hiatus during which Oppen wrote no poetry was "a gestation period for the poetry that was to come," Perloff asserts:

> The assumption behind this argument is that, however firmly the Oppen of the 1960s renounced a life of political action, his Marxist vision remained intact. Certainly, Oppen himself did nothing to dispel this view. (Perloff 2008, 5)

Perloff's subsequent close readings of sections from "Of Being Numerous" try to dispel any such notions. She claims instead that "Of Being Numerous" is "primarily a case 'of being separate'" (Perloff 2008, 6). Although it is plain to see that the poem does tell of withdrawal, distance, reticence, that it never simply embraces numerousness, and questions the place of singularity in the midst of larger numbers, Perloff offers a unilateral reading. First, her assertion that Oppen "did nothing to dispel this view" is worth a second look. He specifically said, referring to those twenty-five years:

> It means we knew we didn't know enough from the poetry that was being written; from the poetry that we had written. And when the crisis occurred we knew we didn't know what the world was and we knew we had to find out so it was a poetic exploration at the same time that it was an action of conscience, of feeling that one was worth something or other. And I thought most of the poets didn't know about the world as a life—so that I fairly easily gave up a great many poetic friends. (MP 25)

As Tom Mandel promptly rephrases, "you realized that you didn't know enough to continue writing poetry, that you had to know more about the world," (MP 25) to which Oppen agrees. Oppen may be using the adjective "poetic" rather loosely when speaking of "a poetic exploration," and of course, the interview in question comes after the facts. This has prompted some to claim that "[p]olitics was in many ways a prison from which poetry could free him" (Hoffman 2008). On the basis of a single reference in Oppen's letters to the possibility for poetry to "be involved in a politics which is radical enough to ask a question of purpose, of desire, to raise the question of our purposes, of our desires" (SL 239), Hoffman concludes that "it is possible for the poet to reconcile artistic and political concerns" (Hoffman 2008). But Oppen's terms, "purpose" and "desire," cannot be said to consist in or describe anything like proper political commitment, which Oppen had sought to differentiate from poetry. It rather sends one back to "poetic exploration," in the sense that past political experience came to count as present poetic data. Hoffman knows this, when he writes that Oppen's "description of his poetic silence as an investigation is true in the sense that during this silence he accumulated material for later work—a life lived from which to write—but only in hindsight," whereas sweeping statements, such as assuming that Oppen's "political commitments became an almost seamless extension of their poetic life" (Hoffman 2008), do not rest on specific demonstrations.

In a similar vein, Tom Fisher finds that "Oppen's silence and political commitments are not opposed to his poetry but are part of its 'exploration'" (Fisher 2009, 88). Fisher then uses Jean-Luc Nancy's *The Sense of the World* to rehearse the now classic conflation of indetermination, negativity, or a nonpredicative stance with leftist or radical or Marxist politics. This is but another instance of what Jameson called the ideology of the text, namely, "the notion of the open work, to which corresponds a similarly moralizing valorization of critical pluralism" (Jameson 2002, 235).

But what was Oppen's own view of his own poem, "Of Being Numerous"? Here is how he described its progression in another interview:

> [...] and then the social, the fact that one does live historically, argued out, that we speak of Crusoe as rescued, and it's argued out, the matter of age, people do feel some metaphysical connection. The old men knew their own lives not the end of the world, ... returning on a different level to the political issue. (Amirkhanian and Gitin 1975, 24)

Oppen's poem "Pro Nobis," one of the last from *This in Which*, describes a similar journey:

> I believe my apprenticeship
> In that it was long was honorable
> Tho I had hope to arrive
> At an actuality
> In the mere number of us
> And record now
> That I did not.
>
> Therefore pray for us
> In the hour of our death indeed. (NCP 157)

In light of this poem, "Of Being Numerous" seems much closer to the genre of the eulogy than to a political call to arms. Nicholls writes, "It is curious that Oppen's emphatic concern with death in 'Of Being Numerous' has never been fully acknowledged in accounts of the poem" (FM 87). Thus, not only does Oppen admit failure, but chooses to speak from that very vantage point to address the hopes of his generation along with those of the new. The poem reads very differently as a testament, which Oppen was reluctant to make for fear that his child might read it too soon (SL 156). Yet political failure is not thematized as exemplary, nor transposed as "a defeat *by politics*" (Nealon 2011, 11) and no insular linguistic plane is suggested where to withdraw. No higher political truth is either expressed or aimed at and what form remains is the Latin phrase of the title taken up in "pray *for us*." Oppen's desired sense of actuality is no longer directly connected to political action and it is now conditioned on a precarious quorum asked to pray for the dead. Oppen objected to sanctimonious declarations—he refused to count as another signature in *New Masses*—and literally sought to number among the people he so often called "us." He chose the contingency of community action—a community now extended to Oppen's readership as those who will "pray for us." The "actuality" in question then takes on a special sense: it is a failed one in terms of implementing change through "the mere number of us," and it only succeeds in giving a sense of actuality to the poem's meaning. Yet one should not jump to the conclusion that these formal features will succeed where historically "I did not." The poem records and does not redeem. The actuality at which the poet did not arrive and the measure of actuality at which the poem does arrive should not be confused, for then the testamentary nature of the poem is lost. In his interview with Dembo, Oppen develops that aspect of his writing:

> We care about the idea of what's going to happen to humanity, including after one's death. […] There are other situations any of us could imagine in which people would not be willing to live, would find it impossible to live, without some concept of sharing in history or humanity—something which is happening after their death. (Dembo 1972 179)

Contrary to this assertion, Perloff's article focuses on Oppen's abstractedness: the poem is, Perloff first declares,

> […] a poem about exile—specifically, the acute sense of pain and disorientation attendant upon the exiled American poet's attempt to relearn "a language of New York," to make his way through the new "city of the corporations." The "journey," which is not temporal but spatial, erasing all or almost all autobiographical traces, is through a landscape of dislocation, of absence, a visual "landscape" of short, abrupt lines ("From lumps, chunks," as Oppen put it in "Image of the Engine," NCP 42), surrounded by white space. (Perloff 2008, 6)

Although she eventually comes very near to wanting to dismiss the work because of its abstractions, Perloff is quite right in saying that "Of Being Numerous," as she puts it,

> […] stands at the opposite pole from Frank O'Hara's New York poems, with their fierce concentration on the perceptual and the particular, their fear of losing the particular or of finding that there is nothing beneath the surface. Oppen, in contrast, cares little about New York and its characteristic images but a great deal about the phenomenology of the mind. (Perloff 2008, 8)

But instead of delving into the poem's ambiguities, Perloff seems intent on exposing Oppen's limitations, as though consciousness and politics could not mix. The spectrum of Oppen's interrogations is reduced to units of sincerity verging on solipsism—themselves deemed unworthy of serving the higher political role some have claimed for this text. In the process, Oppen's poem is said to be both too referential (it is too preoccupied with the self to be accepted as adequately radical), and not referential enough (its abstractions testify to a guilty disconnectedness with his subject). Only when, in Perloff's final comments, Oppen's "realism" has been properly converted to "textual productivity" can it be somehow salvaged for the reader. Demonstrating that this is not a poem about social unison or a univocal plea for social change has been made necessary by the many facile political generalizations that have been made about Oppen. Oppen himself noted that "'the poem was written [...] in despair of the historical, the sense of continuation'" (FM 84). But Perloff goes from noting that sense of despair and historical discontinuity (in a generational sense, but not only) to saying that the poem offers only disconnection and solipsistic estrangement. The problem with drawing such a conclusion is that it does away with the whole test the poem wants to put the reader to.

Perloff is really addressing two issues at once. The first is Oppen's indisputable propensity to use abstract nouns. Perloff calls the adjective in the title "abstract and impersonal" and there is everywhere, Perloff writes, "a concentration on the abstract, the conceptual, the function word" (Perloff 2008, 2). But does this unilaterally translate into remoteness, impersonality, aloofness or seclusion? Taking another, but perhaps not so different nor disconnected example, what of the word "multitude"? Surely it sounds more abstract than people, and yet the King James Bible is full of it. If Oppen's perspective is testamentary, it could be so on that level as well. On the other hand, statements such as Tomlinson's, who wrote about *Seascape: Needle's Eye* that Oppen "still seems to recall Williams' concern for a democracy of language where the smallest units take on substantial meaning" (Amirkhanian and Gitin 1975, 18), cannot be taken absolutely at face value either, as these lines from "Myth of the Blaze" will show:

> dark tho names   the names   the 'little'
>
> adventurous
> words   a mountain   the cliff
>
> a wave are taxonomy I believe
> in the world (NCP 248)

Oppen's tendency to use words generically, as a form of "taxonomy," is an increasingly pervasive practice in his poetry, but this need not be either a reminiscence of Williams or an allegory of language as a social body of words, or yet an implicit sign that Oppen had lost faith in the image. One needs to understand Oppen's specific position. It cannot be deduced from Oppen's generic nominalism that he has gone against Williams toward some kind of disembodiment of knowledge, as Perloff seems to suggest, or that Oppen's image had in any way been so very close to Williams' images. Oppen's praise of Reznikoff's poetry always hinged around the disclosure involved in pressuring the generic into absolute singularity—which is the opposite of universals or generalizations. Talking about Reznikoff, Oppen spoke thus:

> The first *Testimony* is an extraordinary thing, just that ending of it, going along on this testimony from the courts and then those last lines, "ships, harbors, rivers." Just things, just things there, and it's amazing what they do. (MP 44)

As Perloff points to Frank O'Hara's lists and taste for proper nouns, so Oppen, while slightly misquoting Reznikoff's concluding "inlets, rivers, harbors and ports" (Reznikoff 1976, 54–56), does not retain Reznikoff's "Whitmanian catalog of ships and their names cargoes and ports" (Davidson 1997, 166) in the section entitled "Rivers and Sea Harbors and Ports." Instead, he isolates three words, "ships, harbors, rivers" as "things there." A precise account of what takes place with Oppen's nominalizations is as follows, in the words of Robert Hass:

> In the middle of that dilemma what happens with the nouns in George Oppen's poetry, it seems to me that you can actually watch, as the words are laid down on the page, the process from which the perception of the thing gets born into its numinous quality as a word, an abstraction out of the thing. (Hass 1985, 39)

Or, as Oppen himself points out to Dembo:

> The little words I like so much, like "tree," "hill," and so on, are I suppose just as much a taxonomy as the more elaborate words; they're categories, classes, concepts, things we invent for ourselves. Nevertheless, there are certain ones without which we really are unable to exist, including the concept of humanity. (Dembo 1972, 175)

Perloff's second point revolves around assessing referentiality. The question is implied in the issue of genericity, or rather it results from Oppen's nomination practice. It raises more debatable issues because, as always with matters of referentiality, words will be words and can never be univocal and point solely in this or that direction. A good example is the fifth section in "Of Being Numerous":

> The great stone
> Above the river
> In the pylon of the bridge
>
> '1875'
>
> Frozen in the moonlight
> In the frozen air over the footpath, consciousness

Which has nothing to gain, which awaits nothing,
Which loves itself (NCP 165)

Here is Perloff's reading, which needs to be quoted at some length:

> Oppen's focus is not on the bridge or even the pylon of the bridge, but on a single stone in it, bearing the inscription '1875.' The date, placed on a line all by itself, surrounded by two-line blocks of white space, has a peculiar pathos. It is as if the poet's cognizance of the inscription exhausts whatever interest he may have had in the history of the bridge and, by extension, in the city: one bare fact and he has had enough. "Frozen in the moonlight / In the frozen air over the footpath" (note the complex sound repetitions here) accordingly refers, not only to the bridge but to the consciousness "which awaits nothing, / Which loves itself."
>
> How to escape such mental gridlock? (Perloff 2008, 9)

The idea that the poet's knowledge of the inscription hyperbolically exhausts his interest in both bridge and city, while his consciousness retracts on the frozen footpath, seems rather excessive. The dynamic of the poem does not express any sense of satiety. The binary rhythm kept up along the first three lines, building up a massive presence from "great" to "above," then distributing this weight from the erect "pylon" to the horizontal bridge (and implicitly, the twin pylon), culminates in "1875," the date when the Brooklyn bridge was completed. There is an element of dejection in the ensuing lines, which turn the towering "o" in "pylon" and "above" into the twice "frozen" "consciousness" below, "over" the "footpath," met only by apparent solipsism ("loves itself," awaiting "nothing" twice). It is only apparent because the test of consciousness that Oppen performs is an ongoing, gradual, serial one. Oppen is aware of the risk for his perceptions to solidify into words alone, and upon that risk rests much of the poem's dynamic:

> I'm trying to describe how the test of images can be a test of whether one's thought is valid, whether one can establish in a series of images, experiences ... whether or not one will consider the concept of humanity to be valid, something that is, or else have to regard it as being simply a word. (Dembo 1972, 175)

In fact, dejection may be what is in store in the end:

> And yet I don't know that poetry is not actually destructive for people, because what you are implying is true. It does lead to the growing isolation of the poet; there's no question in my mind about it. (Dembo 1972, 186)

But it is too soon to settle that issue, which requires that the whole poem and indeed Oppen's whole work be taken into account. Oppen's choice of the Brooklyn bridge itself is not devoid of meaning. The last section in "Of Being Numerous" consists in a quotation from a letter by Walt Whitman, with its last word, "curious," oddly set apart from the rest of the text. In reference to this, John Peck has already called attention (MP 77–78) to Whitman's "Crossing Brooklyn Ferry," which opens with these lines:

> Crowds of men and women attired in the usual costumes! how curious you are to me!
> On the ferry-boats, the hundreds and hundreds that cross, returning home,
> are more curious to me than you suppose; (Whitman 1982, 308)

Apart from the repetition of the word "curious" as a possible hint that Oppen had this poem in mind, Whitman's poem could be read against Oppen's "Of Being Numerous" in an effort to contrast the poet's sense of community (Oppen's poem is also built, at first, on the sense of a flow of people), namely through the stark difference in their choice of address. Whereas Whitman gradually builds up to his final "We" through an ambiguous, multi-directional second person singular or second person plural, Oppen's focus seems to be entirely on "we," set against the first person singular, and constantly trying to negotiate a locus for "us." Likewise, the consciousness which "loves itself," after all, could very well be Oppen's comment on Whitman's centralizing "we love you" in the twelfth stanza of "Crossing Brooklyn Ferry." More to the point, as Peck argues, Oppen could be pitting his populism against Whitman's, across Hart Crane's *The Bridge*. Oppen's last lines in this section could then also be read as a plea for the crisp, cold, clear consciousness of those who do not await the lending of myths, to paraphrase Crane's final lines in "To Brooklyn Bridge" (Crane 1986, 44). The self-love in question would come as the reassurance that no disproportionate epic desires are at play here at all, and that one is simply, after Reznikoff, walking by the waters of Manhattan. Still another explanation would send one back to Oppen's "Chartres" poem from *The Materials*, which focuses on single stones supporting one another (NCP 77), and offers little of the famous cathedral's design but "The bulk of it / In air" (NCP 77), and the occasional "door" or "doorways." In "Chartres" as well as in section 5 above, Oppen has little taste for structures seeking to build bridges or arches over more than they can chew or sing. What is systematically conveyed, on the other hand, is a sense of the magnitude and the material resistance of stones, not as monuments but as the particulars of people's work. The date inscribed points to that celebration: not the bridge, which did not open until 1883, but the Brooklyn tower alone gets mentioned, as though this were one more "girder."

Therefore, Perloff's conclusion about this section does seem, in its turn, like a case of wishful thinking. She claims that "[…] since that world is so distasteful to the poet—even a simple date like 1875 can intrude only intermittently on a 'consciousness / Which loves itself'—any possibility of social transformation evaporates. 'We have chosen,' says Oppen bravely, 'the meaning / Of being numerous,' but it is not a 'meaning' he can bring himself to accept" (Perloff 2008, 11). Yet Nicholls quotes at length from Oppen's papers on the subject: "the poem, says Oppen, 'does not mean to solve such a problem [the problem of the concept of humanity], but to permit the problem to remain a problem while giving MEANING, if I can, to its terms'" (FM 105). Or again: "'Of Being Numerous: whether we are bound each to each other: this question is the content and meaning of our lives (the poem does not succeed in answering the question——nor did I expect to answer. It remains the question'" (FM 105). Dismissing that very meaning on the grounds that the poem is suffused with a loss of commonness testifies to a very narrow approach to Oppen's poem. If the poem "proposes a condition of numerousness *and* singularity" (FM 108), then trying to pit occurrences of singularity against any possibility of numerousness constitutes an inappropriate reading.

A worse example of Oppen's remoteness, according to Perloff, is apparent in this reference to Oppen's World War II experience:

> Among them many men
> More capable than I—
>
> Muykut and a sergeant
> Named Healy,
> That lieutenant also—(NCP 171)

The accusation is the same. The poem apparently lacks referential veracity:

> The speaker says he "cannot even now / Altogether disengage himself / From those men / With whom I stood in emplacements, in mess tents, / In hospitals and sheds," but the roll call yields no real image. Aside from the two proper names, Muykut and Healy, and the reference to their respective ranks, he does not provide us with a single identifying feature of his fellow soldiers. (Perloff 2008, 12)

In spite of an unusual degree of explicitness here in Oppen's poem, these specific names and ranks are considered insufficient information. One wonders what Oppen should have written to give his fellow soldiers properly identifiable features. Why refrain from accepting Oppen's dog tag introduction of these men? The limited identification it allows amply serves Oppen's purpose here, and it provides the reader with precious insight into another aspect of Oppen's generic use of nouns, from "people" to "men." In the case of his fellow soldiers, maintaining a sense of relative anonymity adequately translates the soldier's status as replaceable unit, while limiting the disclosure of any identifiable details both exhibits the name in uniform, as it were, and preserves that name as the near anagram of any man, any fallen fellow man whose name identifies a grave. Oppen actually wrote, in a 1973 letter to John Crawford, that reading his poem as an image of "the comradeship of war," the idea of a bond of shared suffering, was an interpretation he strongly rejected (SL 254). Oppen's minimal presentation of his fellow soldiers, the impossibility for the reader to identify them and identify with them, is meant to preclude the possibility of any such interpretation. In other words, Perloff finds fault with exactly what Oppen wanted to convey, refusing the fake feelings of comradeship common in war poems. As she continues, her comment veers toward moral judgment:

> This withdrawal from human contact also characterizes the sequence's Vietnam War poems (#18–#20). Completed in the pivotal year 1968, it would seem appropriate that "Of Being Numerous" would make some reference to the war. Yet despite all the talk of "atrocity," "Insanity in high places," and "Failure and the guilt / Of failure," there is curiously little personal passion or absorption in Oppen's indictment. (Perloff 2008, 12–13)

All this raises a crucial issue. Whereas assessing "withdrawal from human contact" is no simple task when words on paper are concerned, the idea that "Of Being Numerous" makes no or little reference to the War in Vietnam, and that Oppen shows neither "personal passion" nor "absorption" is easy to dispute, and refute. In section 18, which contains the word "atrocious" Perloff quotes above, one finds:

> It is the air of atrocity,
> An event as ordinary
> As a president.
>
> A plume of smoke, visible at a distance
> In which people burn.

Section 19 continues:

> Now in the helicopters the casual will
> Is atrocious
>
> Insanity in high places,
> If it is true we must do these things
> We must cut our throats
>
> The fly in the bottle

Insane, the insane fly

Which, over the city
Is the bright light of shipwreck
(NCP 173)

Not only is there evidence, as Nicholls points out, that the war "almost took Oppen back to his decision to abandon writing in the thirties" (FM 85), but these lines make explicit reference to the war. As Jeremy Hooker writes, pointing to the ambiguity between airwaves and airstrikes:

> The 'air' is the appearance; it is also the air on which we and all living things depend for our existence, and the air carrying presidential words and images. 'The air of atrocity' is 'A plume of smoke, visible at a distance': the image of the war, seen on TV screens by millions of Americans and people throughout the world, and even by combatants [...]. The appearance is 'a plume of smoke'; the reality is people burning [...]. What the eye sees is 'a distance / In which people burn'—it is that 'distance' which makes possible both the atrocity and the evasion of meaning and responsibility. (Hooker 81)

I would simply add that Oppen's choice of the unspecified word "people," instead of being proof of his disconnectedness with the monstrous ordeal of the Vietnamese people, was chosen exactly because these are people, any people, you, and me. The ordinariness of the word prolongs and reveals the ordinariness of the atrocity: its namelessness illustrates that *these* people burning are not us, at the same time as it shocks one into realizing that these are *people* burning. So that in that small word, Oppen's dialectic of we/us/I become exemplified, and quite explicitly so. The flies, Oppen's rendition of the bombers flying over Vietnam, "the insane, poisonous Johnsonian flies" (SL 177), cannot be shown the way out the bottle. In the face of this situation, Oppen's statement is again a blunt and direct one: "If it is true we must do these things / We must cut our throats." One cannot say there no passion nor personal involvement in these lines. What of section 20's "Farm animals, / Draft animals, beasts for slaughter," (NCP 174)? Is that not a clear enough reference to the draft and the ensuing massacre? The lines from the lengthy 26th section, already quoted in the previous chapter, "How shall one know a generation, a new generation? / Not by the dew on them! Where the earth is most torn / And the wounds untended [...]" (NCP 178), clearly address the younger generation being sent to Vietnam. It echoes section 14, in which Oppen recounts his experience in World War II. The paradox is that even at that time he was not part of the young generation, being well in his thirties when his fellow soldiers were barely twenty (Hoffman 2013, 54). So that his situation during the Vietnam war strangely mirrors his own past. One can hardly think of a more potent sign of personal "absorption." But Perloff finds the poems lacking in specific images, and when they do occur, they are neglected, or misunderstood:

> Arresting as such images are, they mark a retreat into a private life—the life of the nuclear family—that protects us from the condition "of being numerous." (Perloff 2008, 16)

Perloff is speaking of the more intimate sections, from 28 onward. But if one agrees that this poem is partly concerned with generations and the fate of each generation's fights, within the overall frame of this poet's generation, then certainly it would be absurd not to include some mention of his own family and its own generation's history. In the sense that "Of Being Numerous" is also addressed to the young generation—Oppen was curious about the 60s youth movements and was being more and more solicited by younger poets and critics—it is also addressed to his daughter. The poet's decision to join the army in 1942 was a source of much anxiety and later guilt because it meant leaving his wife and child. Thus, far from being a "retreat" or a "protection" from "being numerous," these intimate moments find a place in the poem sometimes as a haven, yes, but also as reminders of what is and was at risk. I do not mean to show Oppen's poem to be the poetic continuation of his past actions. Supplying the necessary biographical context does not automatically suggest that one is providing general political cause for a given poetic effect. But turning Oppen's poetic economy against itself to accuse its sparseness of being a sign of dereliction of poetic duty clearly manipulates the texts beyond what is possible.

In the end, Perloff's main point reaches even further. Reading the word "numerous" in the title also as "a reference to pure number, and a punning reference at that ('numerous' also referring to the poet's 'numbers' so that we can read the title as being 'Of being a poet')" (Perloff 2008, 2), Perloff sees Oppen's success as deriving from "the other meaning of 'numerous' [that] comes into play—that one can make poetry of one's experience" (Perloff 2008, 6). To that effect, she concludes:

> What is finally affirmed in this beautiful and difficult long poem is not, I think, any sort of "populist vision," much less the possibility of social transformation. Rather, "Of Being Numerous" is a testimony to the need for—but difficulty of—survival—survival won by the "curious" ability of poeisis itself to make the "numbers" interlock. (Perloff 2008, 18)

This oddly Zukofskian apology for Oppen's poem reveals a larger underlying debate, which Perloff introduced at the beginning of her essay. Perloff quotes from Tom Mandel's letter to Burton Hatlen, after their interview of George and Mary:

> A certain suspicion attaches to George, a suspicion on the part of another generation of poets quite screwed down to what they're spending their lives doing, for having given up the task during 25 years. That is why, in the interview we did, I hoped he would out with having written just not published during those years; just because it seems a questionable move when someone abandons the art as not holding enough for him, 'not the most important thing in the world,' as if, *a seeker*, one would go only to that 'most important thing.' But wouldn't that be just the poet's task, to make it important? (MP 49)

The suspicion in question derives, as the next passage shows, from a narrowing down of the perspective to only poets and poetry, against Oppen's more ambiguous choice, in such instances, to consider what one should do as a poet or as an individual. Mandel goes on to make the Zukofsky reference quite transparent, in a passage not included in Perloff's piece:

> Thus, if you will, another poet might see more virtues in Zukofsky's mole-millenia of digging through and casting aside slough (say *"A"-8*, to keep within the sphere of politics/poetry) toward the resplendent poetics of *"A"-22/3*. No matter that one *leaves* the world in the effort, poetry being written at some remove (that is, such is our history as poets: it need not be so written. ((?)) Not-writing moves it no closer of course). (MP 49)

Mandel's and Perloff's point that "not-writing" moves poetry no closer to the world seems odd regarding Oppen's twenty-five-year hiatus, which was meant to bring him, and not his poetry, closer to the world. In other words, Hugh Kenner's well-known statement will not do anymore. Further down in Tom Mandel's letter to Burton Hatlen, one reads: "Nor does Kenner's 'in short it took 25 years to write the next poem' help at all, since that's *not* what happened but rather a metaphor enabling one to look away from what happened" (MP 49). Oppen himself, though he constantly used, and maybe hid behind, that metaphor, provides this account of Kenner providing him with that line: "We visited Hugh Kenner. Our politics (the plural means Mary Oppen and I), somewhat awkward. Kenner being far to the right, and I sort of wanted to keep poking at these things." Then talking about the shock of the Depression:

> You either did something or you didn't do something. In the arts even as a poet I (you could imagine how small a public even those I looked up to as established poets had at this time), well, I was saying to Kenner about populism. I was well launched and Kenner interrupted and said: 'In brief it took you twenty-five years to write the next poem.' (Amirkhanian and Gitin 1975, 23)

I would argue that Kenner's interruption and censoring of "what had happened," allowed Oppen, albeit paradoxically, to maintain the strict dichotomy he so adamantly advocated between poetry and politics. Instead, when attempting to make Oppen's poetry political—either to praise or question it—his work becomes the example everyone had been looking for, allowing one to finally move beyond the paradox that opposes committed writing to committing to action. While Oppen always refused the idea that poetry could be politically effective, the time-lapse in his biography has allowed critics to contradict him on one of his core beliefs. Whereas this gap stands as living proof that Oppen denied any political efficacy to poetry, it is surreptitiously turned into an instrument of political legitimation for his poetry, on the basis that Oppen did not compromise by writing an ode to Lenin or by being the "Whitman of the factories" (FM 84) he refused to be. Oppen's strict separation between politics and poetry becomes the main argument that justifies commenting on how his poetry reflects and is informed by his politics, as though, according to the logic of an absurd analogy, having kept them apart precisely allowed for comparisons.

Note

1. I borrow this title from Oppen's poem (NCP 346).

References

Amirkhanian, Charles and Gitin, David. 1975. "A Conversation with George Oppen." *Ironwood* 5 3/1: 21–24.

Crane, Heart. 1986. *Complete Poems*. New York: Liveright Publishing.

Davidson, Michael. 2011. *On the Outskirts of Form: Practicing Cultural Poetics*. Middletown, CT: Wesleyan University Press.

Dembo, L. S., and Pondrom, Cyrena N., eds. 1972. *The Contemporary Writer: Interviews with Sixteen Novelists and Poets*. Madison: The University of Wisconsin Press.

Dembo, L. S. 1988. *The Monological Jew: A Literary Study*. Madison: University of Wisconsin Press.

Eagleton, Terry. 2005. *The Function of Criticism*. London: Verso.

Filreis, Alan. 2008. *Counter-Revolution of the Word. The Conversative attack on Modern Poetry, 1945–1960*. Chapel Hill: The University of North Carolina Press.

Finkelstein, Norman. 1981. "Political Commitment and Poetic Subjectification: George Oppen's Test of Truth." *Contemporary Literature* 22/1: 24–41.

Fisher, Tom. 2009. "A Political Poetics: George Oppen and the Essential Life of the Poem." *Arizona Quarterly* 65/ 2: 83–98.

Fredman, Stephen, ed. 2005. *A Concise Companion to Twentieth Century American Poetry*. Malden, MA: Blackwell.

Freeman, John, ed. 1985. *Not Comforts / But Vision: Essays on the Poetry of George Oppen*. Budleigh Salterton: Interim Press.

Hass, Robert. 1985. "George Oppen: A Tribute." *Ironwood* 26 13/2: 38–42.

Hoffman, Eric. 2008. "Of Hours: George Oppen, Albert Camus and the Illuminated World." *Jacket*. http://jacketmagazine.com/36/oppen-hoffman.shtml

———. 2013. *Oppen: A Narrative*. Bristol: Shearsman Books.

Hooker, Jeremy. 1985. "'The Boundaries of Our Distances': On 'Of Being Numerous.'" *Ironwood* 26 13/2: 81–103.

Jameson, Frederic. 2002. *The Political Unconscious. Narrative as a Socially Symbolic Act*. London: Routledge.

Nealon, Christopher. 2011. *The Matter of Capital. Poetry and Crisis in the American Century*. Cambridge, MA: Harvard University Press.

Perloff, Marjorie. 2008. "The Shipwreck of the Singular: George Oppen's 'Of Being Numerous'." http://marjorieperloff.com/articles/oppen-numerous/

Wilkinson, John. 2010. "The Glass Enclosure: Transparency and Glitter in the Poetry of George Oppen." *Critical Inquiry* 36/2: 218–238.

CHAPTER SIX

A Realist Poetry

When Oppen does express his views about the function of poetry within the commonplace, and discusses all the necessary political ramifications, they receive little attention. There is indeed no better catalyst than Oppen's essay "The Mind's Own Place" to reveal how strongly the critical consensus can sometimes resist a much-needed and very basic sense of the commonplace. Oppen's one published essay, "The Mind's Own Place,", which originally appeared in *Kultur* 7 (Autumn 1962), along with reprints of five essays by Louis Zukofsky, including his early objectivist critical prose, illustrates the (re)birth of post-World War II objectivist poetics. Yet lately called "a poor performance," "rambling and confused," and "an evasion of the poet's deepest insights" (Weinfield 2009, 26), it has yet to be taken seriously enough. Henry Weinfield's vehement rejection stems from a perceptible disappointment at the thought that Oppen should have still rehashed "a crude and narrow empiricism" which "by now, in 1962, is a shop-worn group of ideas" (Weinfield 2009, 27). Although I will argue against Weinfield's dismissal of Oppen's essay, it is important to wonder why that essay is in fact generally received as pretty anachronistic. The reasons depend for the greatest part on one's views on objectivism, and on Oppen's own trajectory before and after 1960. A palpable discomfort with venerable notions like sincerity and truthfulness—both questionable and even impractical critical tools to be sure—has everyone trying to label Oppen a former objectivist, now turned existentialist, philosopher, thinker, ontologist, political poet or not enough of a political poet: in short, anything but an objectivist, anything but a supporter of some "crude and narrow empiricism." In that sense, Weinfield's argument that the mind's own place must be the mind and nothing but the mind, showing "the depth and intensity of the thought process that unfolds" as a kind of "dialogue the poet carries with a pantheon of other thinkers" (Weinfield 2009, 40), requiring the "setting aside of 'objective reality'" as now deemed unworthy of the general conversation, is only an extreme example of a much broader issue.

Empiricism is viewed, throughout Weinfield's reasoning, as a fraudulent aspiration: "Objectivist theory [...] wants to give priority both to the poem and to the world of objects (which constitutes reality and to which it has immediate access); and in conflating these two domains, it manipulates the criterion of sincerity, so as to make it appear to apply to both of them in the same way" (Weinfield 2009, 29). Weinfield sees an insurmountable contradiction in the fact that "while Objectivism's metaphysical perspective (by which I mean perspective on what constitutes reality) implies the priority of a world of objects—objects that act upon the sense of the poet, who then serves as a transparent medium for rendering the world—its aesthetic commitment implies the priority of an artistic shaping process" (Weinfield 2009, 28). This logic certainly illustrates the opposition between the two notions of sincerity and objectification, but it does not explain or resolve it in any coherent fashion. For even if Zukofsky makes a distinction, in his 1931 essay "Sincerity and Objectification," between three quotations from Reznikoff, one illustrating sincerity, the other two objectification (Zukofsky 2000, 195), the difference is in degree, not in kind. Moreover, asking who came first, the hen-world or the egg-poem, can never lead to any satisfying answer. Worse, it supposes that the long-standing ambiguities of the word "object" in the Latinate West could be settled once and for all and that a single meaning should be assigned to the word. I would rather insist, along with the dictionary, that an "object" may be grasped in the hand and the mind without it being the sign of a guilty and shameful "sleight of hand" (Weinfield 2009, 28). Yet even Eleanor Berry, who carefully differentiates between the several evolutions in Oppen's syntax and metrics, finally opposes sincerity and objectification as well when she presents the following conclusion:

> It becomes apparent that the principle of sincerity can lead to results contrary to the principle of objectification—or, at least, to results that require a reinterpretation of objectification. Even as Oppen's poetic line is perforated and submerged in the seventies, so his poems cease in the seventies to be palpable as made objects. What is objectified in Oppen's recent poetry are the very processes by which language makes and unmakes meaning. (Berry 1984, 322)

Oddly enough, in the previous paragraph Berry quotes Oppen saying that objectification meant "the objectification of the poem, the making an object of the poem" in the sense of "achieving form" (Dembo 1972, 173). In other words, language processes were always the implied object. For which of Oppen's poems could be said to fall in the category of the palpable made object in the first place? Unless one mistakes objectification for the writing of calligrams, sincerity does not stand in the way. Think of Oppen when he speaks of testing nouns, of trying "to lay down the substantive for its own sake" (Dembo 1972, 174) in the hope of providing access to "the life of the mind" as a feeling "that the thing is there and that it's quite something to see. It's an awareness of the world, a lyric reaction to the world" (Dembo 1972, 177). Describing *Of Being Numerous* as "a series of images, of experiences...whether or not one will consider the concept of humanity to be valid, something that is, or else have to regard it as simply being a word" (Dembo 1972, 175), Oppen is experimenting with the reality of a collective noun inside a clear dialectical frame that tries to tie in what can be thought, what is, and what can be said. Contrary to his critics, Oppen never differentiates so abruptly between world and word. Commenting on a line from Michael McClure's *Dark Brown*, in the rare occurrence that is Oppen's "Three Poets" review for *Poetry* (1962), he writes: "This verse simply does not achieve words at all, or disperses them into excitement, intoxication, meaninglessness, a destruction of the sense of self among things" (SP 27). How to achieve words and a sense of self among things are explicitly connected in Oppen's remark.

These issues are at the heart of Oppen's poetry from the late fifties and early sixties, and are largely expounded in "The Mind's Own Place." But the essay has mostly been discussed for the few definitive statements it offers in connection to Oppen's politics and not as a coherent piece. The one specific point which has been acknowledged is that the essay was written in reaction to a poem by and an argument with Denise Levertov, the issue being whether Levertov's assertions in a poem from *The Jacob's Ladder* (1961) were substantiated in that poem or not (FM 55)—the poem Oppen mostly reacts to is entitled "During the Eichmann Trial." What I would like to address now is the essay's poetics, which have too seldom been studied as a whole because of the essay's apparently rambling progress.

In his essay, Oppen tells the story of his generation's historical consciousness, and investigates the fundamental paradox upon which it lies. Whereas the development of a national, vernacular, and secular literary landscape had laid the foundations, in Europe, for the modern concept of literary autonomy, Oppen's own *Grounding of American Poetry*, to use Stephen Fredman's excellent title, lays bare this new literary field, which from the start is conceived from a heteronomous perspective, as subject to historical and cultural impositions. In other words, issues of aesthetic autonomy have become matters of historical inscription. As the influence of foreign models (English and European in general) faded, the American idiom could become the vital domestic resource poets required and upon this shift was predicated the belief that something real was being perceived at last. That seminal association of "reality" with "America" is Oppen's first point in the essay. He opens on the opposition between Impressionist painters and "the art attitudes of the academy" (SP 30), which leads him to insist that art must let go of the "cocoon of 'Beauty'" and embrace the need "to know and to disclose" (SP 30). Such was the birth of modern American poetry—tellingly, Oppen does not use the word "modernist":

> [...] the determination to find the image, the thing encountered, the thing seen each day whose meaning has become the meaning and the color of our lives. (SP 30)

Oppen then momentarily abandons the pictorial parallel, and focuses on modern poetry and modern American poetry. A definitive condemnation of "Philistia and Bohemia" follows, along with praise for "a skill of accuracy, of precision, a test of truth" (SP 30) which one has come to know as the Pound-Williams strain of modernism. But Oppen introduces a word upon which his own departure from these two figures may be said to depend, "the word *reality*." Although Oppen cautiously points out that the word "has long since ceased to mean anything recognizably 'real' at all" (SP 30), he concludes that the English language is "stuck with it." So that the poet's task must be "to restore meaning to the word" (SP 30). Two quotations, one from Russell and the other from Heraclitus, are brought in to restore the word's meaning: "If I were to describe reality as I found it, I would have to include my arm," from Russell, and "'If it all went up in smoke,' that smoke would remain,'" from Heraclitus (SP 30–31). For Oppen, "the shock of that sentence" (SP 31) from Heraclitus becomes palpable in "the arbitrary fact, and not any quality of wisdom literature, which creates the impact of the poets" (SP 31). Both sentences, that is, quotations—Russell's about how our sense-data testify to our own impingement upon them, and Heraclitus's about our perceptions' resilience and adaptability to a fragmented universe—are heavily reworked by Oppen to bring about a greater "'shock of recognition'" (SP 31). The next page or so is dedicated to a brief periodizing of American modernism, again through an introductory reference to painters—here the Ash Can school. In doing so, Oppen proceeds to single out what he calls Williams' populism—"his insistence on 'the American idiom'" and his care for "the image derived from day-to-day experience" (SP 31). In each case, either the philosophers' two quotations or Williams' contribution, Oppen emphasizes the same idea on two different levels.

First, reality is restored to meaning through a shocking awareness of the facts. These facts, from what the two quotations offer the reader, both point to instances when consciousness becomes aware of itself as a form of confrontation with "'the things that exist'" (SP 31). Secondly, the arbitrariness of these facts, which equates one's knowledge of them with a form of initial shock, relies on idiom, daily life, "freedom from the art subject" (SP 31)—in other words, in these being American facts, the facts of American life. From Oppen's appropriation of Heraclitus to the very name "Ash Can school," the same iconoclastic relationship to tradition is advocated. Idiom is reality—the linguistic fact of reality. One needs to bear this in mind when reading the much-quoted *ars poetica* that follows:

> It is possible to find a metaphor for anything, an analogue: but the image is encountered, not found; it is an account of the poet's perception, the act of perception; it is a test of sincerity, a test of conviction, the rare poetic quality of truthfulness. (SP 31–32)

As though morphologically enacting his own poetic process, Oppen's paronomastic reduction goes from encounter to "account," then to "act," before repeating his test of the "data of experience" as "the sense of a[n American] poet among [American] things" (SP 32), if I may so insist. These lines rephrase some of Zukofsky's words from the *Poetry* issue of 1931, but with greater emphasis placed on idiom as fact than on composition. The plea Oppen makes for "the concrete materials of the poem," for "confidence" in the poem itself "and in its materials," is pitted against "performance" as "histrionics" or "desire for the trick of gracefulness" (SP 32). Oppen's example is Levertov's "Matins" (Levertov 1968, 57), which he praises for the idiomatic clarity of its details, "the events of a domestic morning" (SP 32). Oppen then returns to rapid periodizing, this time focusing on the Beats and the San Francisco school, heirs to Williams, "the most American of the American poets of his generation" (SP 33). Now Oppen himself reflects upon his own poetic education, and writes: "I belong to a generation that grew more American—literarily at least—as it approached adult estate: we grew up on English writing—and German fairy tales—as I think no American any longer does" (SP 33). The diminished prestige of England and Germany is not only a fact of the times for an American in the early sixties. Oppen is explicitly describing his own early instruction as a form of Americanization of himself, as he was "tired of Invocation to Someone Else's Muse" (SP 34). However, Oppen does not sacrifice to American literary folklore either:

> I myself was not the barefoot American boy. Having been born near New York, like many of these young poets, I was undoubtedly shod by the age of three months. But neither the barefoot boy nor Robert Frost is really the most American thing in the world, and there are facts to consider beyond orthopedic. (SP 34)

Neither Twain, whom he mentions previous to this statement, nor Whittier nor Frost is deemed "really the most American thing." Oppen thus positions himself against part of the new American tradition as a twentieth century New York born poet aware of other facts to consider, although what these facts could be remains elusive at this point. He then proceeds with a sketchy account of Puritan values, their usefulness in developing American prosperity, their ultimate limitations and the need to reinvent the social covenant at the time of the "Freedom Rides" and the "Peace Marches" (SP 35). Now these facts appear: Oppen's reference to the Civil Rights movement and to the Cold War, followed by a circuitous reminder—through a quote from Bertolt Brecht—of the Great Depression and World War II, both decisive periods in Oppen's life. Yet if war and socio-economic disaster are now "the most American things," they are things that challenge one's capacity to write, for "[t]here are situations which cannot honorably be met by art, and surely no one need fiddle precisely at the moment that the house next door is burning" (SP 36). Indeed, "the question can only be whether one intends, at a given time, to write poetry or not" (SP 36). The argument, if it is well documented by critics, needs to be located within Oppen's discussion of his formative years against the background of America's coming of age. The reason why the connection is difficult to make is precisely because it is an arduous one. At the exact moment when Oppen is about to divulge what facts a poet must respond to, free from inherited foreign influences as well as from early domestic classics, the question takes on another dimension. If an American focus proves liberating for otherwise untold present realities, which may now pour into the poem, the urgency of these very facts pleads against the writing of poetry. Budding modernity comes crashing against a moral dilemma, which Oppen may be said to have solved by strictly separating the realm of aesthetics and the world of moral action.

In conclusion, Oppen does not put his own experiences forward, but rather "declares [the poet's] political nonavailability" (SP 37) before suggesting that the one statement needed at the time—a peace treaty between Russia and the United States—would have to move beyond the euphemisms in "the language on both sides" (SP 37). Oppen asks who could write that poem, "write that she opened her front door, having sent the children to school, and felt the fresh authentic air in her face and wanted—*that*?" (SP 37). One wonders indeed what the poem would sound like, since one must not "give political statements the aura of eternal truth" (SP 36). The solution implies bringing together the two dimensions of "The Mind's Own Place"—its abstract aesthetic concerns and its basic sense of historical context. Nowhere is this connection more apparent than in the two philosophical quotations, which seem like attempts at wording that difficult poem of today, in the sense that Heraclitus, Russell, and the two parties in the Cold War make up a single continuum. "'If it all went up in smoke,' that smoke would remain," is Heraclitus rewritten in the light of the atom and Auschwitz, in the American idiom of the day. Similarly, the need to include one's arm in the description of reality suggests a form of maiming when accounting for the actual ground of one's perceptions, which is always also "the terrible ground" (NCP 81), to use Oppen's words about his war experience.

Only then may one fully grasp the meaning of Milton's lines from *Paradise Lost* that refer to Satan and which Oppen adapts for his title—"A mind not changed by place or time! / The mind is its own place and in itself / Can make a Heaven of Hell, a Hell of Heaven" (Milton 2005, 10). It has been noticed that Milton's lines point in opposite directions: "the second half of the argument ('[t] he mind is its own place') is Cartesian in its absolute separation between mind and matter, the first part ('[a] mind not to be changed') is Stoic" (Gillies 2007, 49). The contradiction is addressed in Book Four, when Satan "now in prospect of Eden" (Milton 2005, 77) despairs of ever changing his condition, since "from Hell / One step no more than from himself can fly / By change of place" (Milton 2005, 78), thus showing "the hollowness of his boast" (Gillies 2007, 50) in Book One. However, Milton's lines may be said to have been altered by Oppen to mean that the mind must find its sense of place elsewhere than within its own boundaries. Oppen's replacement of "is its own place" with the genitive "The Mind's Own Place" requires rephrasing to complete the statement either as a question (asking *what* is the mind's own place) or an answer (*this* is the mind's own place). Syntactically, the segment's truncated aspect, compared to the original, points outside itself: the genitive noun phrase begs for an attribute.

Within the general architecture of *Paradise Lost*, it may also be true that Oppen follows Milton's vision of Satan's seclusion by saying that when the mind's own place is itself, one is truly in Hell. As he rewrote that title into section 7 from "A Narrative," Oppen insisted again: "His mind / Is its own place; He has no story. [...] Let it alone! It is deadly. What breath there is / In the rib cage we must draw / From the dimensions // Surrounding, whether or not we are lost / And choke on words" (NCP 153). So that instead of concluding that "the elimination of the verb in the title of Oppen's essay turns the solipsistic energies of Satan and Hamlet into a cozy euphemism that prevents us from even *hearing* the Miltonic echo and hence from grasping the epistemological problem to which Satan's assertion is connected" (Weinfield 2009, 27), I would suggest that Oppen's title already points toward the argument in "A Narrative": namely, that the cozy solipsistic euphemisms of Satan or Hamlet choking on words prevent one from hearing and grasping "the dimensions // Surrounding." To put it another way, the place the mind must find is its own, and its own place is the mind's own time, its own circumstances, which will "rid the poem of false impositions, false / impositions: to trust the *content.* To speak as clearly / as it can of TIME. *A* TIME" (SP 45). Outside that difficult equation, Oppen's essay merely seems to praise Williams abundantly but somewhat too vaguely, and not to look back explicitly enough on Pound's role, or indeed Zukofsky's in shaping Oppen's early poetic landscape. These may be the shortcomings of an occasional piece, after all, which should not be dealt with as definitive or excessively authoritative. Still, it is worth detailing Oppen's reasoning because this is a revealing text. In it, the notion of idiom becomes so plastic as to enclose, or shift, from words themselves to the poet's living conditions. Putting it differently, Oppen's interest in what he calls reality is not limited to the reality of his words, their capacity to embody a form of knowledge after Williams, to achieve Pound's historical pigment, or to bring the rays of a linguistic object to a focus after Zukofsky. Oppen does not speak of clothing language in more reality—whatever that could practically mean—but hopes that language may restore reality to a sense of reality.

At this point, one should note that critics who favor the phenomenology of the mind over perceptions and actual phenomena are not alone. The idea of a break from "realistic" and historical concerns in favor of ahistorical or abstract thinking in Oppen's poetry is even oddly paralleled by the idea of an underlying continuity, all along Oppen's career, between formal and politico-historical concerns. While the two approaches might seem at odds, they share a common disregard for Oppen's realism—in the name of philosophy for the first approach, in the name of politics for the second. Michael Davidson's wish for an "objectivist continuum" (Davidson 1997, 21) illustrates this supposed continuity between formal strategies and political ones, which would be the hallmark of "an investment in the materiality of [one's] medium to achieve social ends" (Davidson 1997, 27). But the idea of a continuity from culture to politics grasped as forms is no less philosophical than other, perhaps more traditional, ontological claims, for it enacts "[t]he progressive relinquishment of economic or political structures as the central concerns of theory[,] accompanied by a basic shift in the whole centre of gravity of European Marxism toward *philosophy*" (Anderson 1976, 49). Once "the material word" stands for "formalism as a material agent within the social" (Davidson 1997, 239), the "structural divorce" of "Marxism from political practice" (Anderson 1976, 29) becomes effective. In other words, according to Anderson,

> The organic unity of theory and practice realized in the classical generation of Marxists before the First World War, who performed an inseparably politico-intellectual function within their respective parties in Eastern and Central Europe, was to be increasingly severed in the half-century from 1918 to 1968, in Western Europe. (Anderson 1976, 29)

A perfect example of this severance parading as continuity would be Ruth Jennison's views on Oppen's first book, *Discrete Series*, when she writes:

> *Discrete Series* [...] makes its political and aesthetic assertions [...] on a formal level. This emphasis allows the poems to dwell in spaces traditionally considered non-political, while still crafting progressive forms that testify to the deeply social nature of perceptual life. (Jennison 2012, 76)

Jennison believes some of Zukofsky's, Oppen's, or Niedecker's work from the thirties to be the epitome of a "materialist poetics [which] constructs an aesthetic enactment of the Marxian comparative historical method" (Jennison 2012, 15), which is summarized as "a historical methodology that highlights the constructed and mediated character of cultural life" (Jennison 2012, 14). The paradox one is meant to accept is that the more formal the work, the more materialistic it really is. This logic reveals the entrenched syllogism that goes: all language is social activity, all social activity is political, therefore all language activity is political—which thus equates the material nature of any activity with historical materialism, and reveals the materialistic fallacy already denounced by Jameson when he warns that "Marxism is, however, not a mechanical but a historical materialism: it does not assert the primacy of matter so much as it insists on an ultimate determination of the mode of production" (Jameson 1982, 30). Oppen himself never uses the word "Marxism" with such New Left ambiguity. Consider Oppen's discussion of his poem "Chartres":

> what the world   cried out above the mountain was I Am What   Is the marvel
> of the fact, the marvel of the real,   not the whole Christian or Hebrew orthodoxy - -
> (as for your point: what 'produces a cathedral' is a thousand men hauling stone
> and cracking stone for one man 'carrying by hand'   H Adams's is a pretty book, but
> what do you suppose he knew about handling stone (SL 254)

No matter how tempting it would be to allegorize the grammatical structure of the poem, laid bare like the visible arches inside a cathedral, and to compare these small words to the many workers who produced the cathedral, this would be a biased and reductive reading. The poem's architecture tries to give a feeling of weightlessness to the hollowed and massive building blocks that compose it, but the ekphrasis stops there. What the poem does is focus one's attention away from what the cathedral points to, and back to how it stands and what it stands on. Not any "orthodoxy" but the marvel of the fact of it standing. Still, some will maintain, including Weinfield, commenting on section 27 from "Of Being Numerous," that "Oppen is here developing a Marxist conception of poetry" which he then illustrates, after a detour through Adorno, as "one in which poetry depends on a relationship (veiled and attenuated, to be sure) between the poet and the 'productive forces'" (TP 265). Weinfield says this on the basis of Oppen's line in section 27 about the "workman" and his relationship with the poet. But "Marxism" as concreteness is not an analogy Oppen makes—whereas many will use that connection to extend his Communist activities into poetical ones. Oppen's remark in "Chartres" about "what produces a cathedral" is again quite straightforward. The poem did not make the thing, the workers did. The poem's observation, however constructivist in its own poetically productive right, never amounts to "hauling stone and cracking stone." The poem is neither an exposé of ideas nor the thing itself. In mistaking Oppen's perspective for their own, critics extend the definition of intellectual labor to any other labor. Jameson's remarks about this are again perfectly adequate:

> One cannot without intellectual dishonesty assimilate the 'production' of texts [...] to the production of goods by factory workers: writing and thinking are not alienated in that sense, and it is surely fatuous for intellectuals to seek to glamorize their tasks [...] by assimilating them to real work on the assembly line and to the experience of the resistance of matter in genuine manual labor. (Jameson 1982, 30)

"Marxism" is, at best, Oppen's word for community, commonplace, humanity or the people. When prompted by John Crawford's enquiries, Oppen retrospectively considers *Discrete Series* and writes simply: "The 'Marxism' of *Discrete Series* is, was felt as, the struggle against the loss of commonplace" (SL 254). Otherwise, "Marxism" means what it means most often and literally for Oppen, namely "'active' Marxism - - - Marxism in action" (SL 255), as when he chides Crawford thus:

> your marxism is too 'scholarly'   Marx's books are Marx's books, but the Marxist political parties are ways to relieve the suffering,   and simple ways they are,   or they are abominations---   are or will become so - - IF they are not, to get the dams built, to save the people - - -
>
> Marxists who don't get the dams built will sure as hell be lynched in a 'People's Republic'   Which means nothing at all about a new Socialist man or a new art or anything of the sort, it means getting the dams built--- and, no, I don't want people to be hungry. (SL 255)

The habit of mistaking the means of production for the production of meanings—an oddly persistent sleight of hand—should not be extended to Oppen's work, but rather be limited to, for instance, Jerome McGann's doctrine in "Contemporary Poetry, Alternate Routes," when he writes that Ron Silliman's *Tjanting* "does not tell the/a 'story' of 'class struggle.' [...] Rather *Tjanting* is a localized instance of class struggle itself: not merely Silliman's personal act of struggle, but his deployment of an artistic occasion within which such struggle may take place" (Hallberg 1987, 271–272). Charles Altieri's "Without Consequences Is No Politics: A Response to Jerome McGann" meticulously deconstructed these "pious analogies claiming to link art as a mode of production and the psychic economies governing basic forms of social life" (Hallberg 1987, 303). Oppen's response to Crawford's reading of section 20 from "Of Being Numerous" is adamant about the fact that he is "not going to say thank god for the poor, the suffering, they supply us with 'moral action'" (SL 254). Given Oppen's condemnation of what he calls "all the search for a morality of altruism, all the dependence on the poor to confer value" (Dembo 1972 177), "Marxist" or "materialistic" readings seem definitively inappropriate. Yet even Lyn Hejinian writes that "Oppen's testing of the character and 'truth' of reality is a conceptually materialist, thus at least implicitly Marxist, undertaking" (TP 51), when presenting otherwise precious and detailed context on how *Discrete Series* came about.

On the contrary, as Michael Heller puts it, "[t]he cry of the poem, its revolving trope, is the voicing of its own inability to conform to the hegemonies of the Marxist thinking of the thirties" (Heller 2012, 32–33). Moreover, as Heller insists, it is not as though the notion of materiality had travelled intact from the thirties onward:

> So perception, rending it accurately into speech, gives way to the understanding that words must be "treated as enemies" or "ghosts" (Oppen 2002, 116) [NCP 116]. They no longer have "thingness" or materiality or even any of the Poundian "gists" and "piths" of the language Oppen took up when he wrote *Discrete Series*. (Heller 2012, 134)

Heller is not insinuating that *The Materials* fails to live up to its title, but rather warns that the title involves a search or a fight for those materials, and not their immediate celebration. The word "materiality" has been used to apply an oddly compounded critical template onto Oppen's *Discrete Series*. Jennison's chapter on Oppen in *The Zukofsky Era* reads Oppen's first book as a paratactic, materialistic precursor of Silliman's *New Sentence*, while others praise the materiality of language in *The Materials* after the very same logic that has "the New Critical doctrines of the heresy of paraphrase and the fallacy of intention start to look indistinguishable from what Perloff and Hejinian describe as language poetry's commitment to the material form of the text and readerly participation in it" (Ashton 2005, 27). Both approaches aim to reinforce the "myth of Objectivist continuity" (Heller 2012, 133), and to allow literary history to remain separate from world history. In other words: "Oppen speaks of the 'concrete materials of the poem,' but can he any longer mean something so simple as the words' referential character?" (Heller 2012, 134). Only if one neglects that specific context does Oppen's essay seem an anachronistic attempt to repeat old early modernist tenets. In a 1969 letter to Robert Duncan, Oppen develops the idea that his empiricism is closely connected to historical turmoil:

> And in Materials, a poem *Narrative*, which reports an experience in war: it is a recognition of sky and earth, a rebirth of words in war that you speak of also in the introduction ... I write but cannot hope to live in what is written: I mean to find, not create, the handholds [...] I feel we must *find* We are native, hopelessly native . . Hopelessly *included* (SL 183)

There is no such poem in Oppen's *Materials*—"A Narrative" appears in *This in Which* but does not directly report a war experience, nor does the unpublished "Narrative" (NCP 319–320). Is Oppen alluding to "Survival: Infantry"? Or already suggesting some of the content of "Myth of the Blaze"? The most thorough war reporting takes place in "Route," in *Of Being Numerous*. What matters is that to Duncan's "leap, the leap into the music," Oppen opposes his "dedication to 'realism,' to the proof in the image rather than the creation of image for the first time" (SL 183). Duncan's work is especially challenging, Oppen acknowledges with admiration, and perhaps for this reason allows him to articulate more fully his own standpoint. Once more, inclusion or nativeness testifies to where the mind resides, but that recognition, as opposed by Oppen to invention, amounts to a kind of rebirth only as it takes place in war. Far from any sense of phoenix-like destructive creativeness, or some nostalgic taste for ruins, what materials Oppen will find are ambivalent instances of the finite.

Why the sterile opposition between speculation and reportage lives on partly depends on how one chooses to read Oppen's statements about poetic inception such as this one, in which he evokes "place in another sense; place without the words, the wordless sphere in the mind - - Or rather the wordless sphere with things including a word or so in it. ... That I still believe to be, as they say, Poem: the thing in the mind before the words to be able to hold it even against the language - - - " (SL 236). Place as historical circumstance and "place without the words" seem impossible to reconcile, as though the divide between inception and perception could not be bridged. Yet I would maintain that what Oppen is doing in describing "the thing in the mind" is in fact referring to things (including words) as they stand before his eyes, but still "in the mind" only in the sense that they stand "before the words." By holding 'it'—the perception of things and of words as things—"even against the language," the poet thus dramatizes the process of expression as a form of response to the existing world.

In the last text in Oppen's *Selected Papers*—a reply to a letter from Reinhold Schiffer, in preparation for an interview, published posthumously in *Sagetrieb* in 1984—Oppen makes this point quite explicit. In discussing his revisions of some lines from his poem "To Make Much" (NCP 271–272), Oppen states: "The word, the right word, it seems to stand outside of us" (SP 48). Further down he adds that "[t]he word in one's own mouth becomes as strange as infinity—even as strange as the finite, strange as things" (SP 48). Crucially to Oppen, conquering the externality of words requires that one has first confronted the facts which Oppen so consistently argued stood outside the poem as well, which was to him the hallmark of being "a realist, a realist in the sense that something exists outside the poem" (Heller 2012, 94), of practicing "a Realist poetry: Realist in that it is concerned with a fact that it did not create" (SL 140). Those outside facts are, in spite of Oppen's phrasing, no abstractions. Yet Oppen's empirical and "realist" position has been downplayed, along with the role of perception in his poetry, to make room for a poetry of the mind. It always seems as if reality had been found lacking in some way, and the mind needed to reassert its control over it. The label "existentialist" perfectly encapsulates that strategy, and reveals its ultimate agenda. Nicholls, for instance, argues for "the irruption of the existential in the political" (FM 52), in the sense that post-war Marxism used the idea of consciousness to reinvigorate the notion of ideology. In "George Oppen, Albert Camus and the Illuminated World," Eric Hoffman reminds us (Hoffman 2008, 1) that L. S. Dembo went even further and wrote, "When Oppen put pen to paper again, it was... as an existentialist, not as a socialist" (Dembo 1988, 137). In the end, "existential" or "existentialist" may be just a conveniently vague term, as Susan Thackrey warns, in her introduction to *George Oppen: A Radical Practice*, when she writes that it would be "easy, given his reading in Heidegger and Merleau-Ponty, to label this 'existentialist' and be done with it" (Thackrey 2001, 9). When Stephen Fredman quotes from George and Mary Oppen's interview with Kevin Power, in which Oppen claims that the prose section from "Route" could have been written "by any of the Existentialists" (Power 1978, 197), Fredman carefully includes Oppen's own clarification, from that interview, according to which the word is taken to mean only, "Existential in the sense that you do what you do and that is the answer ... Simply that you are yourself" (ON 290). Despite such precautions, the desire to deny Oppen's realist stand sometimes proves too strong. A recent and consistent existentialist reading of Oppen, Robert Baker's 2012 *In Dark Again in Wonder: The Poetry of René Char and George Oppen*, shows how far one may go in that direction. Baker's agenda is made apparent from the start:

> One could characterize this, I think, as late romantic, existentialist poetry, one refracted by the objectivist emphases on a certain phase of modernism and by the phenomenological currents in modern phenomenology. (Baker 2012, 58)

Oppen's poetry is indeed viewed by Baker as a form of ancestral romanticism in objectivist, modernist, or phenomenological disguise, although it must be said that Baker does not always seem to differentiate between the terms. At the same time, Baker claims that "the language of empiricist philosophy and objectivist poetics are not adequate to an understanding of what he is doing in his poetry from the late fifties on" (Baker 2012, 91). So that in the end, Oppen's original poetic context gets written off to make him "one of the last romantics of the fifties and sixties" (Baker 2012, 103). The basic premise, reminiscent of Dembo's phrase, is that "Oppen holds to an existentialist position, itself an inflection of an older liberal position" (Baker 2012, 81). Though parts of Baker's discussion certainly testify to appropriate concerns, when for instance he focuses on the notion of faith in Oppen, thereby relocating Oppen in the larger frame of American transcendentalism, Baker undoubtedly overstates his case. One simply cannot take it for granted that "[Oppen] finds a sort of connection between the openness of vision and the openness of care. He belongs in this respect to a long romantic tradition" (Baker 2012, 87). Such generalizations as "to think is to walk abroad; to think is to enter the world further" (Baker 2012, 67), push Oppen's sense of disclosure too far out of bounds.

The gist of Baker's take on Oppen resides in the way he isolates a tension in Oppen "between a populist concern with the value of active building and a romantic concern with the value of meditative wonder" (Baker 2012, 113). But Baker does not try to see how the two interact. Because his perspective is exclusively a meditative one, Baker's reading is at times helpful in keeping closer to the text than others have done, as with his reading of section 26 in "Of Being Numerous" (Baker 2012, 85–86). But in his reading of Oppen's poem "Eros," Baker's angle effectively obscures a relatively straightforward poem. Looking at "Eros," I would like to show that an empirical, perception-based realism constitutes a valid approach to Oppen's work.

Concentrating only on the items in the poem testifying to "the built world" (Baker 2012, 79) which in spite of their degradation "are nevertheless emblems in Oppen's work of the shared project of constructing a habitable human world" (Baker 2012, 79), leading all the way to "the full resonance of wonder, of curiosity: the openness of Eros longing to discover what matters, searching for sources and horizons to live by" (Baker 2012, 80), Baker endows the poem with an uplifting confidence that is absent from it. The poems' lines used by Baker simply speak of "A devoutness // Toward the future / Recorded in this city / Which taught my generation / Art / And the great paved places / Of the cities" (NCP 120–121). Baker connects these lines to others, in Oppen's work, that remind one of Reznikoff's "girder" poem. The lines I have quoted from the poem

"Eros" do seem to hint at such poetic concerns, intimately related to Oppen's New York experience in the 30s—his generation's time and place. But this poem's emphasis is on Paris as the place which served as a momentary refuge and point of reference for that same generation of American poets, writers, or painters. Not only that, but Paris is exclusively seen in the poem through the prism of its largest innercity cemetery. Baker quotes from "Eros" only as far as "the great places / Of the cities." But the next lines go "Maze // And wealth / Of ancestry" (NCP 121), making it unquestionable that one has not left the cemetery. On the contrary, the city of Paris, and to some extent any city, is implicitly taken to be but one big cemetery—the Père-Lachaise cemetery is in fact often referred to as a city onto itself.

The poem opens with a quote from the book of the Second Esdras in italic: "*Show me also whether there is more to come than is past, / or the greater part has already gone by us*" (NCP 120). Oppen's answer, in the final lines of the poem, is an apocalyptic vision of the tongues of the dead speaking in the cities and "the great squares void / Of their dead," reclaiming their lost voices. The cemetery is evoked as "a culture // Mined / From the ground…" (NCP 121), while the Père-Lachaise was introduced earlier with the line "Here above Paris—" (NCP 120). This is literally true, since it lies in the north-eastern part of Paris, geographically higher than the rest of the city, but the image is also that of an inverted world, where the dead lie "above" the living. Lastly, the core of the poem consists in a recollection of specific casualties: "To the plaque of the ten thousand / Last men of the Commune / Shot at the wall // In the cemetery of Père-Lachaise, and the grave / Of Largo Cabarello and the monuments to the Resistance—" (NCP 120). The introductory "To" implies an address in the form of a dedication: the plaque itself is "to them," but Oppen's syntax, "To the plaque," makes his lines a plaque to that plaque. As for the dead, their political significance is overwhelming: the Commune, Paris's most significant people's insurrection; Largo Cabarello, once nicknamed the "Spanish Lenin," who fled to France in 1939 where he died in 1946, in the wake of his return from a German concentration camp; the French Resistance to German occupation during World War II. But why "Eros" then? I am not implying that Oppen's poem should only be read as a form of mourning. Yet one must pay attention to the fact that these deaths are all untimely, violent and tragic deaths, and that they all point toward one's sacrifice of one's own life in the hope of a better one. Here is the lesson in that "Eros." The reader is not asked to let the dead lie in peace and praise the building of the city of tomorrow, but are asked to see that cities are paved with the deaths of many, and that one must speak for them, so that the terror in the almost grotesque opening lines of the poem may be atoned for by the knowledge of these dead men's desires.

Baker likens Oppen's to "the Eros of Freud's later work on civilization" (Baker 2012, 79), which itself exists only "to enforce renunciation or sublimation of those instincts which threaten to tear apart the sustaining activity of Eros in work, relationship, and culture" (Baker 2012, 79), only to point out that while "watching Europe slide toward nihilism and fascism, Freud was pessimistic about the whole enterprise," whereas Oppen, "for all his pessimism, thinks of the energy of our search for value, our Eros at the root, in broader terms than Freud" (Baker 2012, 79). The problem of course is that in this poem, death pervades culture and civilization, the walls, and the squares of which are scarred with the names of those whose "eros" was cut short. It opens on a putrescent picture:

> 'and you too, old man, so we have heard,
> Once ...'
> An old man's head, bulging
> And worn
> Almost into death.
>
> The head grows from within
> And is eroded. (NCP 120)

Baker knows that "the expansiveness of Oppen's later work involves at the same time a deepened sounding of the tragic: of failure, guilt, fear, haunting memory, and the approach of death at the personal level, of extreme disillusion at the political level. Perhaps this is slightly to overstate the matter" (Baker 2012, 94). Unfortunately, refusing to embrace both dimensions at once, Baker tips the scales in favor of a single reading which, as with this poem "Eros," severely understates the issue. As Oppen wrote in "Of Being Numerous," tragedy lies beneath your feet, for "We stand on // That denial / Of death that paved the cities, / Paved the cities // Generation / For generation" (NCP 178). That same denial of death is palpable in existentialist readings that seek to promote an empowerment of consciousness when, as John Seed once remarked, "[it] is a recurrent theme of Oppen's writing, the powerlessness of consciousness" (Freeman 1985, 17). But it is also present in formalist readings which consider formal strategies as commitments of a different yet equivalent type. From the powers of the mind to the power of literature, a similar hopefulness writes off the poem's actual humility. A clear example of this critical wishful thinking is Blau DuPlessis's statement when she writes: "Oppen's art is political in this way: commitment has migrated into form" (TP 187). If Oppen's commitment has "migrated into form," his choice not to write from the early 1930s to the late 1950s begs the question: why was that committed form not at hand before, and if it needed to be earned in some other, non-poetic way, then how can it all be turned over to form now? Another way of asking the same question would be to wonder whether this is a singular problem or not—it was not available for Oppen, but could have been or was for others. If one cannot write while the house next door is on fire (SP 36), and one resumes writing after the fire, what has happened to the fire? Form as a putting out of the fire as well as an extension of it, now transferred and absorbed by the work, would account for what happened between that fire alarm in the thirties and his 1972–75 *Myth of the Blaze* collection. What I wish to emphasize in the paramount importance of one's historical perspective when discussing this type of "migration." As readers, and even more so as critics, one desires the migration from political commitment to poetic commitment to become palpable, whereas chronologically, to put it very bluntly, it was no migration toward a better place, but a form of exile and defeat. Blau DuPlessis' words quoted by Oppen in section 9 from "Of Being Numerous" point to that same fact: "'Whether, as the intensity of seeing increases, one's distance / from Them, the people, does not also increase'" (NCP 167). The intensity of seeing, if understood as a greater conceptual—and hence also formal—accuracy, causes distance, and that remoteness is not bridged by the migration—it *is* the migration.

Blau DuPlessis's full statement reveals further implications. She states: "An artist must understand [...] that the political has 'migrated into' all art, and work with this situation and its implications. Oppen's art is political in this way: commitment has migrated into form" (TP 204). Reference is given to Adorno's 1962 article "Commitment," where the phrase "migrated into" may be found in the last paragraph. Adorno's text, from the very end of "Commitment," reads as follows:

> This is not the time for political works of art; rather, politics has migrated into the autonomous work of art, and it has penetrated most deeply into works that present themselves as politically dead, as in Kafka's parable about children's guns, where the idea of nonviolence is fused with the dawning awareness of an emerging political paralysis. (Adorno 1992, 93–94)

According to Adorno, the political has specifically migrated into the autonomous work of art, which is not the same as the notion of art or form alone. The autonomous work of art epitomizes an aporetic political situation and stands for a refuge against it. To Adorno, the autonomy of the work was forced rather than conquered, which distances it from high-modernist conceptions of autonomy as well as from the postmodern notion of form as ubiquitous political vehicle. Historically speaking, one cannot substitute an actual political failure at defeating fascism at the time it took power for a trans-historic avant-garde's politically appealing achievement. The implications of the phrase "politically dead" are, in this respect, quite illuminating. Likewise, Kafka's parable, which is Adorno's model, offers little evidence of any successful migration. The text itself is a sketchy fragment from the *Notebooks* (Kafka 1991, 5–6), entitled *Der Aufruf* [The Calling] in German, which Kafka continued here and there but never completed. It begins with an appeal to take arms and fight but the weapons in question are declared useless. As a parable on the combined necessity and vanity of man's efforts at resisting a downpour about to swallow the tenement house in the story, Kafka's short text may well exemplify the kind of desperate autonomy Adorno thought was redeemable: no well-wrought urns here, but inefficient broken-up toys, rusty and inadequate children's guns that are in insufficient number, and which no one wants to register to use. Unlike Kafka, Oppen did not write of useless children's guns but of the use of guns on children. I would suggest that what has migrated was that change: that, using the famous phrase, however seemingly pacified it may seem, form is never more than an extension of conflict, and not an escape from it.

Oppen seems to go back to this very idea of an inevitable distance in an unpublished poem, presumably from the late sixties or seventies, which begins:

> 'Without self-mutilation there can be no withdrawing from our fellows'
>
> Reading, I mis-read that. I thought: therefore we must accept mutilation
>
> I will not answer. A man in war or a man tortured knows of another world.
>
> They show him that his wife and his children have been killed.
> They were killed so easily.
> […] (NCP 341–342)

Such a misreading typically suggests how Oppen himself is misread. First, one wonders whether the self-mutilation is necessary, adequate, or inevitable, and whether the withdrawal implies isolation, integrity, or impotence. Then one realizes that the analogy between withdrawal as a kind of self-mutilation and the actual mutilation of "our fellows" implies that the misreading Oppen warns against is precisely believing that "withdrawing from our fellows" is ever possible, because it would mean self-mutilation. At the same time, the poem seems to suggest that the analogy itself misreads the facts, since it relies on incommensurable realities: the poet's degree of connection or disconnection is proportionate to one's knowledge of the torturing of the man, but the tortured man's knowledge (of his own torture and of the killing of his wife and children) is beyond one's grasp—he "knows of another world." However, the next line in the poem—"There is not this world and that world"—reveals that Oppen understood these distances as dialectic. The statement is then not so atheistic as it seems, and rather points to the idea that there is no world of the mind into which to withdraw from the world of hurting bodies, while making it clear that for the mind to encompass the tragic historical world, it must first acknowledge its own limitations so as not to exceed its grasp through questionable analogies. Oppen's rewriting of Russell (SP 246) in "The Mind's Own Place"—"Bertrand Russell wrote 'If I were to describe reality as I found it, I would have to include my arm'" (SP 30–31)—already points to a form of maiming. This image is tested, in this poem, against the backdrop of actual disfigurement—which is Oppen's test of a realist poetry.

References

Anderson, Cynthia. 1985. "Disasters: Versions and Notes." *Ironwood* 26 13/2: 146–147.

Adorno, Theodor. 1992. *Notes to Literature* (1974), vol. 2. Translated by Sherry Weber Nicholsen and Rolf Tiedemann, ed. New York: Columbia University Press.

Ashton, Jennifer. 2005. *From Modernism to Postmodernism. American Poetry and Theory in the Twentieth Century*. Cambridge: Cambridge University Press.

Baker, Robert. 2012. *In Dark Again in Wonder. The Poetry of René Char and George Oppen*. Notre Dame: University of Notre Dame.

Berry, Eleanor. 1984. "Language Made Fluid: The Grammetrics of George Oppen's Recent Poetry." *Contemporary Literature* 25/3: 305–22.

Davidson, Michael. 1997. *Ghostlier Demarcations: Modern Poetry and the Material Word* Berkeley: University of California Press.

Dembo, L. S., and Pondrom, Cyrena N., eds. 1972. *The Contemporary Writer: Interviews with Sixteen Novelists and Poets*. Madison: The University of Wisconsin Press.

Dembo, L. S. 1988. *The Monological Jew: A Literary Study*. Madison: University of Wisconsin Press.

Fredman, Stephen. 2009. *The Grounding of American Poetry: Charles Olson and the Emersonian Tradition*. Cambridge: Cambridge University Press.

Gillies, John. 2007. "Space and Place in *Paradise Lost*." *ELH* 74/1: 27–57.

Von Hallberg, Robert, ed. 1987. *Politics and Poetic Value*. Chicago: The University of Chicago Press.

Heller, Michael. 2012. *Speaking the Estranged. Essays on the Poetry of George Oppen*. Bristol: Shearsman.

Hoffman, Eric. 2008. "Of Hours: George Oppen, Albert Camus and the Illuminated World." *Jacket*. http://jacketmagazine.com/36/oppen-hoffman.shtml

Jameson, Frederic. 1972. *The Prison-House of Language. A Critical Account of Structuralism and Russian Formalism*. Princeton: Princeton University Press.

Jennison, Ruth. 2012. The *Zukofsky Era: Modernity, Margins and the Avant-Garde*. Baltimore: Johns Hopkins University Press.

Kafka, Franz. 1991. *The Blue Octavo Notebooks.* Translated by Ernst Kaiser and Eithne Wilkins. Cambridge: Exact Change.
Levertov, Denise. 1968. *Poems 1960–1967.* New York: New Directions.
Milton, John. 2005. *Paradise Lost.* Edited by Gordon Teskey. New York: W. W. Norton & Co.
Power, Kevin. 1978. "An Interview with George and Mary Oppen." *Montemora* 4: 187–203.
Thackrey, Susan. 2001. *George Oppen: A Radical Practice.* San Francisco: O Books.
Weinfield, Henry. 2009. *The Music of Thought in the Poetry of George Oppen and William Bronk.* Iowa City: University of Iowa Press.
Zukofsky, Louis. 2000. *A Test of Poetry.* Hanover: Wesleyan University Press.

CHAPTER SEVEN

Germane Questions, German Concepts

Oppen uses a remarkable phrase in a letter he wrote to Philip Levine in 1974, after he had read Levine's 1974 book of poems entitled *1933* as well as, apparently, his 1972 collection *They Feed They Lion*. Oppen praises the poems, while expressing concerns about the "novelistic quality in the poems," and concludes, speaking of Levine's work, as follows:

> Flabbergasted by the poems.
> (a poem including if not questionable history, at least you, me, Zayda's and other matters we might know something about
> A Pound of flesh.   And blood   Always: every line. (SL 275)

The reference to Zayda is actually to "Zaydee," the opening poem of *1933*, about Levine's grandfather. Interestingly, the other two direct references to Levine's poems in that letter are to another poem from *1933* called "Grandmother in Heaven" (the second one in the book) and to the title poem "They feed they lion," which is a combination of incantatory images of human suffering, the proletariat gathering strength, with biblical undertones of a second coming. This sheds some light on the "other matters we might know something about," matters from the 1930s' Great Depression, factory work, with a reference to their Jewish ancestry, against the specific backdrop of the significant title year 1933. The surprising part of the letter is the last line, beginning "A Pound of flesh," with the word "Pound" capitalized. The bloodiness implied prolongs the image of the lions in Levine's poem, while the reference to flesh and blood testifies to the veracity of the whole enterprise. Levine said in an interview he borrowed the title from a fellow black worker in Detroit, around the time of the 1967 riots. But Oppen's emphatic use of those words takes one away from orality, or Detroit orality, back to Shakespeare's *Merchant of Venice*. In the first scene of Act IV, Shylock asks for his bond in the form of a pound of flesh from Antonio, only to be fooled out of his reading of the law by a disguised Portia, when she declares that Shylock must manage to extract exactly a pound of flesh and without shedding any Christian blood. Turning the Shylock caricature on its head, Oppen applies it to Pound, confounding him with the same literalist reproach for, as the "Pound of flesh" image insists, extractions, samples, and grafts can cause senseless dismemberment. Given the incredible extent to which the practice of theoretical generalizing, based on the aphoristic sampling of poems and essays alike, has contaminated the interpretive procedures relevant to the study of poetry, Oppen's phrase stands out as a brutal reminder that the game of hermeneutic cherry-picking can lead one to attempt the riskiest kind of textual surgery.

What I hope to do here is to prove that the proportionally excessive and often exclusionary interest literary critics place in philosophy as purveyor of both the conceptual tools and the overall frame of their thinking causes serious interpretive problems when it comes to the reality of the poems at hand. Projecting their own institutional Weltanschauung onto the poems, their pantheon of choice is already predetermined and oriented toward those poets who explicitly preach that theirs is *The Scholar's Art*, to quote from Von Hallberg's study of Charles Olson, originally from Wallace Stevens' *Agadia*. A more direct way of putting this would be to say that "[…] there is a danger that literary critics seeking help from philosophy may take philosophy a bit too seriously" (Rorty 1991, 78). I insist on philosophical readings, because much of the scholastic bias that I confront stems from the field of philosophy, both literally—the references are to philosophers—and figuratively—that type of bias is echt philosophical. As Richard Rorty also pointed out, the very "*weakest* way to defend the plausible claim that literature has now displaced religion, science, and philosophy as the presiding discipline of our culture is by looking for a philosophical foundation for the practices of contemporary criticism. That would be like defending Galilean science by claiming that it can be found in the Scriptures […]" (Rorty 1982, 155). Literary critics will use philosophical texts as scripture, hoping to authoritatively underwrite their claims. In doing so, critics sample their way through the work they are commenting, looking for conceptual catchphrases, instead of offering valid descriptions. One might argue that there is certainly nothing new in literary criticism's reliance on philosophy, or theoretical thought of any kind. Similarly, enrolling eminent figures to assert one's legitimacy by selecting self-serving quotations is as old as the invention of rhetoric—and possibly an inevitable feature of any substantiated critical writing, *including this book*. In my defense, I will say that my approach was "therapeutic rather than constructive" (Rorty 2009 7). It is only negative in the way that negative theology means to be: pointing out what may not be said. If it may appear unashamedly negative at first, I am not being gratuitously antagonistic. I accumulate a great many don'ts, in a playful wink at Pound's *A Few Don'ts*, but this is by no means a preparation for any proselytism on my part. Over the past two decades, there has been substantial critical interest in George Oppen's work, yet either for the sake of Capital, of the Other, or of Being, causing interpretation to become secondary to the study of an implicit object.

George Oppen's poetry has thus repeatedly been tested for trace of the works of philosophers, and essentially the writings of Martin Heidegger. Nicholls devotes large segments of his study on Oppen to the Heidegger connection, the gist of which is also available in his article entitled "Oppen's Heidegger" (2009). The basis for Nicholls' reading of Heidegger into Oppen's work would appear to be quite indisputable: much of the data Nicholls provides in the precious "Appendix A: Oppen's Reading of Heidegger" (FM 194–196) to his study is highly valuable. However, if it documents Oppen's interest in Heidegger, especially when Oppen was writing *The Materials* (1962) and *This In Which* (1965), indicating interest is not the same as demonstrating lineage. Nicholls ends "Appendix A" by quoting Mary Oppen's statement from an interview with Burton Hatlen and Tom Mandel, in which she says in June 1980 that "those were ideas that were digested. [...] Heidegger somehow isn't there anymore" (MP 35). But Nicholls chooses to insist on Tom Mandel's previous remark in the interview that he had recently seen a book of Heidegger's on Oppen's desk, and concludes that this "testifies, perhaps, to the symbolic significance that the philosopher's work still held for him" (FM 196). Bio-bibliographical evidence, however slight, is in and of itself symbolically significant enough to trump Mary Oppen's point. The reason for such a fascination in finding the source of symbols of significance lies partly in Oppen's specific use of quotations, and partly in many a critic's scholastic bias.

Nicholls insists repeatedly that there are "larger patterns of congruence" (76 FM) between Oppen and Heidegger's thinking, yet he is acutely aware that "Oppen's attention often seemed to focus more on particular words and phrases than on the larger outlines of philosophical or political argument" (76). Nicholls also warns against "the published form of much of Oppen's originally unpublished writings, with 'daybooks' and notebooks seeming to represent their author more as an aphorist and master of the memorable phrase than the insistent and endlessly self-critical thinker that he actually was" (FM 147). He agrees with Michael

Heller's perceptive remarks, which he quotes, that Oppen would "read not for omnivorous knowledge of a subject but to find a passage or even a phrase which would show him an opening or way out of intellectual, emotional or even philosophical impasses" (Heller 2012, 65). As reported by both Kathleen Fraser and Frances Jaffer, Oppen himself said: "'I don't read philosophy for the systems. I read for the language'" (DuPlessis 2015, 89, 184). But instead of drawing the conclusion that one should then be careful not to seek to acquire such omnivorous knowledge of the subjects that were of parallel interest to Oppen, Nicholls finds a way to turn this into another reason why Oppen and Heidegger should be paired: "*Rather like Heidegger himself*, Oppen was often fascinated by a single phrase or sentence which seemed to promise illumination, and possibly access to another world of thought" (FM 76 *emphasis mine*). What is one to think, then, of Oppen's way of opening "the original texts to rereadings and even misreadings governed by chance and coincidence" (FM 77)? Surely, Oppen could hardly be read through Harold Bloom's categories that make misreading such a key feature in poetic composition.

This is even more disconcerting since Nicholls is careful to warn us that Oppen's use of philosophical fragments does not imply one could ever recompose a global, coherent mental picture of the poem's inception. When discussing Oppen's poem "From a Phrase of Simone Weil's and Some Words from Hegel's," Nicholls explains how, in spite of such an enticing title, Oppen's borrowings, "their sensuous embodiment or objectification in the poem undermines their original status as connected 'ideas,' suspending them [philosophical concepts] in the promise of an immanent meaning rather than subordinating them to the demands of thematic or propositional development" (FM 130–1). But instead of offering an analysis of the poem that might emancipate the reader, and allow one to discard the inevitable conundrum presented by the title, Nicholls offers a biography of Oppen's intellectual and philosophical journey. Another example would be Oppen's account of a dream after which he remembers having written down a quotation from Heidegger, from memory, which is to say from that dream, and later could never find the original quote. Oppen discusses the dream in his letters (SL 134–7, 156–7). It is also featured in Susan Thackrey's *George Oppen: A Radical Practice* (2001), one of the few critical texts to deal with the presence of Heidegger in Oppen, as Nicholls points out. This episode takes up a large portion of Nicholls' own "George Oppen: The Poetics of Quotation" (2005). The lines written by Oppen are: "'Substance itself which is the subject of all our planning' // And by this we are carried into the incalculable" (NCP 201), from *Of Being Numerous* (1968). Nicholls helpfully provides the actual missing sentence from Heidegger, one he says he "located with surprisingly little difficulty" (FM 79). But quite typically, Oppen's long and detailed account of his dream is left aside, though it takes up a full page in the *Selected Letters*. Oppen's description of the dream's narrative is an extremely vivid and specific one, down to Oppen's remarks that in the dream he was taking notes on the same kind of paper he used in real life, although it was "difficult to find room for what I was writing on these partly covered sheets, and tore off several pages from the very back of the sheaf—which then seemed rather to be a 'tablet'—expecting them to be blank paper" (SL 135), then exclaiming, as if making a joke, "NO books have any blank pages" (SL 135). Volunteering enough material for page after page, if not session after session, of analysis, the account is left untouched.

Nicholls nonetheless goes on to show that after due comparison, "there is a curious displacement of emphasis, so that it is the notion of 'substance' that now becomes central [in Oppen's lines]" (FM 80), which was not the case in Heidegger's original. He even points out that "Oppen's account of his dream carefully situates it as a remembered event, but his citation of its key terms triggers a series of erasures and reinscriptions which bar access to Heidegger's original text" so that the "'recollection' made it possible for Oppen to find in Heidegger's essay a content which wasn't actually there" (FM 80). Or again, when writing about Oppen's reading of Hegel: "As with his reading of Heidegger, he was not attempting to 'master' the philosopher's work but approached it in his own idiosyncratic and intensely directed way" so that "particular passages or phrases could take on a kind of talismanic significance for Oppen" (FM 120). The purpose of such a habit was always "the discovery of one's own reflection embodied in the 'objective' shape of the poem—yet another twist in Oppen's ongoing definition of Objectivism." (FM 121). This is extremely illuminating, especially regarding how treacherous Oppen's specific use of quotations may prove. For if the word objectification "applied not to the presentation of 'objects' but rather to the objectification of poetic form" (FM 128), which is why Oppen's work differs so radically from Imagist practice from the start, and if that objective form is the embodiment—or objectification—of the poet's thinking, then the critic faces the almost irresistible impulse to jump to the conclusion that these quotations are the closest things to those lost "objects." It is simply a way for the scholarly subconscious, as it were, to put the ideas back into the things, now that those things have gone from red wheelbarrows and white chickens to the more adequate, dependable, philosophic aphorisms. This is the crux, when Oppen's own use of quotations quite uncannily fits the demands of scholarly bias. Aren't critics always on the lookout for "particular passages or phrases" which they may turn into pronouncements endowed with "talismanic significance" (FM 120)? Oppen's poetics of quotation, to use Nicholls' phrase, is precisely appealing to critics because of the reflection of their own habits it apparently offers.

However, Oppen's sense of consciousness—the basis for his poetics and which, he argues, "of itself carries the principle of actualness" (SL 290)—cannot be disassociated from the singularity of its actualized poetic form. Systematically locating the poem's source outside itself results then in two types of errors. First, it dislocates the poem's dynamics, to be reconstructed after-the-facts according to a preconceived teleology, causing the poem's existing process—when it is not completely written off—to become second to a supposedly more significant, quasi-prescient, supposed genetic progress. Secondly, the objectification of the poetic form gets dismantled into templates and other doctrinal fetishes.

For example, Nicholls quotes Oppen's letter to Jerome Rothenberg, about his "own attempts toward the primacy of subject against predicate … Which marks where the subject matter ends" (SL 180), in reference, Nicholls tells us, to Oppen's unpublished notes about "the primacy of the nominative, which Hegel spoke of, the primacy of the subject. *Revelation of the nominative: there can be no predicate of revelation*. It is never which is which" (FM 125). This has been read, mistakenly, as meaning that there is virtually no subject matter in Oppen's poetry, or that it would be somehow beneath Oppen's critics to consider what that may be, or what the poetic matter itself has to offer—as if commenting on Oppen's poems might itself be a predatory form of predication. Hence, many resort to what they hope could be a kind of archeological paraphrase, repeating the subject matter, reconstructing the reader's revelation and re-stating, re-instating it as the nominative paragon that the rest of the subject matter of the poem would be in danger of soiling. But in the process, the subject matter is radically modified: it is reduced to what can be retraced. At the same time, it requires the poem to disown its own words in favor of an effort meant to consecrate whatever speculative authority has been found that predates the thinking in question. Paying tribute to the poet's curiosity in the meantime merely serves to draw attention away from the fact that the more the poet's bio-bibliographical journey is being explored, the less his poetry itself seems to matter. By making the poet's journey a wholly intellectual one, by moving from library shelf to notes and letters and then back to library shelves, one succeeds in actually abstracting poetic form away from the primacy of the subject matter all the way into philosophical predicates.

The ruse some Oppen scholars have resorted to has been to include Oppen's letters and notes in the poetic work as if it were poetic work itself. I am naturally not saying that one should not use all the material at our disposal—as I certainly have done so in this book. Neither am I saying that a rich critical apparatus is not a vital addition to anyone's access to a poet's work. What I wish to emphasize are the dangers in letting genetic criticism be an end in and of itself. Because the physical aspect of Oppen's papers prompts such analogies as noting that "[t]he manuscript for the poem 'The Little Pin' is held together, appropriately enough, by a little pin" (Davidson 1997, 77), with its literal cut-ups, pastings, and bindings made with pipe cleaners or wires which exemplify the notion of the poem as an object in a world of objects, it is difficult to resist pushing the analogy to literal extremes. There is a collector's fixation at work in the fascination with archives, which does not quite agree with objectivist principles of a useful art in an object-world. It is an illusion, which more than anything sums up the need to be aware of one's own professional bias. The regressive extension of a poet's work from publications to archives mirrors the critics' expanding scope of investigation from one to the other, and may well be, in the end, but an expected professional hazard. The problem, with Oppen, is that this tendency pushes the poetry too far in the direction of aphoristic prose, and drives the poems away from the reader toward the reconstructed reading that may or may not have taken place before or during the writing, thus manufacturing bibliographical content in place of poetic process. Methodologically speaking, philosophical outsourcing proceeds in two stages. It first involves isolating the most aphoristic lines in the text, picking out the statements or near-statements that may most readily be converted into actual propositions, to be subsequently adequately paired with their philosophical counterparts. Given Oppen's quoting habits, the problem rapidly becomes a crucial one. The specific progression and proper dynamic of any given poem get suspended, forgotten, or made to fit the choice asperities always-already awaiting transcription into critical prose. However, the number of different ways one text can borrow from another—allusions, echoes, reminders, sources, rewriting, paraphrase, borrowings, quotations, misquotations, collage, montage, and pillage—seems of little importance. The mode of extraction is second to the refining process, which constitutes the second stage. Once the fragments have been sampled, they are distilled into the intellectual narrative the critic intended to package from the start. The given narrative has precedence over the examples, which now effortlessly present themselves to support it. In short, the methodology of scholastic bias may be said to amount to a two-stage decontextualizing process: the poem as a whole gets decontextualized first into comment-ready items, then into the self-justifying critical account that supersedes it.

Such a logic becomes most paradoxical when, in addition to neglecting poetic texts in favor of philosophical ones, philosophical subtexts themselves are ignored and rewritten. Consider an actual quote from Heidegger, used as one of the two epigraphs to *This in Which* and which often works as a key to open the door for Heideggerian readings of Oppen: "… the arduous path of appearance" (NCP 92). It originates, as Nicholls remarks (FM 64), from *Introduction to Metaphysics*. Here is the full paragraph:

> The path to being is inevitable.
> The path to nothing is inaccessible.
> The path to appearance is always accessible and travelled, but one can go around it.

> A truly sapient man is therefore not one who blindly pursues a truth, but only one who is always cognizant of all three paths, that of being, that of nonbeing, and that of appearance. Superior knowledge—and all knowledge is superiority—is given only to the man who has known the buoyant storm on the path of being, who has known the dread of the second path to the abyss of nothing, but who has taken upon himself the third way, the arduous path of appearance. (Heidegger 1959, 113)

Here, Heidegger is interpreting Parmenides' second fragment, outside of which nothing in these lines makes any sense. Alexander Mourelatos, a philosopher and Oppen's son-in-law, provides this "strict translation" of the Parmenides passage:

> Come now and I shall tell you, and do you listen and preserve the account, what routes of quest alone there are for thinking [knowing]: the one, that _is_ and that it is not possible that _be not_, is the course of Persuasion (for she attends truth); the other, that _is not_ and that it is right that _be not_, this I point to you as being a path from which no tidings ever come; for you could neither come to know that which is not_ (for it cannot be consummated) nor could you single it out. (Mourelatos 2008, 55).

A. H Coxon's translation reads:

> 'Come now, I will tell you (and do you preserve my story, when you have heard it) about those ways of enquiry which are alone conceivable. The one, that a thing is, and that it is not for not being, is the journey of persuasion, for persuasion attends on reality; the other, that a thing is not, and that it must needs not be, this I tell you is a path wholly without report, for you can neither know what is not (for it is impossible) nor tell of it for the same thing is for conceiving as is for being.' (Coxon 2009, 56–58)

The philological, grammatical, and philosophical controversy surrounding the issue revolves, to put it succinctly, on the number of paths implied in Parmenides. From two originally, to three, even to four according to some commentators (Couloubaritsis 2008), interpreting the cosmological picture which accounts for those paths has kept critics busy since the time of Parmenides. The word itself (the Greek *hodos*) leads to many variations: Mourelatos speaks of "path," "road," "course," and mostly "route," while Coxon uses "way" or "journey." Does Heidegger's hierarchy between these paths structurally apply to *This in Which*? Is there in Oppen's poems a sense of superiority acquired through superior knowledge? Of course the answer to these questions would be no every time. Is Oppen concerned with the visible universe, and does he seek to navigate between appearance as illusion and appearance as astonishment? In this case, the answer is yes, but this is neither surprising nor specific to Oppen. Indeed, even if one knows how Heidegger liked to play with the notion of—and the word—"appearance," the idea that some measure of ambiguity is to be expected when dealing with appearances is certainly nothing new. In the index to their new translation, Gregory Fried and Richard Polt reference no less than thirteen possible readings of the word in Heidegger, among them appearance (*Erscheinung*) or appearance as appearing (*Erscheinen*), appearance as apprehension, appearance as Being, Dasein as site of appearance, appearance of humanity, appearance and *idea*, appearance as *phusis*, appearance and seeming, setting-into-work of appearance, appearance and space—with a final reference to the related entries on seeming and semblance. Needless to say, these terms make little sense outside their Heideggerian context. Consider the last words of the previously quoted paragraph, now in the Fried and Polt translation: "[…], and who has still taken over the third way, the way of seeming, as a constant urgency" (Heidegger 2000, 120). The "arduous path of appearance" has altogether vanished, along with its appealing alliteration on the letter "p." Not only that, but the word "seeming"—though closer to Heidegger's reasoning at that point in the text—might in another context connote semblance of a treacherous kind. Had another translation been available, would Oppen have chosen that same epigraph?

Similarly, Nicholls opens his article entitled "Oppen's Heidegger" with Jacques Maritain, whose *Creative Intuition in Art and Poetry* provides the source for the first epigraph to Oppen's *The Materials*: "We awake in the same moment to ourselves / and to things" (NCP 38). The passage from Maritain, as so often with Oppen, is heavily rewritten (TP 91), along with the second epigraph which is a variation on one of Yeats' poems (NCP 362–3). So why, instead of using this text from Maritain as a segue into Heidegger, should one not rather look into Maritain's *De Bergson à Thomas d'Aquin*, for instance? This might in fact shed light on unexpected connections within modernism, since Bergson's theories played an important part in the history of modernism, as Nicholls mentions in *Modernisms, A Literary Guide*, and Oppen's use of the notion of clarity has been discussed in relation to Saint Thomas' *claritas* (Wilkinson 2010). What sense of hierarchy decides what source is relevant to pursue, what is meant to give meaning to the whole and produce the correct intellectual narrative? Bearing in mind what Nicholls calls Oppen's "need to, as it were, rewrite that earlier modernism which had shown itself so inadequate to the challenge of modern barbarism" (TP 92), which is to say make sense of Pound's fascism and his own return to writing with *The Materials* (1962) after *Discrete Series* (1934), Nicholls sees Maritain's role within Oppen's thinking as a chance to bring about a reconciliation with the world, which he discusses in greater detail in chapter two of *The Fate of Modernism*. But the narrative in "Oppen's Heidegger" begins by pitting Pound and Heidegger against one another. Nicholls writes: "Above all, it was Heidegger's elaboration of a philosophical poetics that seemed to him to provide an alternative to the political entailments of Poundian modernism" (TP 93). But I would argue that when Oppen's concerns become Heidegger's, or vice versa, then all sense of context, Heidegger's own or Oppen's, disappears.

If one goes back to Oppen's title, *This in Which*, and to Nicholls' account of its Heideggerian sources, the case seems pretty convincing:

> In the chapter called 'The Limitation of Being', Heidegger wrote that 'The polis is the historical place, the there *in* which, *out* of which, and *for* which history happens.' [...] Oppen's use of his title to signal, as he put it in a letter of the period, a conception of the world 'as something IN WHICH we exist among other existences' both recalled the epigraph he had taken from Maritain and Heidegger's own attempt to break with the emphasis on subjectivity he discerned in Western philosophy since Descartes. [...] This association of *This in Which* with Oppen's reading of Heidegger is further supported by the recent discovery of the poet's paperback copy of *Introduction to Metaphysics*, the title page of which bears the annotation '"This is which" all truth is contained—the universe contains all truth—[illegible]' (FM 64)

Pursuing "phrases which again have a deliberate Heideggerian inflection" (FM 65), Nicholls expands on Oppen's postwar "philosophical poetics" (FM 66) while maintaining that Oppen had "*not* forsaken the political for the existential" (FM 65). In many ways, Nicholls' insistence on the critical relevance of Heidegger for Oppen is justified in the sense that it enables him to dismiss readings of Oppen's work as post-Imagist realism. For the "confining structures which he associated with [...] the legacy of high modernism" (FM 42) also include in Oppen's mind "the bad dream of a modernism he associated primarily with Pound" (FM 38). Nicholls considers Oppen's postwar poetry as a time when Oppen was "rediscovering politics, but this time in the 'existential world' of being and making rather than in that other world in which 'knowledge' had been devalued to the currency of conspiracy and surveillance" (FM 42). Where this reasoning oversteps the mark is when it forgets that Heidegger's aestheticization of politics is both conceptually or historically not very far removed from Pound's—whose aesthetics Oppen so desperately sought to challenge. Ironically, Nicholls uses Heidegger's 1935 text to distance Oppen's 1965 collection *This in Which* from Pound's 1930s political aesthetics. Putting it differently, one might say that Heidegger's journey through the twentieth century bears more than a small resemblance to Pound's in terms of political blindness. In a reading of Heidegger's "*The Origin of the Work of Art*," which Heidegger began as lectures at about the same time, in the mid-1930s, Karsten Harries does not shy away from confronting Heidegger's fascination with National Socialism, now a well-established fact and an openly debated issue, which may be best illustrated from Gadamer's position, thus summarized by Harries:

> Gadamer is here making the following points:
>
> 1. Those who had known Heidegger could hardly be expected to be surprised by the new revelations.
> 2. Heidegger had long dreamed of a radical transformation of European culture, of a post-Christian secular religion.
> 3. The National Socialist movement appeared to answer to that dream.
> 4. Heidegger's dream made him blind to the reality of National Socialism.
> 5. Heidegger's turn to Being has revolutionary implications, as does his talk of the end of philosophy and the overcoming of metaphysics.
>
> Gadamer, too, sees an essential relationship between crucial aspects of Heidegger's philosophical thinking and his entanglement with National Socialism. (Harries 2009, 33–34)

Though Oppen may have been insufficiently aware of that side of Heidegger's heritage, at least for a time, it remains that pitting Heidegger and Pound against each other today creates the illusion of contrast when it would be much more appropriate to draw a parallel. Moreover, as Hans Sluga points out, one should remember before reading Heidegger's *Introduction* that "[t]he correspondence between poetry, thought, and politics remains, however, largely unthematized in the *Introduction to Metaphysics*, and is only made explicit a year later in Heidegger's essay 'On the Origin of the Work of Art'" (Fried and Polt 2001, 212), where "concern with politics is pushed increasingly aside and subsumed under a concern with the work of art" (Fried and Polt 2001, 213). Heidegger's book is essentially a prolonged commentary on passages from Parmenides, Heraclitus, and Sophocles. Indeed, Heidegger's line quoted by Nicholls as a possible origin for Oppen's title—"The *polis* is the historical place, the there *in* which, *out* of which, and *for* which history happens" (FM 64)—comments on "the first chorus from the Antigone of Sophocles" (Heidegger 1959, 146). In it, Heidegger offers one of his customary etymological inventions, as Sluga explains:

> Where Sophocles seems to *contrast* the man who is high in the city (hypsipolis) as someone who applies "the laws of the earth and the justice of the gods" to the outcast from the city (apolis) with whom the ignoble consort, Heidegger *identifies* the two in a daring but questionable grammatical move and translates the Sophoclean verses as saying that man becomes *both* high above the city and without city by "driving between the law of the earth and the sworn justice of the gods." (Fried and Polt 2001, 211)

In Oppen's edition of *Introduction to Metaphysics*, the Ralph Manheim translation, this occurs a few lines after the *This in Which* potential reference. Heidegger's appropriation of the Greeks has already been thoroughly critiqued, and Heidegger himself later reinterpreted his own conclusions on *Antigone* (Fried and Polt 2001, 161–182). What is relevant to this discussion is how, in the *Introduction*, one is made to come to the following conclusion:

> Instead, what we have named is political—that is, at the site of history—insofar as, for example, the poets are *only* poets, but then are actually poets, the thinkers are *only* thinkers, but then are actually thinkers, the priests are *only* priests, but then are actually priests, the rulers are *only* rulers, but then are actually rulers. *Are*—but this says: use violence as violence-doers and become those whose rise high in historical Being as creators, as doers. (Heidegger 2000, 163)

For clarity, I am using the more recent translation of the *Introduction* by Fried and Polt. Yet on the issue at hand, the Manheim translation was blunt enough: "*Be*, but this means: as violent men to use power, to become pre-eminent in historical being as creators, as men of action" (Heidegger 1959, 152). Putting it differently:

> Charismatic and sovereign leadership (in politics as well as in poetry and philosophy) is thereby affirmed as essential to the well-being of the commonwealth and, in particular, to the health of the polis. (Fried and Polt 2001, 212)

Is this how Oppen viewed the polis? Nicholls may caution that Oppen's is an "often idiosyncratic reading of Heidegger" (FM 63), his tracing *This in Which* back to Heidegger's *Introduction* implies a connection. As I have shown, if one pursues the quotation further, if only a few lines down the page, all comparison becomes impossible. If the connection is so idiosyncratic, then its critical weight seems most debatable. One thinks of such statements as the one made by Randolph Chilton, who explains, "It is not my intention to transform Oppen into a philosopher, but rather to look at the ways in which philosophy helps to explain his poetry" (MP 105). In his discussion of the differences between Oppen and Williams, especially comparing Williams' over-quoted "no ideas but in things" and Oppen's "things explain each other, / Not themselves" (MP 101), Chilton also considers Heidegger to have been a means for Oppen to come into his own, not unlike Williams used Whitehead (MP 89), but never explains why poetry needs any philosophical help in the first place. Susan Thackrey also devotes a chapter of her book on Oppen to "Oppen and Heidegger" (Thackrey 2001, 33–45), one that provides a valuable introductory overview of Oppen's use of the philosopher. However, as often with Heidegger, Thackrey gets carried away. Quoting from Oppen's letter in which he states he wanted to arrive in his poems "at the concept of Being from an account of experience as it presents itself on its own terms" (SL 410), she concludes that when "Oppen was trapped in a fox-hole with his dead companions" and "recited, over and over again" lines from Reznikoff and Wyatt, as Oppen tells us in "Myth of the Blaze," "[h]e was arriving at the concept of Being, over and over" (Thackrey 2001, 45). Again, there is a certain embarrassment in reading that Oppen's war experience finds its meaning in Heidegger's concept of Being, given Heidegger's position in that war. Besides, according to Nicholls' "Appendix A," Oppen's encounter with Heidegger's writings dates from the 1950s, not before. Why not at least try and discuss Reznikoff's and Wyatt's poems? Why subsume it all immediately under the convenient heading of "Being"?

More puzzling still is the erasure of context, if not reference, as with Forrest Gander's reading of Oppen's "*If It All Went Up In Smoke.*" Thinking of the echoes which may be found between Oppen's interest in phenomenology and the work of Maurice Merleau-Ponty (which, Gander reminds us, Michael Heller had recommended to Oppen), Gander comments on the difficult syntax of the poem before concluding that "Oppen honors a consciousness interwoven with the world of objects, a consciousness that is nothing if not a collaboration with the world" (TP 126). But the poem is used, after a substantial journey into Merleau-Ponty's concepts, to illustrate a point being made quite outside the poem. So that even though one can but acknowledge the interwoven character of Oppen's sense of consciousness that would include the natural world, along with "the Whitmanesque identification with grass blades and touch" (TP 125), the context of that poem in *Primitive* is not mentioned at all. As Davidson notes, several poems from *Primitive* "were reprinted as a series under the title, '*If It All Went Up in Smoke*,' in *Voices Within the Ark: The Modern Jewish Poets*. Eds Howard Schwartz and Anthony Rudolph (New York: Avon, 1980)" (NCP 407). Speaking of a "world of objects," this poem is surprisingly devoid of any, unless one is using the word object not as material thing but as the thing to which a specific thought is directed. The only things that can be touched are the grass-blades, which also occur in "The Natural"—"I am // of that people the grass / blades touch" (NCP 281). Gander quotes from Oppen's notebooks, where one finds him stating "I see what the grass (blade) would see if it had eyes" (TP 126), and grass is often Oppen's image for minute perception. But what exactly is being perceived?

The title phrase and line one of the poem, "*If It All Went Up in Smoke // that smoke would remain*" appears in Oppen's essay, "Of the Mind's Own Place" (SP 31), as Oppen's heavily adapted translation of Heraclitus' fragment 7. Heraclitus writes: "If all existing things were to become smoke the nostrils would distinguish them" (SP 246), the idea being that if all visual data were to become invisible, one's sense of smell would still guarantee the primacy of the perceptive self. The original fragment from Heraclitus, which appears in Aristotle, has received various interpretations, among them that Heraclitus is here discussing the impingement of the senses upon the mind, and vice versa, to show the unity (the smoke) and—or within—the multiple aspects (the different smells) of reality. The phrase is used in Oppen's essay to demonstrate a restoration of "the meaning of the word" (SP 31). But in *Primitive*, the poem is said to begin "neither in word / nor meaning but the small / selves haunting // us in the stones" (NCP 274). In that case, Gander's idea of "a consciousness that is nothing if not a collaboration with the world" seems inadequate. The world as it appears in that poem is one of "sources" and "wells," "footprints" and "small distances" (NCP 274). It is a perforated, emptied, lonely world, revolving around a definition of the poem as "less // always than that," an unanswered cry, "help me I am / of that people the grass // blades touch" (NCP 274). In Oppen's poem, and in Oppen's rewriting of Heraclitus, the doubling of visual perception—seeing everything, then seeing it all only as smoke—makes the case for a highly ambiguous sense of permanence which would imply destruction. The subtext pointing back to Heraclitus therefore needs to be qualified all over again, which is what Oppen does, so that if the whole poem does not read as a poem "about" the Holocaust, the first lines of the poem answering the title, "that smoke / would remain," cannot but also be read as a possible reference to the chimneys of Auschwitz. Going even further, one could also reconsider the grass image through the following biblical texts:

> Therefore their inhabitants were of small power, they were dismayed and confounded; they were as the grass of the field, and as the green herb, as the grass on the house tops, and as corn blasted before it be grown up. (2 Kings 19 26)

> Thou shalt know also that thy seed shall be great, and thine offspring as the grass of the earth. (Job 5 25)

> For they shall soon be cut down like the grass, and wither as the green herb. (Psalm 37 2)

In the much earlier poem, "From Disaster," in *The Materials*, Oppen had already pitted the disaster of the Great Depression against "the small lawns of home" (NCP 50). Either as promise of abundance, or warning of pending destruction, the presence of these blades of grass, along with the lines from "The Natural" referred to above, and the inclusion of "*If It All Went Up in Smoke*" in an anthology of Modern Jewish Poets, suggest a specific people and a specific enough disaster.

Contextual distortions equally affect philosophical contexts, such as when Heidegger and Adorno are made to agree. To show that Oppen needed Heidegger to avoid Pound's predatory predication, Nicholls resorts to Heidegger's distinction "between 'calculative' and 'meditative' thinking" (TP 95): "Against the idea of a 'distanced' subject, aloof from the world in its objectivity and intent on manipulating and judging what is before it, Heidegger—and Oppen with him—seeks an elision of thinking with being" (TP 98). Nicholls is right to insist that Oppen equates the words "Dasein" or Being with the sense of presence that constitutes the "cadence of disclosure" (SL 97) he wished his poems to achieve, so that "[t]his, finally, is the objectification of the poem, as thought becomes present to itself as 'being'" (FM 100), when the "the subject-object dualism" (FM 99) has been overcome and the experience of thinking can be recorded, as Oppen puts it in his notes (FM 100). But this is done poetically, not philosophically, and in Oppen's prosody, not through Heidegger's concepts. One might also wish to add that to present Heidegger as the epitome of the subject that is *not* "aloof from the world" seems at odds with several episodes in the philosopher's biography. Moreover, the insistence on the difference in Heidegger between "calculation" or "computation" and "essential thinking" (TP 95), here as elsewhere in Nicholls' article, comes dangerously close to suggesting that Adorno coauthored his critique of instrumental reason with Heidegger rather than Horkheimer, a step that Allan Marshall is willing to take in *American Experimental Poetry and Democratic Thought* (2009), when he writes, after quoting these lines from Oppen:

> Closed car—closed in glass—
> At the curb,
> Unapplied and empty:
> A thing among others
> (NCP 13)

> This seems like textbook Heidegger, pared down in Oppen's distinctive style. But of course the poet was not reading *Sein und Zeit* when he wrote this—it would not be translated for another thirty years. He is just bringing his existential metaphysical proclivity to bear on something like Marx's notion of use-value. But the effect is the same. (Marshall 2009, 245)

It comes to this: Oppen's poetics "pared down" to a "distinctive style" as though the content were Heidegger's and the form Oppen's—as though poetry were never more than the stylized extension of a philosopher's content. The disclaimer that follows hardly calls into question the connection being made. It is only there to preempt the expected counter-argument, whilst it does not address it. Instead, Marshall moves to Marx, whose "notion of use-value," by the virtue of a surprising sleight-of-hand, seems to have become Heideggerian as well. It might be necessary at this point to emphasize that I do not intend to disqualify Heideggerian readings on purely political grounds, though I do believe that the methodological problems I am raising are made more blatant because of the political divide between Heidegger and Oppen. Apart from the expected words of caution, that divide has not been discussed at length when reading Oppen through Heidegger. Nicholls discreetly mentions "Heidegger's controversial politics" (TP 93)—a characteristic euphemism when it comes to Heidegger—or quotes Mary Oppen's very brief comment that it was indeed a problem, then moves on to quote an enigmatic acknowledgement, from Oppen's papers, according to which Oppen saw a "risk" in Heidegger's powerful "awareness of the world" (TP 93). Nicholls takes up those notes at the very end of his article, in reference to a previous version of a few lines from "The Book of Job." The presence in the poem of the sun's tremendous flames (NCP 241), the raw vividness there does appear verbatim in the passage from Oppen's papers (TP 110). But Nicholls' conclusion that "The vision here is Heidegger's" (TP 110) follows a difficult line of reasoning. Assuming that the risk Oppen says is worth taking is actually the risk of reading Heidegger, or of following Heidegger one step too far, what is one to make of Heidegger's presence in a 1970s poem about the Freedom Summer of 1964 and the murders of civil rights activists Andrew Goodman, James Chaney, and Mickey Schwerner, to whom the poem is explicitly dedicated? Quoting from Lacoue-Labarthe, Nicholls shows, albeit euphemistically again, that he is well aware of the "dubious charms" (TP 93) of some of Heidegger's concepts and "fantasies of 'dwelling'" (TP 111). But those aspects, far from being worked into the analysis, remain allusive, while the article, quoting Heidegger in *On the Way to Language* (1959), gives Heidegger the last word. Nicholls sees the "rawness" in Oppen's poem as a tribute to Heidegger's vision of "embracing '*both* gentleness *and* destructiveness'" (TP 111) in Heidegger's words from his reading of Georg Trakl's "Grodek." Strikingly, the last words of the passage are: "Flame is growing lumination. What flame is the *ek-stasis* which lightens and calls forth radiance, but which may also go on consuming and reduce all to white ashes" (TP 111). Perhaps due to the fact that Nicholls does not go into the detail of Heidegger's language and concepts, their proper context or their proper philosophical definitions outside of any discussion of Oppen, one cannot but remain skeptical. In this particular case, neither the specific phoenix imagery of the radiant ashes, nor indeed the larger narrative of Oppen's escape from Pound through Heidegger, seem appropriate, when commenting on a poem chiefly concerned with the figure of Job and the lynching of "children" (NCP 240), within a book of poems heavy with references to the death camps, written in the context of the cold war shadow of the Bomb and the smoke of napalm over Vietnam.

Heidegger's language in the passage about Trakl's "Grodek" and the meaning of those "flames" has already been discussed at length as highly problematic by

Jacques Derrida, who outlines Heidegger's uses of the word "spirit" (*Geist* and its declensions) in *Of Spirit, Heidegger and the Question*. Derrida follows the chronology of the word within Heidegger's work, from *Sein und Zeit* (1927) to the now famous Rectorial Address of 1933, the *Introduction to Metaphysics* from 1935, the subsequent classes on Nietzsche, the courses on Hölderlin (from 1934 to 1942), up to Heidegger's piece on Trakl from 1953. Derrida summaries his point in the following remarks:

> What is spirit?
>
> Everything suggests that, from as early as 1933, the date at which, lifting at last the quotation marks, he begins to talk *of spirit* and in the name *of spirit*, Heidegger never stopped interrogating the Being of *Geist*.
>
> What is spirit? Final reply, in 1953: fire, flame, burning, conflagration.
>
> *Twenty years later*, then, and what years! (Derrida 1989, 83)

The implications in Derrida's exclamation about those twenty years discourage against any immediate connection between Heidegger's fiery spirit and Oppen's Blakean blaze. There is no doubt but a very thin line at times between finding a connection and making a connection, yet therein lies, in many ways, the heart of any argument. For instance, when quoting from Oppen's notes on Heidegger's *Poetry, Language, Thought*, Nicholls picks up on Heidegger's "idea of the 'rift' (*Riss*) between world and earth" (TP 107), and combines Oppen's notes—"The poem must conceive the world or it is 'a thought[,]' a remark" (TP 109)—with Heidegger's words about the "earthy character" (TP 109) language must not lose. By putting forward the primary quality of language for Oppen, against what would be the secondariness of comment, Nicholls is making a perfectly valid point, which he then illustrates with a quotation from the poem "Semite" (FM 190–192):

> the proofs
> are the images the images
> overwhelming earth
>
> rises up
>
> in its light (NCP 251)

"The image now becomes the rift itself," Nicholls writes, "for, like Heidegger, Oppen is not thinking of it in a representational sense, as the secondary presentation of an object [...] and that act of pure nomination is also a withholding of what we would normally think of as the function of the image (to be an image *of* something)" (TP 109). Presenting his case thus, Nicholls cannot but misread much of this poem. The word "image" crops up repeatedly in Oppen's later poetry. Making sense of this phenomenon is crucial if one is to come to terms with Oppen's late take on his objectivist debuts, as reference to William Carlos Williams's "image" makes clear in "To Make Much" (NCP 271). But how does one move, in *Primitive*, from "an image," then "image," to "the image," and "image image" or "images images"? The whole spectrum of Oppen's perceptions seems contained in this shift from the indefinite to the definite article, then to these mirror pairs, but Nicholls' focus is only on the earth's rising up, such as can be found in Heidegger's *On the Way to Language* (TP 109). However, Davidson's notes indicate that "Semite" was originally entitled, "Reznikoff's Reading: The Quiet Earth Rises" (NCP 404), and Reznikoff's use of Heidegger has yet to be established. The immediate connection that comes to mind when thinking of Reznikoff and Oppen and earth is again the line about the girder "still still itself in the rubble" of that "terrible ground" (NCP 81). Another common denominator, hidden in the poem "Semite," are those "distances // my distances neither Roman // nor barbarian" (NCP 251), which become "my heritage *neither Roman // nor barbarian*" (NCP 257) in "The Lighthouses," dedicated to Louis Zukofsky "in time of the breaking of nations" (NCP 256). One is reminded of Reznikoff's poem "Hellenist," "As I, barbarian, at last, although slowly, could read Greek" (Reznikoff 1976, 107). As for Heidegger, Harries comments at length on Heidegger's notion of earth, in *Art Matters*:

> It is in the *Rectorial Address* that the conception of the earth that was to become so central in Heidegger's thinking makes its first public appearance. He had encountered it in Hölderlin's hymns; these must have made him receptive to the Nazi rhetoric of *Blut und Boden* and it is not surprising that shortly after *The Rectorial Address* "the earth" should figure prominently in the lecture course *Hölderlin's Hymn "Germanien" and "Der Rhein,"* given in the winter semester 1934/1935. (Harries 2009, 44)

The remainder of the passage after "rises up // in its light" reads as follows:

> in its light nostalgia
> of the mud guilts
>
> of the foxhole what is a word a name at the
> limits
>
> of devotion
> to life the terrible knowledge
>
> of deception (NCP 251–2)

Immediately, the word "nostalgia" stands as the ambivalent reminder of the soldier's nostalgic longing for home and the veteran remembering that ground of loss, rather than as an instance of pure nomination. Moreover, "Semite" is the one poem in Oppen's work which most explicitly alludes to the extermination of the Jews. The lines are: "demeaned thrown away shamed / degraded // stripped naked Think // think also of the children / the guards laughing" (NCP 252). Oppen's short prose text *Non-Resistance, etc. Or: Of the Guiltless*, published in *West End* 3, no. 1 in the summer of 1974, and reproduced by Stephen Cope, contains another version of these lines, leaving no doubt as to what is meant:

> Thrown away, unloved, shamed, degraded
> —stripped naked, herded into the gas ovens. Think
> Think also of children. The guards laughing. (SP 46)

The specific reference (the words "herded into the gas ovens") is omitted in "Semite" in favor of a repetition of the verb "think." Oppen's emphasis on thinking, however, is certainly not synonymous with a lack of empathy. It is rather a way for him to offer a visual representation and moral interrogation simultaneously as the reader is twice summoned to "think," as an outside witness, of the unthinkable. Going back a little, in "Semite" one also reads:

> [...] the sky the low sky
>
> of poems precise
> as the low sky
>
> that women have sung from the windows
> of the cities sun's light
>
> on the sills a poetry
>
> of the narrow
> end of the funnel proximity's salt gales in the narrow
>
> end of the funnel the proofs (NCP 251)

These lines are exemplary in terms of the scope and range of Oppen's poetry, but they are also instructive in terms of Oppen's overall poetic trajectory. By praising precision, Oppen is praising Reznikoff's poetry "on the sills" of the windows of Manhattan, as it were. But as always, Oppen rewrites as he remembers, and Reznikoff's underlying lines take on a more abstract—which is not to say non-representational—nominal quality, which may be what made Nicholls choose these lines to make his point. Once more, Oppen is returning to the first poem in

Discrete Series, which opened with a woman at the window. The lines are in fact made to depend on the redirection of the gaze away from the view and back to the frame. From this vantage point, a dialectical movement combines the view from "the narrow / end of the funnel" and the view of the ocean and "proximity's salt gales," possibly indicated by a funnel-shaped cloud, also called a funnel cloud, foretelling a coming tornado, until one gets to the other meaning of the word funnel, that of a pipe, stack, or metal chimney, to be found for instance on a boat to carry off smoke. The picture could be said to end on this maritime note, very familiar in Oppen, but the "end of the funnel" ultimately calls to mind the light one awaits at the end of the *t*unnel: here, the funnel would represent a kind of optical device, bringing the picture to a focus, bringing the poem to the proof that was found in the image, in those "poems precise" such as Reznikoff's. However, the "gale," like the "weather-swept" world in *Discrete Series*' inaugural poem, is Oppen's common metaphor for history. As such, the lines, "end of the funnel the proofs // are the images the images / overwhelming earth"—given the context of this poem—urge the reader to picture those images. The idea that "the proofs // are the images" may imply something more than a reminder of Pound's insistence on direct treatment. One of the proofs of the death camps, beyond survivors' testimonies, was indeed for the public "the images the images" of that "overwhelming earth," which could read as Oppen's remarkably economical combination of one being overwhelmed by images of mass graves and the literal overwhelming of the earth, in the transitive sense of the verb—the overturning implied in the burial in mass graves and the overturning of the earth to uncover those mass graves. Heidegger's jutting earth may well have been what Oppen had had in mind when the words came to him, but only just as the last words of Hamlet, in scene two of act I, "Foul deeds will rise, Though all the earth o'erwhelm them, to men's eyes," may be the first thing that comes to someone else's mind when reading Oppen's lines. When Nicholls interprets the "rift" on a syntactical level, he writes that "as the prosodic 'gap' induced by Oppen's emphatic use of the caesura had banished the speaking voice, so now the author is effaced in the 'blaze' of the world's disclosure" (FM 191). My contention is not that this prosodic gaping does not take part in the poem's surging images of violent disclosures, but that the remarkable feature in "Semite" is precisely that while "the speaking voice" has largely been "banished" by those syntactical blanks, the last lines of that poem are, "in the open the moving / edge and one / is I" (NCP 253). Nicholls refers to Oppen's "dilemma" (FM 183) regarding his own Jewishness, but without calling into question the belief that "Oppen's 'images' are now generic ones which do not evoke particular objects but which point toward a 'world'" (FM 183). Rather than speaking of a "purging of the particular" (FM 182), I would argue that Oppen did not gradually erase particulars in his late poetry. Their position or their role has changed, from that of receiving primary visual and syntactical focus to becoming rhythmic and symbolic units within a different type of construct. Oppen's late poetry is one of partial particulars. Nouns—not that nouns should necessarily be equated with particulars, but for the purpose of this argument, I limit my scope to nouns—may seem to take on an unusual allusiveness (which is not to say blurriness), but only if one forgets that Oppen uses them for their associated connotations and weight not so much in the language as within his own previous work. Therefore, there may seem to be a decrease in the deictic nature of Oppen's particulars, but only insofar as they are simply pointing in another direction—that of the poet's past work and life. The transition is a logical one if one bears in mind that Oppen's work after *Discrete Series* was always in part involved in taking a backward look at the life he had led. The use of the definite article, for instance, often lends the line a tone of abstraction, but these articles never open onto universals. Thus, if one may suspect a form of symbolism is taking hold in Oppen's late poems, each of those symbols would be but an instance of split particulars, pointing partly to perceptions now de-actualized into memories and partly toward halting statements of reported truth that in turn revisit what actually took place.

At times, Heidegger's views seem so at odds with Oppen's that the gap is unbridgeable. Nicholls quotes from a note of Oppen's in which the poet speaks of "[t]he idea, in Heidegger, that man may have to discard humanity in order to live" (TP 98). These words, which suggest a paradox, if not a provocation, require serious consideration. In a note, Nicholls refers to another of Oppen's notes about the uncertain "permanence of man" in Heidegger's view (TP 114). But the question is Oppen's, from the fact that he was unable to "discard humanity in order to live" but instead discarded poetry, to the haunting question of survival in wartime (when being alive meant one had discarded humanity by not choosing self-sacrifice), to Oppen distancing himself from political struggle to live as a poet. His possible estrangement from the world, however attenuated by the fact that the twenty-five years spent out of poetry took place within this very world, pervades Oppen's poetry from *The Materials* on to *Primitive*. As Nicholls otherwise notes (FM 85), the Vietnam War was a time when Oppen thought he might no longer succeed in forgetting humanity in favor of poetry. Why then does Nicholls assimilate Oppen and Heidegger's view?

> Oppen gives no source for this idea [that man may have to discard humanity in order to live], but it is likely that he is alluding again to Heidegger's essay "What is Metaphysics?" There we find an elaboration of what is called "essential thinking." Whereas calculative thinking "uses everything that 'is' as units of computation," essential thinking "expends itself in Being for the truth of Being": "The need is: to preserve the truth of Being no matter what may happen to man and everything that 'is'" (*Existence*

> *and Being* 388, 389). Heidegger thus argues that "this sacrifice is the *expense of our human being* for the preservation of the truth of Being in respect of what-is" (389; my emphasis). (TP 98)

By conflating source (of which there is, avowedly, no actual instance) and allusion, Heidegger's statement becomes a means of explaining Oppen's poetry. When Oppen looked back on the lines he rewrote from Heidegger in section 13 of "Route" (NCP 201) about the "incalculable," he wrote that the "reference, in Heidegger and, now, in the poem, was simply the acceptance of the inevitable final death of mankind—an actual acceptance, a dealing with it—" (SL 136), not so far from the "vision of a non-human world" (Nicholls TP 81) as presented in "Time of the Missile" (NCP 70). Heidegger's meaning, however, is radically different in this instance, which is one of the main reasons why Emmanuel Levinas eventually disapproved of Heidegger's philosophy:

> My view is opposed to the tendency of one whole portion of contemporary philosophy that prefers to see in man a simple articulation or a simple aspect of a rational, ontological system that has nothing human about it; even in Heidegger, the Dasein is ultimately a structure of being in general, bound to its profession of being, "its historic deeds of being," its event of being. The human is not the entire meaning of being; man is a being who comprehends being and, in that sense, is the manifestation of it, and only thus does he concern philosophy. (Levinas 2000, 111)

Levinas further states:

> What I admire in his work is *Sein und Zeit*. It is a peak of phenomenology. The analyses are brilliant. As for the later Heidegger, I am much less familiar with him. What scares me a little is also the development of a discourse in which the human becomes an articulation of an anonymous or neutral intelligibility [...] They say that in my view—I am often criticized for this—there is an underestimation of the world. In Heidegger, the world is very important. In the *Feldwege* there is a tree; you don't find men there. (Levinas 2000, 116)

Neither in "Oppen's Heidegger" nor in *George Oppen and the Fate of Modernism* does Nicholls pursue the point any further, although one cannot but wonder what that "sacrifice" at "the expense of our human being" could possibly entail. Upon closer examination, Nicholls conflates this discarding of humanity with "[t]he primacy assigned to poetry" (FM 70), writing that "Oppen shares Heidegger's view that poetry is the privileged means by which we might recover our sense of being" (FM 69). As far as Heidegger's views on the matter are concerned, as Lacoue-Labarthe writes in *Heidegger and the Politics of Poetry*, Heidegger's famous trinity of "Dichtung," "Sprache," "Sage," involves a very definite primacy assigned to poetry (namely through Heidegger's very personal readings of Hölderlin and Trakl): "[i]n the 1950s Heidegger may say the *Sage* is not the *Heldensage*, the saga of heroes—and in fact, there is no Siegfried here; Heidegger's anti-Wagnerism was always unshakable, which does distinguish him, after all. It is nonetheless the case that *Sage* translates nothing other than *muthos*. And there is something fundamentally *dubious* about this" (Lacoue-Labarthe 2002, 33). Whenever such questions are raised, Nicholls reminds us that Oppen "was not about to succumb to Heideggerian mystifications of 'nation' and 'folk'" (FM 82). This may be true of Oppen but, by definition, not of Heidegger. It is therefore regrettable to keep referring to some of the most famously debatable—dare I say detestable—notions in Heidegger while never engaging with them on that level. Lacoue-Labarthe (whom Nicholls occasionally quotes) is nonetheless very explicit (Lacoue-Labarthe 2002, 161) on the connotations of such a "sacrifice" as Heidegger speaks of, and refers it through Kantorowicz's *The King's Two Bodies* to the ultimate sacrifice for the fatherland and the logic of *pro patria mori*. With Charles Bambach's *Heidegger's Roots. Nietzsche, National Socialism, and the Greeks* (2003), Holger Zaborowski's yet untranslated "*Eine Frage von Irre und Schuld?" Martin Heidegger und der Nationalsozialismus* (2010), Richard Wolin's *The Politics of Being: The Political Thought of Martin Heidegger* (1990), or simply *The Heidegger Controversy: A Critical Reader* (1991), to quote but a few in the long list of authoritative in-depth academic studies which have now accumulated, one has had ample opportunity to consider the problem with Heidegger as, at the very least, a very serious problem, requiring specific contextualizing and conceptualizing. Even the very slow publication of Heidegger's complete works has now seen the release of Heidegger's notebooks, which has made it officially impossible to pretend one might ever again neglect Heidegger's consistent commitment to everything Oppen ever fought against.

Once more, I am not claiming that there is never a philosophical ring to Oppen's images. One often finds very tempting lines in Oppen's letters, such as the following:

> suppose, instead of an 'instant archeology' that imagines a personification of things already known, one imagines the first objects to become *object* to living consciousness - - their force in that among sensations they emerged as *objects* ----- can we suppose, in the history of the Sacred, a greater moment ? (SL 248)

Not a thing being grasped, but a force emerging, a moment happening—as if indeed the aim of the poem should be to try and recreate the very conditions of that inception. Or when Oppen speaks the ineffable and writes:

> But I would like to get to the first moment, the crucial moment in which one has not yet found the terms and has, for the moment, stopped the noise in one's head

> ----- that moment which is held before the mind which searches for terms -------
> Does it not happen? (SL 115)

My critique of the excessive philosophical slant among critics seeking to explain Oppen's poems away does not imply, I must insist, that Oppen's poetry asks no philosophical questions. But if one reads these two passages closely, one will realize that here, as in many of his poems, Oppen is interested in the process of conceptualization for its own sake, and not so much in connection with any preexisting concept. In dealing with Oppen's images as symbols for concepts, one loses sight of Oppen's primary concern for the mechanisms of consciousness. Moreover, these processes are, in Oppen's poetry, changing and ambiguous—very far from a static doctrinal set of beliefs. Critics who insist on the Oppen and Heidegger connection and provide their readers with a necessarily limited view of Heidegger's philosophy would do no harm, poetically speaking, if Heidegger's texts were only summoned through Oppen's eyes. However, they are not. As academics, critics are versed in Heidegger in a way that Oppen would have found both inaccessible and undesirable. In saying this, I neither intend to question Oppen's judgment or abilities, but wish to stress the fact that a trained academic and a poet who was an avid reader cannot be said to have the same relation to a famously difficult German philosopher. Take such an openly Heideggerian cry as "the infant first sees, not objects, but being" (SP 117), and apply that statement to a reading of Oppen's image of "boatness"—another transparently philosophical neologism—at the end of "Product":

> The boat soars, finds the waves
> The hull accepts. Once someone
> Put a bowl afloat
> And there for all to see, for all the children,
> Even the New Englander
> Was boatness. What I've seen
> Is all I've found: myself. (NCP 61)

Although the surprising word, "boatness," has an unmistakably conceptual, and indeed Heideggerian ring, the poem's specific New England context—biographically significant to Oppen—and rhythmic depiction of boats in the plural before the final neologism, all like salt erode conceptual astonishment into sensory experience, as "boatness" never ceases to be a product, indeed, of "the dry tools / And the dry New England hands" (NCP 61). The children in the poem may be said to see being and not objects, yet that vision is channeled by the poem's imitative balance—the lines afloat with the same tug and hull—buoying the poem up on an even keel with the poet's perception, as a child and then as a man familiar with New England. The recognition which causes "boatness" to overlap with "myself" in a final chiasmus redirects the conceptual awakening toward the self's point of view and personal history. Thus, the apparent metaphysical strain in Oppen's poetry should never obscure the fact that Oppen was careful to point out that metaphysics meant to him "a language that talks *about* physical facts" (SL 84)—physical facts or, which is often the same for Oppen, history.

Oppen, however, is not the first poet to whom this happened. It is worth noting that Paul Celan has suffered from the same critical illusions, which now plague Oppen's work. Since critical proof reading, as it were, is often confused with *ad hominem* polemics, I now propose, by way of comparison, and as a conclusion to these remarks, a rapid overview of the much-commented relationship between Celan and Heidegger. As will be made clear, the exact same methodological problems arise. In chapter one of James K. Lyon's study, *Paul Celan and Martin Heidegger: An Unresolved Conversation, 1951–1970*, aptly titled "The Repulsion and Attraction of Opposites," one is reminded of how acutely and explicitly aware Celan was, contrary to Heidegger it would seem, of the divide that existed between them, learning as early as the late 1940s about Heidegger's compromised position during the war from Ingebor Bachmann (Lyon 2006, 2). This alone speaks volumes regarding the critical habit of using poets on the other end of the spectrum to vouch for Heidegger's open-mindedness and "unfortunate," as some will argue, anti-Semitism. Overall, Lyon's book is very straightforward about Heidegger's commitment to the Nazi party. As such, it widely differs from efforts made to establish a connection between Oppen and Heidegger. Moreover, there was a relationship between Celan and Heidegger: they read each other's work, they corresponded and met. Yet some of Lyon's positions seem surprisingly close to those of Peter Nicholls. Lyon actually begins the second section in his first chapter with an analysis of a "six-and-one-half-page prose piece [Celan] wrote during his six-month stay in Vienna entitled 'Edgar Jené and the Dream of a Dream'" (Lyon 2006, 3). In this very early piece of poetic theory written at the age of twenty-seven, Lyon tells us, "Celan uses diction that sounds as if he were appropriating Heidegger's" (Lyon 2006, 4). While the detail of these similarities, which Lyon presents extensively, falls outside the scope of this study, I would draw attention to the idea that "[a]lthough he clearly was not imitating an author he had not read, such similarities in diction are a few of the elements that suggest a preexisting kinship to or affinity with certain aspects of Heidegger's language use" (Lyon 2006, 4). Dismissing chronology along with the concrete evidence he himself provides, Lyon asserts the existence of an anachronistic kinship between Celan and Heidegger based on the text of the "Dream of a Dream," much in the same way as Oppen, and his critics after him, takes for granted the "superstition" (SL 156) that the word "boredom" in the first poem from *Discrete Series* was already Heidegger's.

There would be much to say about the distinction between Heidegger's language and Heidegger's concepts as far as Celan is concerned. In *The Poetry of Thought*, George Steiner noted that Celan's interest in Heidegger was probably more linguistic than philosophical. In similar fashion, Lyon explores Celan's misgivings about his command of German, noting that "his confidence in his control over the language lagged far behind his actual abilities" (Lyon 2006, 26), in connection to Celan's "markings of numerous individual words throughout the text" which "give the over-riding impression that on one level this chapter of *Wrong Paths* served him as a means of vocabulary building" (Lyon 2006, 27), bearing in mind Celan's livelihood at the time depended on his translations from French into German. One may even venture that Celan also used Heidegger's conceptual vocabulary as a stimulating treasure trove rather than as philosophical gospel. I would suggest this was decidedly the case for Oppen, which should discourage one from working backward from word—a necessarily translated word—to concept. Outside those limits, the critical ground for any association becomes dangerously slippery. Commenting on Celan's markings "on chapter 5, section 34" of *Being and Time*, Lyon points to Celan's focus on Heidegger's distinction between "linguistic utterance/discourse and acoustic perception/hearing" (Lyon 2006, 12), then states this

> may have echoed Celan's own awareness of the phenomena of the semi- or unarticulated voices of his dead that inhabited his poetic world. [...] What we first hear are *unintelligible* words but words nevertheless and not just tone-data (*G* 2:218). In Celan's specific world these were unintelligible or muted words emanating from the Holocaust dead, words that he was trying to recover from speechlessness and forgetfulness. (Lyon 2006, 12)

Lyon makes this point one page after quoting Steiner's comments about writing in a language "that had given hell a native tongue and left parts of the language unusable" (Lyon 2006, 11). The only way to move past the glaring contradictions in Celan's use of Heidegger's distinctions about the intelligibility of words to refer to "Celan's dead" is to assume that the appropriation amounts to a corrective. Although the impression Celan was using Heidegger's *Being and Time* as a kind of sophisticated toolbox concurs with this interpretation, introducing Celan's "search for verbal strategies compatible with his own developing sensibility" (Lyon 2006, 15) comes very close to typecasting poet and philosopher in respectively the role of he-who-feels and he-who-thinks. Lyon is mostly careful not to overstep the mark, but not always, as when he compares Heidegger's use of hyphenation and Celan's "in his 'Meridian' speech of 1960" (Lyon 2006, 16), saying that "Celan did not learn this device from Heidegger, but in him he found validation of one of his own literary and stylistic propensities" (Lyon 2006, 16). Is Heidegger's antecedence really so absolute that even when the poet is said to have come up with something on his own, the philosopher must always loom in the distance, allowing and legitimating the poet's own devices? A similar problem occurs when reading Lyon's conclusions on Celan's use of the German verb for translation. Lyon tells us Celan discovered the German word's specific polysemy when reading *Wrong Paths* "in August 1953" (Lyon 2006, 34), namely that:

> In spoken German the past participle of the verb *übertragen* functions like and is synonymous with the term *übersetzen*. When accented of the third syllable, it means to "translate" or "transcribe." Accented on the first, that syllable becomes a separable prefix, and the word means "to carry over, transport, or transfer." (Lyon 2006, 41)

Quoting from several poems from 1954 to 1967 which contain variations on this key image of transfer, transportation, translation, transmigration (thinking especially of this word's former reference to "the removal of the Jews into captivity at Babylon" [OED]), if not deportation, Lyon concludes that these "illustrate the power that a single concept, which Celan discovered in Heidegger in 1953 and 'translated' into his own poetic world, continued to exert on his writing over the course of fourteen years" (Lyon 2006, 41). But is it still Heidegger's concept, once it has been so translated into Celan's poetry, especially given the sometimes radical morphological reshuffling the German words *übertragen* and *übersetzen* endure in these poems, as they so often do in Celan? And does the emphasis on the "power" of Heidegger's concept not almost imply that the conception is really all Heidegger's? Pushing this precedence too far causes one to envisage even worse absurdities. Still about *Being and Time*, in a section entitled "Learning about 'Truth' from Heidegger," Lyon discusses Celan's notes on Heidegger's use and variations on the word "truth," in relation to Celan's letters to his wife, where the word often appears: "For him it meant openness, candor, sincerity, genuineness or, in negative terms, the opposite of deceitfulness, falsehood, insincerity, dishonesty, meretriciousness, shallowness. In confirmation of Heidegger's observation, it was precisely these 'untrue' characteristics that he found in postwar German society" (Lyon 2006, 17). Except that such characteristics of postwar German society—the general denial of the Third Reich—far from simply confirming Heidegger's 1927 observations from *Being and Time*, were characteristics of Heidegger himself in postwar Germany, a fact of which Celan, Lyon tells us, was painfully aware. Regarding

Heidegger's 1956 pamphlet *On the Question of Being*, which Celan read at that time, Lyon writes that Celan marked many passages "dealing with forgetfulness and memory" (Lyon 2006, 64), quoting from one of them. He then proceeds to make the following summary, which to my mind exemplifies much of the difficulty in extrapolating from Heidegger's influence on any poet, which is why I quote it in full:

> Whether the poet accurately grasped Heidegger's total meaning in this passage or others is immaterial. For him the immediate sense was more than enough. His own concept of forgetfulness had a specific point of contemporary reference—the forgetfulness he saw working overtime in post—World War II Germany to obliterate memories of the Third Reich and the Jews exterminated in the Final Solution. Heidegger's observation that forgetting is all-pervasive in Being not only resonated with him; it could only have intensified his desire to cultivate memory in his poetry in order to recover from oblivion the voices lost in 'that which happened.' (Lyon 2006, 64)

Once again, the poet's probably inaccurate understanding of the philosopher's concepts, and presupposed satisfaction with "the immediate sense," paints a very distorted picture, implementing a sense of hierarchy one cannot ignore. More surprisingly, reading Heidegger's concept of forgetfulness [*Vergessenheit*] as a reminder, for Celan, of the silence in postwar Germany about the Final Solution, seems paradoxical to the point of being absurd. Was Celan thus turning Heidegger's concepts against Heidegger himself? Was Celan writing history into a body of work which had always been careful to de-historicize itself by way of distancing its author from his past Nazi affiliation? This would have to be made crystal-clear to the reader. In the absence of any such clarification, one has to infer that the critic failed to realize that he was promoting Heidegger's vocabulary as a potential tool in raising awareness about the Final Solution, in the eyes of Celan at least. Immediately afterward, Lyon documents Celan's close reading of another passage about "unconcealment," clearing the issue:

> Though he seems to have generally accepted the general thrust of Heidegger's argument, he made the connection between "unconcealment" and the immediate Nazi past much more specific by a small but significant editorial change that suggests he was reading very attentively. Focusing on the Heideggerian coinage Gewesende, he crossed out the letter d in the text and entered in the margin a proofreader's notation to delete it. In so doing, he transformed an untranslatable word meaning roughly "past beings or entities" (das Gewesende) into "what was [in the] past" (das Gewesene). The revised term is almost surely a variation on similar circumlocutions Celan employed that referred obliquely to the events of the Third Reich generally as "that which was" or "that which happened" (das, was geschah, GW 3:186). For him,

> memory and the past centered on specific events, among them the death of his parents, and a specific historical time, and he emended Heidegger's text to conform to this view. (Lyon 2006, 65)

Lyon's work captures these profound and, sometimes, overwhelming contradictions, yet never seeks to resolve them. Arguably, this was perhaps not the task he had set for himself. Yet it remains methodologically illuminating that a similar measure of scholastic bias, concerning the same philosopher, can be demonstrated.

Similarly, one learns from the chapter entitled "The Dialogue Continues: Heidegger Reads Celan's '*Meridian*,' 1960–1961," that in his notes in the margins of Celan's *Meridian* address, Heidegger tried to bring Celan's thinking closer to his own. For instance, when Celan speaks of the poem standing "in the encounter" (Celan 2011, 9), using the German term *Begegnung* (Celan 1999, 9), Heidegger writes alongside "'In what region?' (Im welcher Gegend?)" (Lyon 2006, 152), implying "an etymological wordplay by connecting the root of the term *region* (Gegend) with its identical root in the word *encounter* (Begegnung)" (Lyon 2006, 152). Lyon adds that Heidegger may be here "responding to Celan's recurrent use in *Meridian* of the term *site* (Ort), the indeterminate metaphysical or metaphorical locus where an encounter of any sort—between two people, between the poet and unspoken language [...]—takes place" (Lyon 2006, 152). Celan's key notion of encounter takes up much of his *Interview on the Mountain*, a prose piece that precedes the *Meridian* address and in some ways anticipates it. Interestingly, it was written in memory of a failed encounter with Adorno. But Heidegger chooses to twist Celan's sense of site as encounter to make the notion and the text's reasoning fit his own philosophy of poetic dwelling. Though it may rely on an innocuous enough wordplay, the shift is actually very consequential, from Celan's encounter between two Jews and the dialogue that ensues to Heidegger's Hölderlin-derived (or Hölderlin-imagined) regionalism. Lyon also reminds his reader of Adorno's attacks on Heidegger, and namely on that word "Begegnung," "that also enjoyed favor in the vocabulary of National Socialism" (Lyon 2006, 206). According to Lyon, Celan did not agree with Adorno on this point, though he was grateful for the lexical unveilings undertaken by Adorno in *Jargon of Authenticity*. Last, as the clearest example of the conflict I have been addressing, I should mention Celan's much-commented poem "Todtnauberg," which recounts Celan's first encounter with Heidegger at the philosopher's cabin near the mountain village of Todtnauberg (Lyon 2006, 163). Lyon manages a very balanced treatment of this poem, which has received many competing interpretations. When commenting on Celan and Heidegger's second encounter in June 1968, little less than a year after their previous meeting, Lyon expands on a specific episode: "in the vicinity of Tiefenhäusern in the Black Forrest," "Heidegger and Baumann made good on their promise to show Celan a mountain moor, which they had attempted to visit the previous summer before being rained out" (Lyon 2006, 204). Here is Lyon's account:

> Based on what Celan told him, Pöggeler claims that in a moor he saw the luminescence that arises from death and decay, a light that calls into memory what is dead and yet still present. He compared this emanation to the memory of those who perished in the Holocaust yet whose presence was still noticeable for him in various manifestations of light from the moor. One might easily see a connection between the luminescence of the unseen, light-producing decomposition, one of many images of light found throughout Celan's poetry, and the light phenomenon reflected both linguistically and conceptually in Heidegger's term "forest clearing" (Lichtung). Though not identical, each might be read in Heideggerian terms as a manifestation of the unconcealedness involving Being. The difference, of course, was that for Heidegger this unconcealedness involved Being, whereas for Celan it related to specific memory, insight, and understanding of those who perished in the Nazi genocide. (Lyon 2006, 204)

If the reference diverges so greatly from poet to philosopher, why maintain, even after the precautionary mention that these are "not identical," that "each might be read in Heideggerian terms"? How could Celan's terms in this instance be Heideggerian still? As I hope to have shown at length, these questions are not only a matter of opinion or method. They resonate far beyond, and impinge upon the meaning of one's words.

References

Charles Bambach, Charles. 2003. *Heidegger's Roots. Nietzsche, National Socialism, and the Greeks.* Ithaca: Cornell University Press.

Celan, Paul. 2011. *The Meridian. Final Version, Drafts, Materials.* Edited by Bernhard Böschenstein and Heino Schmull. Translated by Pierre Joris. Stanford: Stanford University Press.

———. 2003. *Die Gedichte. Kommentierte Gesamtausgabe in einem Band*, hrsg. und kommentierte von Barbara Wiedemann. Frankfurt am Main, Suhrkamp.

———. 2001. *Selected Poems and Prose.* Translated by John Felstiner. New York: W. W. Norton.

———. 2005. *Selections.* Translated by Pierre Joris. Berkeley: University of California Press.

———. 1999. *Der Meridian. Endfassung, Vorstuffen, Materialien.* Edited by Bernhard Böschenstein and Heino Schmull. Frankfurt Am Main: Suhrkamp.

Couloubaritsis, Lambros. 2008. *La Pensée de Parménide.* Bruxelles: Ousia.

Coxon, A. H. 2009. *The Fragments of Parmenides: A Critical Text with Introduction and Translation, the Ancient "Testimonia" and a Commentary.* Las Vegas: Parmenides Publishing.

Davidson, Michael. 1997. *Ghostlier Demarcations: Modern Poetry and the Material Word* Berkeley: University of California Press.

Derrida, Jacques. 1987. *De l'esprit. Heidegger et la question*. Paris: Galilée.

———. 1989. *Of Spirit. Heidegger and the Question*. Translated by Geoffrey Bennington and Rachel Bowbly. Chicago: The University of Chicago Press.

DuPlessis, Rachel Blau, ed. 2015. *The Oppens Remembered: Poetry, Politics, and Friendship*. Albuquerque: University of New Mexico Press.

Fried, Gregory, and Polt, Richard, eds. 2001. *A Companion to Heidegger's Introduction to Metaphysics*. New Haven: Yale University Press.

Von Hallberg, Robert. 1978. *Charles Olson, The Scholar's Art*. Harvard: Harvard University Press.

Harries, Karsten. 2009. *Art Matters: A Critical Commentary on Heidegger's "The Origin of the Work of Art."* Springer.

Heidegger, Martin. 1959. *An Introduction to Metaphysics*. Translated by Ralph Manheim. New Haven: Yale University Press.

———. 2000. *Introduction to Metaphysics*. Translated by Gregory Fried and Richard Polt. New Haven: Yale University Press.

———. 1949. *Existence and Being*. Edited by Werner Brock. Chicago: Henry Regnery Company.

———. 1971. *Poetry, Language, Thought*. Translated by Albert Hofstadter. New York: Harper & Row.

———. 1996. *Hölderlin's Hymn "The Ister."* Translated by William McNeil and Julia Davis. Bloomington: Indiana University Press.

———. 1992. *Parmenides*. Translated by André Schuwer and Richard Rojcewicz. Bloomington: Indiana University Press.

———. 1971. *On the Way to Language*. Translated by Peter D. Hertz. New York: Harper & Row.

———. "'Only a God can Save Us': Der Spiegel's Interview with Martin Heidegger." *Der Spiegel*, May 31, 1976.

Heller, Michael. 2012. *Speaking the Estranged. Essays on the Poetry of George Oppen*. Bristol: Shearsman.

Heraclitus. 1954. *The Cosmic Fragments: A Critical Study, with Introduction, Text and Translation by G. S. Kirk*. Cambridge: Cambridge University Press.

Kantorowicz, Ernst H. 1997. *The King's Two Bodies: A Study in Mediaeval Political Theology*. Princeton, NJ: Princeton University Press.

Lacoue-Labarthe, Philippe. 2002. *Heidegger. La politique du poème*. Paris: Galilée.

———. 2002. *Poétique de l'histoire*. Paris: Galilée.

Levinas, Emmanuel. 2000. *Entre Nous: On Thinking-of-the-Other*. Translated by Barbara Harshav and Michael B. Smith. New York, NY: Columbia University Press.

Levine, Philip. 1974. *1933*. New York: Atheneum.

———. 1972. *They Feed They Lion*. New York: Atheneum.

Lyon, James K. 2006. *Paul Celan and Martin Heidegger. An Unresolved Conversation, 1951–1970*. Baltimore: The Johns Hopkins University Press.

Marshall, Allan. 2009. *American Experimental Poetry and Democratic Thought*. Oxford: Oxford University Press.

Mourelatos, Alexander. 2008. *The Route of Parmenides*. Las Vegas: Parmenides Publishing.
Reznikoff, Charles. 1976. *Poems 1918–1936: Volume I of the Complete Poems of Charles Reznikoff*. Santa Barbara, California: Black Sparrow Press.
Rorty, Richard. 1991. *Essays on Heidegger and Others. Philosophical Papers Volume 2*. Cambridge: Cambridge University Press.
———. 1982. *Consequences of Pragmatism*. Minneapolis: University of Minnesota Press.
———. 2009. *Philosophy and the Mirror of Nature*. Princeton: Princeton University Press.
Thackrey, Susan. 2001. *George Oppen: A Radical Practice*. San Francisco: O Books.
Wilkinson, John. 2010. "The Glass Enclosure: Transparency and Glitter in the Poetry of George Oppen." *Critical Inquiry* 36/2: 218–238.
Wolin, Richard., ed. 1993. *The Heidegger Controversy: A Critical Reader*. Cambridge, Mass.: MIT Press.
———. 1990. *The Politics of Being: The Political Thought of Martin Heidegger*. New York: Columbia University Press.
Zaborowski, Holger. 2010. "*Eine Frage von Irre und Schuld?*" *Martin Heidegger und der Nationalsozialismus*. Frankfurt am Main: Fischer Verlag.

CHAPTER EIGHT

Unethical Criticism

Alongside philosophical readings, which use Oppen's poetry as a pretext for ontological extrapolations, there has been another sustained critical effort conducted chiefly through philosophical means, which can be described as an effort to moralize poetics. Joan Retallack's *The Poethical Wager* is a highly representative example, and provides a clear picture, of the justification of literature as a noble, ethical pursuit. She writes:

> To place *ethos* in the foreground of the discussion of aesthetic process is to think about consequential "forms of life" specific to formally distinct experiences of art. What kind of life is one living *in the act of reading* Gertrude Stein? Is it the same as the act of reading Wallace Stevens or John Cage? [...] The most pressing question for me is how art, particularly literature, helps form the direction and quality of attention, the intelligences, the sense we bring into contact with contemporary experience. (Retallack 2003, 12)

This is but one of countless occasions when Wittgenstein's phrase is being used almost magically. As Rupert Read put it, quoting from Putnam, "the volume of the secondary literature on 'forms of life' is out of proportion to what would appear to be its importance in Wittgenstein's actual work, and the sense its invocation makes often in inverse proportion to the claims made for it in any given instance as the lynchpin of Wittgenstein's philosophy" (Read 2007, 10). What is immediately striking about such a statement is its absolutization of literature as the unique provider of "sense" on virtually any occasion. The idea becomes troubling when one considers its consequences. For "the act of reading" is never practically elucidated beyond the proposition that the act of reading and the act of living overlap to the point that they should be considered as equivalent manifestations of the same meaning-making matrix. Using the traditional etymological analogy, Retallack goes on to say:

> A related question concerns the ways in which contemporary poetics invites us into an ethos of the collaborative making of meaning. "Making," poeisis, is always key. This is an imaginative activity that materially affects the life one lives in language, the life of language at large, the world of which language is both made and inextricable part. (Retallack 2003, 12)

The assimilation of "us" as speaking creatures with, all at once, "the life of language" and "the world," rests upon the premise that "an imaginative activity" can "materially affect" anything. As with previously discussed political readings of Oppen, the belief is always that "if you alter the structure of artistic discourse in a decisive way, the realities to which it corresponds will find themselves thereby similarly modified" (Jameson 1976, 242). What is truly remarkable is Retallack's legitimation of her position in a note about the phrase "forms of life," which is, she writes,

> [...] Wittgenstein's phrase for dense cultural practices that can be identified by their "language games"—rule—and use-governed linguistic habits. By foregrounding such practices, one might analyze just how parts of Bourdieu's *habitus* work. Foucault's analysis of "docile bodies" in *Discipline and Punish* is another productive model. (Retallack 2003, 244)

To pair Wittgenstein's phrase with Bourdieu's concept is especially pernicious. The comparison only holds as long as one never defines what those "dense cultural practices" might be, and as long as the resemblance between "habit" and "*habitus*" is allowed to hide the fact that "rule" has a different "use" in linguistics, philosophy, and sociology. Terminological proximity is not to blame, nor the connection itself, and Bourdieu did say he had found in Wittgenstein's work signs of a like-minded endeavor, but Retallack's neutralization of what is at stake in Bourdieu's *habitus* poses a serious problem. What Bourdieu's sociology teaches one is not how art or literature may shape the "quality of attention, the intelligences, the sense we bring into contact with contemporary experience" (Retallack 2003,12), but that one's "quality of attention," one's intelligence and sense of our experiences is radically predicated upon one's social position. Domination, whether it is based on class, gender or ethnicity, and its pervasive structuring role, was always Bourdieu's main concern. Taking domination out of the equation by excessively formalizing this as a pure and hypothetically reversible process—"an ethos of the collaborative making of meaning" (Retallack 2003, 12)—nullifies the entire proposition, while pretending to illustrate it. As for Retallack's example of Foucault's chapter on "docile bodies," it is painstakingly revealing: all semiotics aside, Foucault's example is that of the body of the early seventeenth century European soldier, and his description of the molding of those objectified bodies seems a far-fetched productive model for any "language games." I am taking issue with Retallack's jumble of "many languages, social structures, events, persons," and vague "ongoing poetics of daily life" (Retallack 2003, 12) because of her key argument that literary critics not only can, but should, extend their interpretative activities to the point that all communities ought to be seen as "interpretative communities" in their own right, to use Stanley Fish's phrase (Fish 1982). However, once you accept the existence of these *a priori* interpretive communities, once commonplace or community is but another word for readership, then Oppen's sense of the loss of the commonplace becomes literally inconsequential: it has no consequence outside the realm of interpretation. Foregrounding ethos as what ties together praxis and hermeneutics really disguises the assimilation of praxis to hermeneutics, and makes ethos an empty notion. In order to maintain the illusion that ethical problems refer to "forms of life" alone, to use Wittgenstein ever-popular phrase, and that they should be dealt with on such a formal level, ethos cannot involve anything more specific than a certain hermeneutic attitude. To accept this paradox—for the word ethos first means character, characteristics or characterization—means to accept that absence of characterization as a kind of supreme value, which is in turn epitomized in the plasticity of language as a kind of protective hermeneutic defiance in our troubled world. This amounts to a denial of context—borrowing a line from Oppen one might call it a "denial / Of death" (NCP 178)—which becomes dramatically vivid when reading Oppen's work.

To begin to unravel the secrets of ethical readings and their assumptions, consider this enrollment of Emmanuel Levinas when, concluding "Of Being Ethical; Reflections on George Oppen," Nicholls recommends that one turn to Levinas and his definition of ethics. Nicholls is cautious not to suggest "that Oppen knew of Levinas' work, but only that this way of understanding 'ethics' may help to elucidate Oppen's evolving poetic" (Nicholls 1997, 168). This is then summarized in two steps: "First, a poetics of encounter will assume that the domain of the ethical is also the domain of the ordinary and the everyday, of relationships expressing proximity rather than contemplative or legislative distance [...]. Secondly, the ethical subject is not only open, but vulnerable and in question" (Nicholls 1997, 168). All this has now become standard ethical talk. But categories such as "the ordinary and the everyday" opposed to "contemplative and legislative distance" have very little to do with Levinas' actual body of work, and merely repeat sets of standardized pairs such as concrete / abstract, common / privileged, everyday / rare, action / contemplation, proximity / distance, descriptive / legislative, heterogeneity / homogeneity, others / the self, democratic / authoritarian. The point is to make the readers feel secure that they are on the right side of the implied dichotomy through the use of vague yet recognizable keywords. The next three words and phrases, "open," "vulnerable," and "in question," though they do (especially the middle one) have their place in Levinas, are being used here in the largest connotative sense, while picking up, again, new sets of polarities (closed / open, overbearing / vulnerable, stubborn / in question). The first point is backed by a disconnected quotation from Oppen, "Near is / Knowledge" (NCP 185), while the second point leads to a quotation from Levinas. The balance is meant to establish the connection, and neither Oppen's words nor Levinas' are discussed any further. Tim Woods, whose reading of Oppen and Zukofsky in *The Poetics of the Limit* (2002) is heavily indebted to Levinas, offers a similar pros and cons approach:

> Albeit hesitatingly, one can very roughly schematize Levinas' set of oppositions between the two philosophies as follows:
>
> | | |
> |---|---|
> | ontological (Hellenic) | ethics (Hebraic) |
> | totality (conceptual) | infinity (nonconceptual) |
> | centeredness | dispersal |
> | hatred/war/violence | love/peace/justice |
> | being/sameness | otherwise-than-being/otherness |
> | being-for-self | being-for-other |
> | autonomous freedom | responsible justice |
> | the Said | the Saying (Woods 2002, 144) |

Such binary reasoning seems only designed to satisfy and reassure the reader (for who would choose "hatred/war/violence" over "love/peace/justice"?). Against "Poundian modernism," Nicholls tells us, Levinas's ethics stands for "a relation which presupposes that the self comes into being only by first recognizing its responsibility to others" (Nicholls 1997, 168). That may very well be, but the reason why one should turn to Levinas to explain that Pound's brand of modernism was foreign to Oppen is never made clear. A quick perusal of any biographical sketch devoted to Oppen would suffice to point out crucial differences in each poet's perception of their "responsibility to others." Was this detour through Levinas necessary to be made aware of the fact that Oppen did not follow in Pound's footsteps and that he essentially cared for his fellow-men? The proper motive quickly becomes apparent. After mentioning Oppen's lines from "Of Being Numerous" about "The act of being, / the act of being / More than oneself"

(NCP 159), Nicholls interprets that "more" as pointing toward "a transcendence of self" (Nicholls 1997, 169), which in turn reveals the impenetrability of matter. Levinas comes up again in Nicholls' argument about the necessity for Oppen to undo "a ruined ethic // Bursting with ourselves" (NCP 98), in the name of "a perception of radical heterogeneity" (Nicholls 1997, 168) but what this heterogeneity might be, either in the light of Levinas' work or Oppen's, goes unsaid. Instead, Nicholls evokes Charles Bernstein's sense of "linguistic impenetrability or opacity" (Nicholls 1997, 169) and "the recognition of language as a material and social medium [in which] some sort of 'ethical' frame for writing is to be found" (Nicholls 1997, 169), to put forward the idea that one might "associate an 'ethical' relation with a certain linguistic opacity" (Nicholls 1997, 170). The shift is an abrupt one. In the end, following Bernstein, Nicholls presents the case for language as the prime location of man's political economy, pushing the agenda for language's hegemony over social realities to the point that language becomes the only locus of social reality (alternatively addressed either as political or as ethical). This new turn, or u-turn, to language, could have been introduced by emphasizing the centrality of language to Levinas's philosophical project—though in a very different way—yet no further reference to Levinas is made there.

As this investigation of the sampling of poetical texts into and through philosophical ones, and vice versa, now turns to Levinas as the key figure summoned to help make sense of Oppen's poetry, it is worth noting that for literary criticism to allow so easily for such shift from Heidegger to Levinas in dealing with Oppen's poetry is in and of itself a cause for concern. In spite of obvious connections and of the intimate knowledge of Heidegger that one finds in Levinas, the French philosopher explicitly wished to distance himself from Heidegger's teachings. Thus, the possibility of reading Oppen alternatively with the help of either represents in all seriousness a daunting contradiction. The assumptions I mean to challenge here are neatly expressed by Robert Eaglestone in the introduction to his study, *Ethical Criticism: Reading after Levinas* (1997):

> A Levinasian understanding of the ethics of criticism does not provide a methodology or type of literary theory, but rather a justification of a variety of approaches to literature. Levinas's work offers an ethical justification for the influx into criticism of the new and challenging questions, called 'theory.' (Eaglestone 1997, 7)

A promising justification indeed, which leads Eaglestone to the conclusion that literature is only *apparently* rejected by Levinas:

> Three factors suggest this: first, Levinas's understanding of language in general; second, the use of, and appeal to, literature in *Otherwise than Being*; third, the text's own potential 'literary' status. (Eaglestone 1997, 157).

The first point holds the promise of a syllogism: literary works are made of language, so Levinas' analysis of language—notwithstanding the fact that it occurs within a specifically philosophical work—cannot but apply to, and actually always already includes, literature. It is a common enough syllogism, often used to hide baseless analogies. The second argument, which points to references to literary works in Levinas' texts, is purely incidental. The third point relies on a syllogism akin to the first: Levinas' use of metaphor, or of really any trope, qualifies as literary. Accordingly, any text is literary, in that it uses rhetoric—not an impossible point to be making, but which need clarification. I would much rather note, with Gerald L. Burns, that "The question is whether assimilating poetry to the ethical in this way doesn't just allegorize poetry and therefore reduce it in the usual philosophical style" (Bernasconi and Critchley 2002, 226). In fact, when looking closely, one finds that "Levinas' theoretical discourse on the aesthetic most often asserts an unbridgeable chasm between art and ethics" (Robbins 1999, xxi). Looking into the criticism on Oppen's work, one sees that, as Nicholls adds in a note (FM 105), two critics have offered readings of Oppen through Levinas: Tim woods and Mathew Jenkins. In the first, Tim Woods' *The Poetic of the Limit: Ethics and Politics in Modern and Contemporary American Poetry*, only the penultimate chapter deals specifically with Oppen. The second is G. Matthew Jenkins' *Poetic Obligation, Ethics in Experimental American Poetry After 1945* (2008). Woods introduces Levinas in the following fashion:

> For Levinas, one has access to the meaning of being only by the experience of the invasion of infinity into being. That is, one "knows" being only by the fact that the conception of the self-sufficient bourgeois ego, whose inner calm is based on possession and security, is interrupted by nonbeing, by an excess that goes beyond being, an irreducible "otherness." Oppen clearly inscribed this recognition in his poetry: "The act of being, the act of being / More than oneself." (Woods 2002, 222)

It is indeed one of those lines of Oppen's which a critic can transforms most conveniently into a variety of generalizations. Yet the language used by Woods is faulty in many respects. The central condemnation of "the conception of the self-sufficient bourgeois ego, whose inner calm is based on possession and security," may be appropriate when re-writing a polemical statement from Adorno's *Negative Dialectics*, but it is not to be found in Levinas in those terms (no matter whether he would have agreed with those terms or not). As for "the meaning of being," knowing "being" and the interruption by "nonbeing," which would handily enough be performed by and provide access to "otherness," Levinas does not offer any such binary opposition nor binary solution to these questions. Derrida's main point in his famous article on Levinas' *Totality and Infinity* was to insist that there may not be a language to express the infinite or anything other than being. Levinas certainly answered Derrida in *Otherwise Than Being*, but never presented anything like a kit to get out of Being. Neither does Oppen directly qualify this awareness of "being / More than oneself" as a form of transcendence in the specific sense in which Levinas understands that word. To complicate things even further, Woods adds: "Here one has a materialist poetics rather than metaphysics, yet one finds the world always opening to a nonrepresentational otherness that forces itself into being" (Woods 2002, 222). All this would have to be consistently backed up with poetic evidence. Can any reader honestly deduce from reading Oppen's "World, World—" that Oppen's statement that "the mystery is / That there is something to stand on" (NCP 159) amounts to the recognition of "an unspeakable presence, an absent existence, a trace toward which language can only gesture without making manifest embodiment" (Woods 2002, 222)? Moreover, when Levinas points to the infinite, he does so within the constraints of his own thinking, which was never meant for easy duplication. As early as 1964, Derrida warned: "We will refuse to sacrifice the history of Levinas' thought and works to the order or aggregate of themes" (Derrida 1978, 104). A variation on the same problem occurs in Woods' discussion of Oppen's "Myself I Sing" (NCP 56). Woods concentrates on the aphoristic lines "And all I've been / Is not myself? I think myself / Is what I've seen and not myself" and comments:

> The Other has precedence over the subject, and the subject emerges only through an act of remembrance of the Other in oneself. In other words, subjectivity is not constituted in the present and does not exist as a presence in and for itself. Subjectivity emerges as a delayed being, always out of kilter with self-consciousness. (Woods 2002, 223)

The homage is clearly to Whitman here, as Woods acknowledges, but the poem's satirical tone and several jokes about Whitman are left unexplored. The poem also takes stock of the changes in American history from the time of the pioneers to the 1960s, quotes from crucial lines from a previous poem of Oppen's from *Discrete Series*, includes a passage that clearly points to man's condition as shipwrecked, which will be made so much of in *Of Being Numerous*, and is crucially relevant to one's understanding of Oppen's sense of vision as opposed to imagination. None of this matters to Woods, which probably causes him to misread Oppen's line, for Oppen is not being Rimbaudian, even by way of Levinas. What Oppen is doing is pairing "been" and "seen" to insist that one is the product of one's visible surroundings, that one is made up of what one has come into contact with, although one may be deprived of such contact, as "A man marooned" (NCP 56) or when "we are all housed now, all in our apartments, / The world unattended to, unwatched" (NCP 57). Poking fun at the Hamlet-like pose of whoever believes interiority somehow trumps the material fabrics that clothe our selves, Oppen especially draws attention to how much precise perception can help dispel illusions, such as in the opening lines which go, "Me! he says, hand on his chest. / Actually, his shirt. / And there, perhaps, The question" (NCP 56). On the contrary, Woods uses Oppen's specific images as concepts to such a point that it amounts to a form of thematization of poetic particulars into general abstract ideas. The same is true for other types of generalizations, not only about the subject and the other, but for instance about objects and transcendence. Woods writes:

> Oppen's poetry testifies to the ghostliness of objects—how they tremble before/in our consciousness. The American poet and literary scholar Michael Davidson has argued that this ghostliness may be seen at work in the textual materialism of Oppen's work, in the shape of what Davidson calls his 'palimpsestic' practice. His poetry constantly maintains a clear sense of the 'otherness' of the object, resisting any attempt to cover up the object by a concept:
>
> > What is inexplicable
> > Is the 'preponderance of objects.' the sky lights
> > Daily with that predominance [NCP 89]
>
> It is this sense of transcendence that motivates Levinas so firmly. (Woods 2002, 226)

This concludes the second section of Woods' chapter on Oppen, and epitomizes much of his logic. A series of ambiguities culminate in an extraordinarily rash assumption. The resistance to "cover up the object by a concept" (Woods 2002, 226), which is standard negative dialectics, is promoted at the same time as the poetic object is de facto being covered up by a concept. Oppen's lines are as usual stripped of their context—in this instance, in the poem "Leviathan," the context is that of the corruption of speech and truth, the difficulty to reach political goals and to experience solidarity. The more troubling idea is that these overwhelmingly present objects are the exact opposite of ghosts. Their ponderous presence predominates and gives one pause. It is words, Oppen said, which should be treated as ghosts (NCP 116), if their meaning is to be restored. A veritable climax is reached with Woods' last remark: "It is this sense of transcendence that motivates Levinas so firmly." In an unexplained twist, probably owing to the presence of the word "sky" in those lines, the objects' predominance has become transcendent. However, not only is the sky a common equivalent in Oppen for this world beneath the sky, and not the heavens, and is therefore not necessarily connected to any sense of transcendence, but transcendence is never a matter of objects in Levinas, only subjects. Moreover, it is doubtful that Woods now means to use the word "object" in its philosophical sense as that which is apprehended by the mind. Could it be that Woods is mistaking object for other, or suggesting transcendence be understood in the phenomenological sense, as in Husserl's sense of the transcendental consciousness of the transcendental subject?

These objects could then be phenomenology's intentional objects, in the sense that in "transcendental phenomenology, the experience that is constitutive of intentional objects is perceptual or pre-predicative before it is an experience of thought or judgement" (Bernasconi and Critchley 2002, 84), but Levinas soon distanced himself from Husserl's phenomenology. The very concept of phenomenon is very delicate in Levinas, who first uses it, then changes its definition, and then develops the concept of the other. Woods could have referred to Levinas' understanding of time and its connection with transcendence, in the sense that for Levinas, "it is not immanence but rather *transcendence* that constitutes the essence of temporality" (Bernasconi and Critchley 2002, 92). It would have been worth noting, since Oppen's next line in that poem is "And we have become the present" (NCP 89). Furthermore, Levinas' move away from Husserl on the subject of objects, as it were, consists in a critique "of the primacy of intentional consciousness" and of "Husserl's intellectualism" (Bernasconi and Critchley 2002, 20), one aimed at going "from representation to enjoyment," thus showing "how intentional consciousness is, to put it simply, conditioned by *life*," so that the "self-conscious subject of intentionality is reduced to a living subject that is subject to the conditions of its existence" (Bernasconi and Critchley 2002, 20). On this very topic, Critchley quotes the following passage from *Totality and Infinity* in his introduction: "we live from good soup, air, light, spectacles, work, sleep, etc. These are not objects of representations [but] the sensible, material world" (Bernasconi and Critchley 2002, 20). This leads Critchley to conclude that "the Levinasian ethical subject is a sensible subject, not a conscious subject" (Bernasconi and Critchley 2002, 21). This could have proved a more suitable point of entry for establishing a connection between Levinas and Oppen—except that, again, Levinas' concepts are not Oppen's, even when they might seem more appropriate than Heidegger's.

Levinas' notion of the "il-y-a" is a case in point. Levinas' horror of the impersonal and the neutral, of which he finds an example in Heidegger's *Dasein*'s relation to art and poetry, is well-established. Thus, as Burns remarks, "for Levinas the experience of poetry or art is continuous with the experience of the *il y a*, which *De l'existence à l'existant* describes as an experience of a world emptied of its objects" (Bernasconi and Critchley 2002, 213). Or as Levinas put it, "Dasein is never hungry" (Bernasconi and Critchley 2002, 21). For Levinas, art's deictic gestures imply that the subject's perceptual hold on the world's objects has been hollowed out, so that once deprived of objects in the sense that objects always imply subjects, the world is now only full of *things*. As Robbins writes, "The *il y a* effects not just a loss of world, 'the disappearance of all objects,' but also the 'extinction of the subject' and of the very distinction between subject and object (EE, 67). It is 'the rupture with the category of the substantive' (EE, 67)" (Robbins 1999, 92–93). In Levinas' thinking, the purpose of art is to reveal the *il y a*. Oppen's view of the purpose of art is diametrically opposed: for Oppen, objectness both resists and reveals the subject's substance, the form of which is the poem. But then why attempt such a risky conflation of the two? The answer is that Woods' aim seems to be to conflate Adorno and Levinas:

> This Adornian concern with everyday particulars is the basis for Oppen's ethical poetics. Oppen appears to conceive of ethics as entailing a fidelity to location of one's perceptions—a materialist *location* for things and emotions as understandings. In this respect, the self is removed and an ethical poetics emerges as the negation of the self in the face of the other's existence. (Woods 2002, 231)

Taking up some of Bernstein's remarks in "Hinge, Picture," Woods introduces Adorno into his analysis when Bernstein's own piece did not use the reference. Despite the fact that "fidelity to location of one's perceptions" sounds geographically closer to Paterson, New Jersey than Frankfurt, Hesse, Woods removes the self from the poetic equation so that Oppen's supposed stance may seem like a by-product of Levinas' thinking, thus making the Adorno-Levinas association inescapable. However, there is no removal or negation of the self in Oppen's poetry. Similarly, Levinas never meant to bring subjectivity to an end. The opening pages of *Totality and Infinity* are perfectly adamant about this:

> This book will present subjectivity as welcoming the Other, as hospitality; in it the idea of infinity is consummated. (Levinas 1991, 27)

As Etienne Feron writes in his study of Levinas, one exclusively concerned with the question of language in Levinas:

> It can never be stressed enough that, far from aiming for a disembodied mysticism exalting the other's face, Levinas' project sinks deep into the thickness of the subject's own world experience, and that it is this concrete subject itself which is assigned its being 'for-others.' (Feron 1992, 42)

In contrast to Levinas' ever so complex and careful wording, Woods concludes that "[i]f an ethical stance is articulated in Oppen's poetry at any particular juncture, it is in the insistence on the necessity of the ethical importance of community" (Woods 2002, 232). It is difficult in the end, when reading this, or "Oppen crucially notes that it is interpersonal relations which form the basis of ethics"

(232), to agree with Marjorie Perloff's endorsement on the back of Woods' book, that "ethical concerns, sometimes denigrated as no more than the liberal humanist apology for the bourgeois subject," are not exactly that.

Jenkins, like Woods, focuses on "the nonrational, nonsystematizable Other" (Jenkins 2008, 7) in Levinas' work, while Oppen's poetry is described "as not focusing on the self but as uniquely *other-oriented*" (Jenkins 2008, 36). Unfortunately, if Jenkins' whole book constantly refers to Levinas, only a few lines in the preface attempt to clarify the use of Levinas' terminology. Wishing to distinguish his own "use of the terms *Other*, *otherness*, and *alterity* from those employed frequently in postcolonial, multicultural, psychoanalytic, and feminist theory" (Jenkins 2008, xi), Jenkins offers the following definition:

> By *the Other*, I mean what Levinas would describe as a person which manifests as a face that speaks but who cannot be reduced to knowledge or theme. The synonymous terms, *otherness* and *alterity*, refer to that quality the Other exudes of being beyond knowledge. Because language embodies this ethical relationship for Levinas, his notion of alterity gives us a new way to think of the ethical implications of poetic form. Once we begin to notice these implications, I argue, we can also see that the poetry has already been enacting what the philosophers were merely theorizing. (Jenkins 2008, xi–xii)

The surprising dismissal of philosophy announced in Jenkins' preface prepares the reader for the conclusion to Jenkins' chapter on Oppen, which I will come to in a moment. It may already be noted, nonetheless, that it seems somewhat illogical to ground one's reading of poetry in philosophy only to prove that poets were already *enacting* what the philosophers had been merely *theorizing*. This is especially troublesome from a chronological perspective, since Levinas' writing precedes or is concomitant with much of the work of the six poets studied by Jenkins (only Oppen's *Discrete Series* and Reznikoff's early work predate Levinas' earliest work). In addition, Levinas' philosophy is well known for its textual difficulties and stylistic intricacies, offering the very kind of speculative enactment into or with words that Jenkins only seems to allow for poetry. This particular sense of hierarchy even becomes rather disturbing in Jenkins' final pages about Oppen, when he concludes:

> Oppen gives us, with this linguistic ethics, a different way of "dwelling poetically," to use Heidegger's terms, in a world that is full of people and all that goes with them: exile, isolation, war, atrocity, duties, death, joy, and, most of all, obligation. Such a realism and specificity distinguish his poetry further from Levinas's more abstract ethics, especially because Oppen's poetry seems to more radically enact the very ethics about which Levinas only philosophizes. (Jenkins 2008, 60)

The same opposition crops up between poetical enactment and "only" philosophizing, yet the contours of this enactment remain fundamentally unclear, while the cliché that philosophy is always "more abstract" than it should be and therefore not "radical" enough seems quite out of place. The confusion increases with Jenkins' use of Heidegger's notion of poetic dwelling, which was never concerned with a world "full of people," and stands for the very opposite of the items on Jenkins' list. Going back to the previous passage from Jenkins' preface, what seems conspicuous is how Levinas' concepts are being summoned. Although numerous references to Levinas are made along the way, Jenkins does not take time to provide if only a rapid overview of Levinas' work. However, one of the first difficulties when reading Levinas, if not the main one, is learning to differentiate between such terms as the other [*l'autre*], the Other [*l'Autre*] (sometimes introduced by a definite, sometimes an indefinite article), others [*autrui*] (sometimes capitalized as well), and otherwise [*autrement*]. These are not, contrary to what Jenkins suggests, "synonymous terms," and their use or meaning may evolve from one essay to the next. Similarly, the reader cannot immediately grasp the idea of the Other as "a person which manifests as a face that speaks but who cannot be reduced to knowledge or theme." Not only does the concept of face [*visage*] deserve careful presentation, but equating the Other, with a capital, to a person, encourages many misconceptions. The Other is not other people, one's fellow-man or one's neighbor. Specifying that the Other is not "reduced to knowledge" is not enough to make that clear. Even when taking up this problem and pointing out the fact that "although often figured in everyday metaphors such as 'the neighbor,' 'the widow, the orphan and the Stranger,' the Other for Levinas cannot be completely identified as a 'human being' by traits or qualities because the Other, as infinite, exceeds all possible identification," Jenkins comes back to his choice of the word "person" instead of "human" (Jenkins 2008, 11)—though Levinas also often uses the words human, humans, humanity and man.

In "Levinas and the Face of the Other," Rudolf Bernet insists that *Otherwise than Being* is a "hard text which should not be changed into a soft reading" (Bernasconi and Critchley 2002, 75). In his introduction to the concept of face, Bernet warns that "Levinas initially approaches the face of the other by the double way of *via negationis* and of *via eminentiae*" (Bernasconi and Critchley 2002, 64). In other words, Levinas' concept of face cannot be approached from outside Levinas' specific dual focus, which means it cannot be grasped correctly outside the realm of Levinas' own process of thought or Levinas' own language—which I will come back to very soon. This is true if only because of the relation of the concept of face to the concept of phenomenon, and of how Levinas progresses from a Husserlian and then Heideggerian concept of phenomenon to his own, then to the concept of face as a way out of or beyond the concept of phenomenon. It might also be added that the concept of face changes, in terms both of its definition and its uses, between *Totality and Infinity* and *Otherwise than Being*. Finally, the concept of the face alone makes little sense outside the progress of the work itself: *Totality and Infinity* shows a progression, after the six steps in Plato's *Banquet* (Schnell 2010, 18), in or through seven questions: "jouissance [enjoyment], possession, the feminine, the face, the apologetic I, love and fecundity" (Schnell 2010, 18). To show the place and function of the concept of face within that structure would require an independent chapter, and possibly a complete study. The phrase "a person which manifests as a face that speaks" requires a painstaking analysis of what exactly can be said to "manifest" here, since Levinas' efforts in putting forth this concept were aimed at stripping the concept of face of all the residue inherited from the field of sight, seeing and vision. In short, the "epiphany of the face as face" (Levinas 1991, 75) cannot be reduced to a soundbite ready for critical repetition.

Understanding Oppen's poems then seems secondary, when declaring them to be opaque legitimates the critic's choice to focus on formal or theoretical properties. Conversing about such concepts is in fact made indispensable by that very opacity. Difficulty, or resistance, like opacity, often amounts to a scholarly ruse. The more difficult, resistant or opaque the poem, the easier it is to prefer the better option—that of philosophizing around the poem. Jenkins thus points to "a certain *opacity* to Oppen's language," which reveals that Oppen is attempting "a clarity of uncertainty," amounting to "an ethical event" (Jenkins 2008, 49). Warnings such as the following appear to be defiantly dismissed, when instead it should never be forgotten that "[a]ny approach to the question of the relationship of Levinas's philosophy to literature has also to deal with the incommensurability between Levinas's ethics and the discourse of literary criticism" (Robbins 1999, xx).

Reading *Totality and Infinity*, "*where poetry is described as and aligned with everything that ethics must struggle against*" (Robbins 1999, 88), one is reminded that "[t]he answer that Levinas most often provides to this question—Does the work of art give access to the ethical?—is a resounding *no*." (Robbins 1999, 75). Hence such statements, on Jenkins' part, as "[p]oetry embodies ethics for Levinas, and for Oppen this embodiment becomes his poethics" (Jenkins 2008, 46), must be discarded. When Levinas contemplates the use of literature or art, it is within a restricted frame, which places the Bible as the first textual resource, and devoting one's life to the study of the Book as the final achievement in that respect. Levinas writes in *Difficult Freedom* that "[t]o admit the effect that literature has on men is perhaps the ultimate wisdom of the West in which the people of the Bible may recognize themselves" (Levinas 1991, 53). Putting it differently, Levinas needs to assimilate literature to biblical study before it may be of any illustrative use. When literature is not equated with biblical foundations in the propaedeutic sense, it is only accepted as a reminder, or an extension, of the book of Lamentations. As Robbins argues:

> It is indeed possible to argue that Levinas's rejection of art is to some extent a response to the Holocaust. But it is also necessary to observe that when Levinas does speak positively about art, as he does in the essays on Agnon, Celan, Blanchot, and Laporte, written in the 1960s and the 1970s and collected in *Proper Names* and *On Maurice Blanchot*, that art always has a relation to the Holocaust. Either it is art made by survivors or it is art that deals with the Holocaust in some way. (Robbins 1999, 133–134)

Robbins makes this point very convincingly, when analyzing how Levinas' volume, *Proper Nouns*, is organized alphabetically, in liturgical fashion, to echo the acrostic Hebrew structure of Lamentations (Robbins 1999, 135). In that context, reading Levinas and Oppen alongside poses many similar methodological problems as reading together Oppen and Heidegger, but it has further significance. Levinas' position on art and literature as being only valid if and when it "deals with the Holocaust in some way" (Robbins 1999, 134) is paralleled by Oppen's sense and use of what he called his circumstances. It is therefore the whole question of context that becomes apparent, and with it, the relationship that literary criticism will or will not establish with history. To better understand Oppen's role in this debate, one may turn to Lyn Hejinian's discussion of Adorno's "often cited pronouncement that "'[t]o write poetry after Auschwitz is an act of barbarism'" (Hejinian 2000, 325), in a piece she entitled "Barbarism." She makes the following point:

> The word "barbarism," as it comes to us from the Greek *barbaros*, means "foreign"—that is, "not speaking the same language" (*barbaros* being an onomatopoeic imitation of babbling)—and such is precisely the task of poetry: *not to speak the same language as Auschwitz*. Poetry after Auschwitz must indeed be barbarian; it must be foreign to the cultures that produce atrocities. (Hejinian 2000, 325–6)

Hejinian then quotes from Oppen, and seeks to make him a paragon of the virtues she wishes to promote, using Nicholls' article, "Of Being Ethical: Reflections on George Oppen." The aim is to provide a background to the notion of difficulty, "the notorious 'difficulty,' 'obscurity,' 'opacity,' or 'impenetrability' that is sometimes ascribed to Language and post-Language writing (as to much of the modernist writing that follows, that of Gertrude Stein and the Objectivists in particular)" (Hejinian 2000, 330), rephrased as excessive singularity:

> Such excess is embedded in the poetic device we call "difficulty"; excess creates difficulty even as it erupts from it—in unassimilable surpluses of meaning, in impossible games, in rage, in disruptive and disordering pleasure, in laughter. (Hejinian 2000, 333).

The idea that "difficulty," ever so loosely defined, means "not speaking the same language" as Auschwitz, equates aesthetic autonomy with political opposition in a way that is never so implicit in Adorno, and after having made Jakobson's definition of the poetic function—poeticity as a type of self-reference—into a criterion of historical relevance. Hejinian does not reference Adorno's line that "German words of foreign derivation are the Jews of language" from *Minima Moralia* (Adorno 1974, 110), which could be used to illustrate the resilience and persistence of "difficult" or "foreign" words in that context, if one wanted to pursue Adorno's analogy. By recommending that one should not speak the same language as Auschwitz, Hejinian does not attempt to define what that language could be. The statement apparently refers to the language that led up to it—the distortions of Nazi propaganda, from the language of the Wansee conference, a particular taste for reifying euphemisms, all the way up to the infamous "*Arbeit Macht Frei*" sign—making the historical and political process that resulted in Auschwitz almost entirely an ideational one. Besides, any of the dehumanizing jargon that is the hallmark of the administered world would fit the bill in this case, while a measure of irony lies in the fact that a great many languages were actually spoken in Auschwitz. As historian Raul Hilberg, author of *The Destruction of the European Jews*, declared in one of the last interviews before his death, "In Buchenwald and possibly some other camps as the war ended, the inmates put up big signs that said 'never again.' I think it was really the Communists who were behind that, but I can't be sure. The signs said 'never again' in various languages because there was a Babel of languages in these camps" (Hilberg 2007). In that true Babel of voices, the notion of foreignness is so ambivalent as to preclude theoretical pronouncements aiming at absolving one's speech, as though evil could finally be foreign to humanity. Even the task of defining foreignness at the time looks like an impossible one: from a linguistic point of view alone—which European languages were concerned, the place and role of Yiddish—not to mention from a judicial angle, the loss of citizenship for Jews who until then had *not* been foreign, but sometimes completely assimilated, to list but the most obvious aspects. Even the implication that laughter had no place in Auschwitz is both tragically obvious and historically inaccurate. Steve Lipman's *Laughter in Hell. The Use of Humor during the Holocaust* (1991), among others, like Anne D. Peiter or Andréa Lauterwein, has for instance documented the unexpected role of humor in confronting Nazi horror. The overall claim made by Hejinian seems to be that language on its own might constitute a first step toward "atrocities," at the same time as it is assumed that conversely, language may remove one from the risk of "atrocities." Generalizations of this kind often resurface, as J. H. Prynne remarked about a comment from Peter Handke:

> Whatever the context may have been for the comment attributed to Peter Handke, who in a recent protest against the NATO air-raids over Bosnia is reported

> to have observed that the first victim of war is language, it is hard not to wince at what seems extreme naivety and self-righteousness. Of course it is rather easy to 'see what he means'; and the history of Europe in this century is full of those terrible events supposed to have traduced or contaminated language, along with sorrowful bystanders, perched upon some peak of purity, who can bewail the loss of a model of rational, passionate and poetic discourse that would somehow resist the ruptures of historical process. But, how silly. [...] the idea that there is an innocent or unwounded condition for language in any of its historic or conceptual formalizations [...] is false and dangerous and absurd. (Prynne 2000, 23–25)

Naivety and self-righteousness are unfortunately rampant when it comes to such interpretations as when, for instance, Alan Filreis writes, "Even when writing about her family life, Hejinian is always at least implicitly a political poet because the honesty of her language refuses to reproduce that fraud, and 'fraud produces atrocity'" (Fredman 2005,174). Honesty may well be preferable to fraud, and fraud will produce atrocities—yet how does honesty manage to oppose fraud or atrocities? My reason for reconsidering these statements is that their fundamental assumptions were neither shared by their presumed source, in this case Adorno, nor by the poet to whom they are sometimes applied, that is Oppen. When Hejinian declares that "Poetry [...] must be foreign to the cultures that produce atrocities" (Hejinian 2000, 325–6), she is doing away with the paradox that "producing atrocities" can be part of one's culture. From an historic as well as a geographic perspective, Auschwitz is not foreign to Western or European culture. As a Communist, a Jew and an enlisted man on the European front, George Oppen was in the rare position for an American-born poet in the twentieth century to share in the awareness, the concerns, and the experience of fellow Communists, Jews, soldiers, and indeed the people of Europe at that time. As for Adorno, he was convinced that no escaping from the shadow of that event was possible, when he wrote: "Whereas art opposes society, it is nevertheless unable to take up a position beyond it; it achieves opposition only through identification with that against which it remonstrates" (Adorno 1997, 133). In *Aesthetic Theory*, when Adorno speaks at length about "the culture resurrected after the catastrophe" (Adorno 1997, 234), he expounds on a similar point:

> In its disproportion to the horror that has transpired and threatens, [art] is condemned to cynicism; even where it directly faces the horror, it diverts attention from it. Its objectivation implies insensitivity to reality. This degrades art to an accomplice of the barbarism to which it succumbs no less when it renounces objectivation and directly plays along, even this takes the form of political commitment. Every artwork today, the radical ones included, has its conservative aspect; its existence helps to secure the spheres of spirit and culture, whose real powerlessness and complicity with the principle of disaster becomes plainly evident. [...] Artworks are, a priori, socially culpable, and each one that deserves its name seeks to expiate this guilt. (Adorno 1997, 234)

Guilt pervades Adorno's discussion of art after 1945, but Hejinian does not takes this into consideration, whereas Adorno provides a specific poetic example. When evoking Paul Celan, Adorno declares:

> [Celan's] poetry is permeated by the shame of art in the face of suffering that escapes both experience and sublimation. Celan's poems want to speak of the most extreme horror through silence. Their truth content itself becomes negative. (Adorno 1997, 322)

This has often been taken to mean that silence, or its cognates such as difficulty, resistance, or opacity, could be thematized as content. In a curious inversion of Adorno's position, negativity becomes the truth content—thematized as silence. That silence is then experienced and sublimated as form, doing away with that inescapable element in Adorno's analysis: shame and guilt. The last lines in "Paralipomena," one of the last sections in *Aesthetic Theory*, state how definitive Adorno's position truly was: "Even in a legendary better future, art could not disavow remembrance of accumulated horror; otherwise its form would be trivial" (Adorno 1997, 324). In this respect, Oppen's own position is surprisingly close to Adorno's. Nicholls' sixth chapter in *The Fate of Modernism* considers in great details what Oppen's position was regarding poetry "after Auschwitz," and contains a careful approach to Oppen's thoughts on his own Jewishness, which would sometimes prompt such statements as: "Afraid I'm one of the Jews' Jews, stiff-necked persons in the singular, I'll come to no good end Who however does?" (SL 235). It especially provides an enriching reading of Oppen's letter to "fellow San Francisco poet, Shirley Kaufman" (FM 148), in relation with Kaufman's translation of Israeli poet Abba Kovner's poem *My Little Sister*. Nicholls reads Oppen's letter against his notes about Kovner's poem, in which he privately expressed severe criticism. In these notes, of which Nicholls provides a full transcript in "Appendix B" of his study, Oppen insists: "These experiences are not such as to touch the emotions which were ready and waiting everywhere," which meant that,

> [...] with what had been experienced, this poem had to start fresh, absolutely anew it is terrible, terrible, disheartening for this man, for this poem, to be touched by Pound by Eliot by St John Perse by————O, this is junk, in the holocaust this is junk————He was, after all, afraid to risk failure——or could not face these things without the mediation of another and ignorant poetry———— (FM 197)

Oppen's view that, in the Holocaust, any language "is junk," that will not "face these things without the mediation of another and ignorant poetry," translates into the reader's need to face these things, these poems, without the mediation of another and ignorant critical apparatus. On the same note, Oppen's short essay "Non-Resistance, etc. Or: Of the Guiltless," is evidence enough of the pervasiveness of shame, guilt, and the continued presence of horror in Oppen's memory and in his representations of a warring world. In this, Oppen's position is quite close to Paul Celan's, as sketched above by Adorno. Instead, critics have essentially focused on Oppen's work as the sign that it was not barbarous to write poetry after Auschwitz—that, in Hejinian's words, one had to be ironically "barbarous"—as long as one quoted Adorno's phrase for good measure. As with critics who use Heidegger to ensure Oppen's philosophical resonance, Adorno's thinking is regularly twisted into a political justification for relevance. By way of Adorno as well as, sometimes, Walter Benjamin, it seems the promise of "a counter poetics, a contestatory resistance" (TP 214) is always at hand, since, as Blau DuPlessis writes:

> If culture means affirmations only, we are doomed to those who want to manipulate us. If it means skeptical hope and secular attentiveness—we can, like Oppen, work against wholeness, positive thinking, delusive ideologies, celebratory visions. (TP 213–4)

But in terms of effectiveness, this seems to be rather a characteristic instance of the kind of "positive thinking" that induces the sort of "celebratory visions" attached to the powers of Adornian negativity, once it has been stripped of its historic sense of failure, and of the guilt resulting from the horror that took place. Oppen's 1974 overwhelming essay offers explicit evidence that Oppen did not think he could shed any of these feelings. Stephen Cope introduces the essay as "Oppen's meditation on his decision to join the war effort against Hitler" (SP 46), and most of this one page essay deals with the following double-bind: "If I killed, I would suffer guilt. If I did not, I would suffer … I don't even know a word, a name for what I would suffer" (SP 46). However, the essay offers no solution to the dilemma. Instead, Oppen describes the soldier's guilt as two-fold: it is the guilt of killing and "the guilt of fear, the desire to run, the guilt I've told of, the guilt of that foxhole" (SP 46). So that when he makes a distinction between the guilt of killing and the guilt of not killing—joining or not joining the army—the hypothetical moral satisfaction of having joined the army is tainted not only with the guilt of killing, but with the guilt of having survived the ordeal. Guilt toward the dead who could not be saved and guilt toward the living whom he left behind make up a key cluster of anguish in Oppen's poetry. Any sense of righteousness in taking part in the anti-Nazi war effort is equally undermined by the present context—alluded to at the end of the piece—which is that of the Vietnam war. War itself appears in the end as the epitome of deception, since "He, like us (he, the target) has 'his own' army, the children will display the medals" (SP 46). Nearly thirty years after the end of

World War II, Oppen still felt it necessary to express that everlasting guilt, which has come to spread to all wars.

If one could start from that point, one might remember that the first pages of Levinas' first major work, *Totality and Infinity*, open with a discussion of war, or that the later *Otherwise than Being, or Beyond Essence* begins with a dedication, in French, "To the memory of those who were closest among the six million assassinated by the National Socialists, and of the millions on millions of all confessions and all nations, victims of the same hatred of the other man, the same anti-Semitism," while in the other dedication "in Hebrew," Levinas, "using traditional phraseology dedicates the volume to the memories of his father, his mother, his brother, his father-in-law and his mother-in-law" (Bernasconi and Critchley 2002, 34) who were all murdered in the war. Levinas himself was taken prisoner as an officer in the French army, and spent the war incarcerated while his wife and daughter remained in hiding and barely escaped deportation. It is also commonly acknowledged that Levinas was largely influenced both by Franz Rosenzweig's *The Star of Redemption*, written at the end of World War I, which opens with riveting pages about the experience of dire anguish in the face of death, and by Husserl's last work, *The Crisis of European Sciences and Transcendental Phenomenology*, written between 1934 and 1937 and heavy with the context of those years. Only from these circumstances may one begin to understand Oppen's ethical stand, for they make up his sense of the commonplace and tell the story of why it was lost.

References

Adorno, Theodor. 1974. *Minima Moralia: Reflections from Damaged Life*. Translated by E. F. N. Jephcott, London: NLB.

———. 1997. *Aesthetic Theory*. Translated by R. Hullot-Kentor. Minneapolis: University of Minnesota Press.

Bernasconi, Robert and Critchley, Simon, eds. 1991. *Re-Reading Levinas*. Bloomington and Indianapolis: Indiana University Press.

Bernasconi, Robert, and Critchley, Simon, eds. 2002. *The Cambridge Companion to Emmanuel Levinas*. Cambridge: Cambridge University Press.

Cohen-Levinas, Danielle et Trigano, Shmuel, eds. 2002. *Emmanuel Levinas: Philosophie et Judaïsme*. Paris: In Press Éditions.

Derrida, Jacques. 1978. *Writing and Difference*. Translated by Alan Bass. Chicago: The University of Chicago Press.

Eaglestone, Robert. 1997. *Ethical Criticism, Reading after Levinas*. Edinburgh: Edinburgh University Press.

Feron, Etienne. 1992. *De l'idée de transcendance à la question du langage. L'itinéraire philosophique d'Emmanuel Levinas*. Grenoble: Jérôme Millon.

Fish, Stanley. 1982. *Is There a Text in This Class: The Authority of Interpretive Communities*. Harvard: Harvard University Press.

Fredman, Stephen, ed. 2005. *A Concise Companion to Twentieth Century American Poetry*. Malden, MA: Blackwell.

Hejinian, Lyn. 2000. *The Language of Inquiry*. Berkekey: University of California Press.

Hilberg, Raul. 2003. *The Destruction of the European Jews*. New Haven: Yale University Press.

———. 2007. "Is There a New Anti-Semitism? A Conversation with Raul Hilberg." *Logos* 6/1–2. http://www.logosjournal.com/issue_6.1-2/hilberg.htm

Husserl, Edmund. 1970. *The Crisis of European Sciences and Transcendental Phenomenology*. Translated by David Carr. Evanston, IL: Northwestern University Press.

Jameson, Frederic. 1975–76. "The Ideology of the Text." *Salmagundi*, 31/32: 204–246.

Jenkins, Matthew G. 2008. *Poetic Obligation. Ethics in Experimental Poetry After 1945*. Iowa City: University of Iowa Press.

Kovner, Aba. 1971. *My Little Sister and Selected Poems*. Translated by Shirley Kaufman et al. Harmondsworth: Penguin Books.

Lauterwein, Andréa, ed. 2009. *Rire, Mémoire, Shoah*. Paris-Tel Aviv: Éditions de l'éclat.

Levinas, Emmanuel. 1994. *Beyond the Verse: Talmudic Readings and Lectures*. Translated by Gary D. Mole. Bloomington, IN: Indiana University Press.

———. 1991. *Difficult Freedom: Essays on Judaism*. Translated by Seán Hand. London: Athlone.

———. 1998. *Discovering Existence with Husserl*. Translated by Richard A. Cohen and Michael B. Smith. Evanston, IL: Northwestern University Press.

———. 2000. *Entre Nous: On Thinking-of-the-Other*. Translated by Barbara Harshav and Michael B. Smith. New York, NY: Columbia University Press.

———. 1978. *Existence and Existents*. Translated by Alphonso Lingis. The Hague and Boston: Martinus Nijhoff.

———. 1998. *Of God Who Comes To Mind*. Translated by Bettina G. Bergo. Stanford, CA: Stanford University Press.

———. 1994. *Les Imprévus de l'histoire*. Paris: Fata Morgana.

———. 1976. *Sur Maurice Blanchot*. Montpellier, France: Fata Morgana.

———. 1990. *Nine Talmudic Readings*. Translated by Annette Aronowicz. Bloomington, IN: Indiana University Press.

———. 1978. *Otherwise than Being or Beyond Essence*. Translated by Alphonso Lingis. Dordrecht and Boston, MA: Kluwer Academic Publishers.

———. 1993. *Outside the Subject*. Translated by Michael B. Smith. Stanford, CA: Stanford University Press, Meridian.

———. 1997. *Proper Names*. Translated by Michael B. Smith. Stanford, CA: Stanford University Press.

———. 1987. *Time and the Other*. Translated by Richard A. Cohen, Pittsburgh, PA: Duquesne University Press.

———. 1991. *Totality and Infinity: An Essay on Exteriority*. Translated by Alphonso Lingis. Dordrecht and Boston, MA: Kluwer Academic Publishers.

Lipman, Steve. 1991. *Laughter in Hell. The Use of Humor during the Holocaust*. Northvale, NJ: Jason Aronson.

Nicholls, Peter. 1997. "Of Being Ethical: Reflections on George Oppen." *Journal of American Studies*, 31/2: 153–170.

Peiter, Anne D. 2007. *Komik und Gewalt. Zur literarischen Verarbeitung der beiden Weltkriege und der Shoah*. Köln, Weimar & Wien: Böhlau Verlag.

Prynne, J. H. 2000. 'A Quick Riposte to Handke's Dictum about War and Language'. *Quid* 6: 23–26.

Read, Rupert and Cook, Laura, eds. 2007. *Applying Wittgenstein*. London: Continuum Books.

Retallack, Joan. 2003. *The Poethical Wager*. Berkeley: University of California Press.

Robbins, Jill. 1999. *Altered Reading. Levinas and Literature*. Chicago: The University of Chicago Press.

Rosenzweig, Franz. 2005. *The Star of Redemption*. Translated by Barbara E. Galli. Madison, WI: The University of Wisconsin Press.

Schnell, Alexander. 2010. *En face de l'extériorité. Lévinas et la question de la subjectivité*. Paris: Vrin.

Woods, Tim. 2002. *The Poetics of the Limit: Ethics and Politics in Modern and Contemporary American Poetry*. New York: Palgrave Macmillan.

CHAPTER NINE

Simple and Primitive

History's Children

Critics' inability to deal with Oppen's simplicity due to their disciplinary bias toward conceptual legitimations has contributed to turning that simplicity into a perpetual blind spot. Oppen was quite aware of the problem, as he puts it in section 6 of "Route":

> … One man could not understand me because I was saying simple things; it seemed to him that nothing was being said. I was saying: there is a mountain, there is a lake (NCP 197)

Everything revolves around the way one reads these simple statements. Almost irresistibly, critics are prone to view these facts as comments, thus implying a kind of division between observation and interpretation at the heart of these "simple things." For instance, however simple they might seem, one could say that what makes this instance of deixis remarkable is its secularization of the biblical there clauses one finds in Genesis which function here as paradoxically bare existential clauses that rob the poet of any prophetic tone—an implicit comment on the powers of the poet. However, in putting forward this interpretation, I am merely making the poet's own speculative comment—about "what I was saying"—more explicit, to emphasize the scope of Oppen's simplicity. I am not using that simplicity as an introduction for complexities to come. In other words, if there is a difficulty with Oppen's images, it is not the consequence of an image being a symbol for a concept, but the result of the special investigative role of pictures in Oppen's poetry, as a means of testing one's common sense of place within language and without. Note the four repetitions of the word "picture" in the lines that immediately follow in the poem:

> A picture seen from within. The picture is unstable, a
> moving picture, unlimited drift. Still, the picture
> exists. (NCP 197)

In his notes from *Daybook III*, "[l]ikely bound after the completion of the manuscript for *Of Being Numerous*" (SP 141), Oppen comments on the idea of seeing from within or from without:

> At a certain point we step into water.
> With the word, we know it is the sea, we see the sea. *From outside it.*
> Without the word, we can feel as if from the inside. The taste of an apple, the sensation of sunlight—With the word, we see, *we see from outside.* (SP 148–149)

The two statements, "A picture seen from within," and "Still, the picture / exists," frame the contradictory central statement: the picture is uncertain, as the many reiterations of the word "picture" suggest: it is "unstable," "moving" and drifting, for it is inevitably also seen "*from outside it*," that is with the help of words. Still, the previous clauses, as well as the first and last "picture" here, rest upon the existence of realities experienced "as if from the inside," to use Oppen's notes, in the sense that they are verified through "taste" and "sensation." That aspect of the question may seem to fall outside the linguistic limits of language or poetry, inside which the reader stands. But Oppen is looking at it the other way around: he speaks of words and poetic pictures as standing outside the world of experience inside which he stands. Because of the critical consensus according to which the limits of one's language act as strict cognitive limitations, language's externality to Oppen is one of the most neglected aspects of his writing. In what seems almost a direct comment on his earlier poem, "Image of the Engine" (NCP 40–42), Oppen develops this idea of language as something that remains external to him:

> It is possible to explain an engine. The flywheel actuated the push rods which open the correct valve at the proper moment which—etc; there is no difficulty, it can all be explained. But we are looking at the motor from outside. If there were nothing outside of this engine, and nothing before nor after it, and no laws but those of the motor—if we could conceive of nothing beyond it or before it or after it—we would ask other questions. (SP 180)

Standing both as a part of and apart from reality, the poet is hopelessly included because he is hopelessly native, and hopelessly excluded because he is necessarily word-bound. Such a paradoxical reversal is implicit in that same section from "Route":

> We are brothers, we are brothers?—these things are
> composed of a moral substance only if they are untrue. If
> these things are true they are perfectly simple, perfectly
> impenetrable, those primary elements which can only be
> named. (NCP 197)

Oppen seems to be saying that this common bond of humanity, once put into words, becomes a kind of moral judgment, and would therefore be untrue or unearned. Since, as fact, it predates any argument, it may be acknowledged, but it certainly cannot be accomplished through some magical performative utterance. Oppen makes this forceful claim based on the perfection of "those primary elements" which can bear no predication, and "can only be / named." In other words, instead of differentiating between visual representations and mental ones, Oppen distinguishes between verbal representations and sensory ones. His three adjectives, "simple," "impenetrable" and "primary," describe the whole equation: the thing being said, the image being put forth, seems either too transparent—it is called "simple"—or excessively enigmatic—it is then called "impenetrable"—when it is really "primary." However, understanding Oppen's "things" as "primary" rather than "simple"—or simple in the sense that they are primary—is questionably helpful. The idea seems either too obvious or, again, needlessly puzzling. For what does primary mean? Oppen explains his position in a letter he wrote to his sister June Oppen Degnan, in 1963:

> Bronk is greeted, interestingly enough, as Pound, Williams, Rezi were greeted thirty or more years ago with the feeling that there is something childish about his concerns. [...] There seemed in the late twenties something childish about writing of red wheel barrows, rather than the more stately mansions of the soul. Apparently there seems something childish now about writing of anything else. (SL 84–5)

Although it is at times extremely tempting, as Henry Weinfield has done, to read Oppen and Bronk alongside, Weinfield's focus on *The Music of Thought* alone, to use his title, neglects the crucial tension in Oppen between image and thought, that results from his search for the facts that will allow for a cadence in the first place. What is so striking in Oppen's letter is the continued use of the adjective "childish" to describe, albeit defensively, the concerns of his fellow poets from the 1930s (the list potentially includes Oppen as well) and his contemporary preoccupations in the early 1960s. Both things and the mind are alternatively demoted to "childish." On one level, the idea is put aside, but on another, if Oppen can redeem and even reclaim that word, this may be a hint that there is a continuity among Oppen's concerns regarding "childishness," understood as simplicity and as what leads to what is primary. In "Philai Te Kou Philai," a philosophically titled poem indeed, Oppen speaks of being "Lost in the childish / Here" (NCP 97), which confirms how much he appropriated the notion.

Instead of Oppen and Bronk, I would argue that it is Oppen's relation to Armand Schwerner, which one needs to consider in this respect. Oppen's position is discussed at some length in Finkelstein's "The Sacred and the Real in *The Tablets* of Armand Schwerner" (2005): agreeing with Blau DuPlessis' introduction to the *Selected Letters*, Finkelstein insists that "primitive" is first and foremost Oppen's word for root perceptions, the foundational base of consciousness. For instance, although there have been readings of Oppen's poem "Psalm" as a Christian-Heideggerian compound, there is in that poem no sense of cultural authority being regained through faith, nor does Oppen's poetry ever argue for the bonds of community to be revived through ritual. Not that Schwerner sought to achieve such a revival—he wanted to move "[b]eyond irony and nostalgia, the Scylla and Charybdis of the modern poetic sensibility" (Finkelstein 2005, 261), and "recreate the past itself" (Schwerner 1999, 134). Therefore, the difference is not between a secular poet and a nonsecular poet, even though Finkelstein rightly argues that in Schwerner's *Tablets*, "we are privy to the formation of the sacred from inchoate utterances within the self and between the self and others" (Finkelstein 2005, 267). As Finkelstein points out, quoting what he sees as a key statement in the "Tablets Journals / Divagations" section which concludes the final collected *Tablets*: "The thing is, I wanted not to separate the song from the entropic world. This *and* that" (Schwerner 1999, 157). This "inseparability" (Finkelstein 2005, 275), a notion that one has come a long way from the early modernist desire for inclusion, echoes Schwerner's own statement that the *Tablets* "are not *about* anthropology; they are dramatic, and lyric and entropically narrative evocations of human beings living in such spaces as anthropology has made it possible for us to inhabit as we could not otherwise have done" (Schwerner 1986, 356). Paleographic time even includes Schwerner's own biography, and in particular his experience as an anthropology graduate at Columbia, where he "lived in the work with an absence of self-consciousness which comes near to a definition of happiness" (Schwerner 1986, 356), which makes *The Tablets* a personal narrative as well. In other words, the primitive means of course ancient, and points to non-industrial times, or implies fluency in different types of literacy than post-Renaissance Western literacy. In that, it evokes structuralist attempts at an archeology of humanity's representational powers. But primitive is simply also Schwerner's word for his own preoccupations, as he himself explains his "discovery of the primacy of myth, ritual, linguistics, archeology and ethnography. I was going to say: *the primacy of these interests in my thoughts*, [...] not 'thoughts,' rather apprehensions" (Schwerner 1986, 355). That primacy of the primary, both from an autobiographical and an anthropological perspective that is specific to Schwerner's concerns, is illuminating in that it contrasts radically with Oppen's definition of the primary.

The divergence is most apparent when Schwerner addresses Oppen directly and asks: "George Oppen, tell me, if there's no object constancy, what is the shipwreck of the singular? And how is it that a place to start from implies at the very least a potentially identifiable and receiving thereness..." (Schwerner 1999, 139). Finkelstein understands these questions as Schwerner's effort to distance himself from Oppen because to Schwerner, there is no unshakable singularity to be shipwrecked—or which has not already been tossed by the sea. Furthermore, subjectivity is implicitly assimilated to yet another inconstant object in Schwerner's statement—that points to another, perhaps deeper difference in perspective. The second half of Schwerner's point is understood by Finkelstein as an indication that to Schwerner, Oppen "fails to recognize that in the search for origins" one must acknowledge "thereness" as "one way of conceiving of the divine" (Finkelstein 2005, 266). However, Schwerner's persona in the *Tablets*, and perhaps even more so in the "Journals / Divagations" section, seems uncertain that any sense of sacredness may ever be fully achieved:

> The aim is to get in touch but the object fades. The good society. Poetry is a body invested with rhythmic cells; it is neither the Way nor the object; its appearance makes no difference, but at least it permits the freedom to discover apparently new games. Though one tires of chance itself, and cooks a nice piece of fried zucchini. This or that: hints, the almost conceivable possibility of some transitory order. (Schwerner 1999, 137)

Schwerner's notion of chance and games upon which to build a precarious sense of transitory coherence sets him apart from Oppen, more so than a concern for the divine. Schwerner does not imply that Oppen denies "thereness" or does not recognize its potential to reveal sacred space, but rather believes that Oppen relies too much on a sense of belonging that is simply foreign to his own project. Whether Schwerner is right in this assessment, and how his statement applies to his own work, is beyond the scope of this study. The relevant difference here is not between a supposedly directly accessible primitivity and a highly constructed one. For one thing, Oppen's sense of place is much more dialectic, if not more ambiguous, than has often been construed. Secondly, Schwerner's *Tablets* come across as a much more palpable and tangible object, for all their ironic distance, than do Oppen's restricted disclosures. The matter is one of perspective, as Finkelstein remarks, quoting Oppen's 1968 letter to Jerome Rothenberg in which he writes that "Armand's Tablets of course dis-embowel the nouns but is therefore the account of tragedy" (SL 180), and a subsequent one to Schwerner himself in 1977 in which Oppen objects to what he calls Schwerner's comedic tone in reading his *Tablets*, against his own tragic interpretation of them (Finkelstein 2005, 277). Oppen's choice of words in 1977, underlined by Finkelstein, of "poet-translator" (SL 342) instead of Schwerner's scholar/translator, further clarifies the distance between their two approaches to the primitive. Rothenberg's praise of primitivity as complexity in *Technicians of the Sacred*—as akin to the modernist open form (Finkelstein 2005, 260)—or Schwerner's definition (by no means final though), "The Tablets: formal games and invention give rise to substantive concerns and social reality" (Schwerner 1999, 127), have little in common with Oppen's search for the primitive, which he defines as originary in a different sense—not the search for origins as what gives rise to either the self, society, or a civilization, but the search for what is left of the self, society, or a civilization and which could be the source of a new foundation.

However, Oppen's emphasis on his "childish" concerns and, later, on the primitive as the means to arrive at his own "account of tragedy" has received little attention outside the prevailing critical perspective which tends to de-historicize the matter altogether. Giorgio Agamben's position in *Infancy and History* (1978) is undoubtedly one of the most well-known examples of this trend. Oppen's focus on experience is nonetheless largely incompatible with what Agamben calls the "Destruction of Experience," which after Benjamin's "The Storyteller" he dates back to World War I. The way in which Agamben hopes to justify his belief that experience is now inaccessible precisely requires him to isolate the notion of infancy, against that of history, as a transcendental category, which he presents as follows in his preface:

> Infancy is an *experimentum linguae* of this kind, in which the limits of language are to be found not outside language, in the direction of its referent, but in an experience of language as such, in its pure self-reference. (Agamben 1993, 5)

Experience is never defined by Agamben. It hovers somewhere between the battlefields of World War I and "that humdrum daily life in any city" (Agamben 1993, 13). All one may know of life is a meaningless "jumble of events," which combines the impact of the 1910s on Western society as a whole, in very vague terms, and extends without any transition into Agamben's own 1970s. It prevents one's access to experience, whatever "it" exactly is. What is made abundantly clear though is the rise of language as a new form of the ineffable: the "non-translatability into experience" of "everyday existence" (Agamben 1993, 14) translates into "a concept without a name and knowledge without an object. Ironically, the ineffable in philosophy, which seems to direct us toward pure thinking without language, actually comes to name language for this tradition" (Watkin 2010, 9). Heidegger's involution of being into language transpires in Agamben's "*experiementum linguae*" when it is defined as "language that is content-less speech, pre- or ir- referential language, language that says nothing other than here I am, I am language, experience me" (Watkin 2010, 10). Watkin rightfully notes that "Agamben simply introjects the problem" (Watkin 2010, 10). Introjection is literally how one would go from a poetics of perception to one of inception. If perception can no longer translate into the poem, then the poem will at least translate its own coming into being—its self-perception of itself as a poem. What Agamben calls "experience" thus paves the way for "infancy" as an introjected experience of language, meaning, or thinking. Critics have likewise reframed the supposed "childishness" of Oppen's concerns to fit similar premises as Agamben's, namely, that Oppen's interest in primacy should be understood in the sense of infancy as "*experiementum linguae*." Worse, defining infancy after Agamben prevents one from acknowledging the importance of infancy and childhood in general as important themes in Oppen's poetry.

As a close reading of Oppen's "Psalm" will demonstrate, the introjection of the poem as a philosophical conundrum completely discards the poem's other dimensions, especially the role of the child and of the animal as points of pre- or non-human consciousness. When Nicholls quotes from the end of Oppen's "Psalm," with its startled "wild deer" staring "out" (NCP 99), he refers the poem's Latin epigraph to Aquinas, "which Oppen probably came upon [...] in Maritain" (TP 100), then proceeds with occurrences of deer in Williams and Stevens, and ends with the opening lines to Rilke's "Eighth Elegy": "With all its eyes the creature-world beholds / the open" (TP 101). While the presence of Rilke is transparent in Oppen's poem, Nicholls does not pursue this connection any further. Nicholls only really quotes from the first six lines, and stops at the mention of the animal's gaze when it is opposed to man's. But in line six of his elegy, Rilke introduces the transitory figure of the child as a means to make sense of the man-animal dichotomy. Instead, "Oppen's deer" are interpreted by Nicholls as "similar figures for a nonsymbolizing, non-appropriative approach to the world" (TP 101), which is to say "not objects designated by words but [...] the event of language itself" (TP 101). Oppen did say he aimed at capturing that event (SL 236), yet not explicitly at the expense of the definitional qualities of words. The poem ends, after all, on a remarkable statement about Oppen's faith in words as "the small nouns" (NCP 99). As close attention to Rilke's "Eighth Elegy" will show, Oppen's subtle reading of Rilke's poem[1] also testifies to Oppen's faith in actual poems rather in "language itself."

The choice of the deer in Oppen's poem may very well have been suggested by Rilke's line about a "large brute gaze" (Rilke 1977, 86): depending on the translation, the gaze or the eyes might be said to be vast or wide or big—evoking a deer's round protruding or bulging eye-balls (also an uncanny echo of the German word for animal—*Tier*—as well). But at this point in Rilke's poem those large protruding animal eyes are an image of man's eyes when failing to look at death—"For, nearing death, one perceives death no longer / and stares ahead—perhaps with large brute gaze" (Rilke 1977, 86)—whereas animals, in Rilke's poem, are "Free from death" (Rilke 1977, 86). So Oppen's poem cannot be said to follow exactly the curvature of Rilke's round-about looking away. There is a connection between death and staring in Oppen's earlier poem "Image of the Engine," where "The machine stares out, / Stares out / With all its eyes" (NCP 41). In that poem, mortality is explicitly defined as "The image of the engine // That stops" (NCP 40). The most undeniable parallel is in the last line from Oppen's "Psalm," "stare out," which is literally very close to Rilke's German phrase, "starrt *hinaus*"—staring outside or beyond. But Oppen writes "Startle, and stare out" (NCP 99), which calls to mind another line from Rilke's poem about the child, "A child / sometimes gets quietly lost there, to be always / jogged back again." (Rilke 1977, 86)—which in a literal translation would sound something like, "As a child / loses itself in stillness in this and is / startled." So that Oppen's last line combines the two reactions described by Rilke—the child's and the man's—as one. The contraction is especially significant since in Rilke the opposition is between the child's perceptions and man's. Rilke contrasts the child's perceptions with man's near death or after death stare. Not that Oppen does not choose—but he offers a different choice. While Rilke's elegy is entirely focused on seeing—on eyes turning in and out of their sockets—and on a person turning around and revealing what one may or may not see—Oppen's poem follows a downward movement from eyes to lips, teeth and torn grass, before opening onto the clearing where the deer seem to stand, and returning to the eyes with the final startling moment of contact between the two perspectives, the deer's and the reader's. Is Oppen opening up Rilke's line that "Always facing Creation, we perceive there / only a mirroring of the free and open, / dimmed by our breath" (Rilke 1977, 87)? The dim light in Oppen's "beauty of the forest" "in the distances / Of sun" (NCP 99) would then encompass all one may perceive of creation. For Oppen's "shade" (NCP 99) is a benevolent one, not a limiting one like Rilke's dimness.

Still, a pervading strangeness, especially upon rereading, is palpable in Oppen's poem. The almost grotesque detail of the deer nibbling seems to encourage as well as discourage anthropomorphic projection, thus preserving the sense of confrontation in Rilke's lines, "that a dumb brute's calmly / raising its head to look through and through. / For this is Destiny: being opposite, and nothing else, and always opposite" (Rilke 1977, 87). It is worth noticing, although, that the confrontation, the sense of there-ness expressed in "That they are there!" / "They who are there" (NCP 99) takes place silently in Rilke's "ein stummes, aufschaut, ruhig durch uns durch"—the repeated vowel sounds in /u/ point to "uns," us, and we as being pierced through by the animal's gaze, introduced line one not as "Tier"—animal—but as "Kreatur," so with an echo of /u/, /"uns"/, us creatures. What one hears in Oppen's poem are "The small nouns / Crying faith." This faith stems from one's resemblance with the deer, with whom one shares a similar sense of wonder at "this in which" they are startled by us, as we are startled by them into a new awareness. Going back to Rilke, one reads of a similar experience: "What *is* outside, we know from the brute's face / alone; for while a child's quite small we take it / and turn it round and force it to look backwards, / at conformation, not that openness / so deep within the brute's face." (Rilke 1977, 86). However, the faith one may derive from the animal's face, in Oppen, imply a crying. To understand that cry and its relation to those "small nouns," one should know about the small creature that appears at the end of Rilke's poem. The lines go:

> Oh, bliss of *tiny* creature that *remain*
> for ever in the womb that brought them forth!
> Joy of the gnat, that can still *within*,
> even on its wedding-day: for womb is all! (Rilke 1977, 87)

Rilke's other creature in the eighth elegy is that smallest of creatures—"Mücke" in German being either a midge, a gnat, or a mosquito, used here as a generic insect for a rhyme with "glück"—possibly implying a joke, bearing in mind the German expression "aus einer Mücke einen Elefanten zu machen," literally to make an elephant out of a fly, or make a mountain of a molehill in English. In Rilke's poem, the gnat is happily hopping inside the womb and then fearful at having to learn how to fly. There is no such small creature in Oppen's poem, apparently. The wild deer would not qualify, yet if one listens carefully, could not this "Crying faith" summon the idea of birth through the crying of a newborn? Oppen's poem "Primitive," from *This in Which*, connects primitive fear with a baby crying (NCP 133). Crying faith also evokes, as Weinfield remarks, "the voice of him that crieth in the wilderness" (Weinfield 2009, 187) in Isaiah 40:3, and more generally Adam naming the animals (in Hebrew, the verb translated as naming in Genesis 2:19

also means calling, crying and reading, all pointing to the oral performance of words), which sends one back to the title, "Psalm." From singing to crying, or vice versa, the poem is the place—this in which—both processes may take place. From this perspective, Oppen's achievement here consists in articulating the two opposites—psalming and crying—holding language at that level, combining the psalmist's harmonies and the child's inarticulate outcry into a single poem.

If one now returns to what Nicholls says about the poem as pointing to the event of "language itself," it appears that this is both true and false. True in the sense that the poem revolves around issues of language (and is, in many ways, a case or rewriting), but misguided insofar as Nicholls sees it only as an illustration of Heidegger's concerns about language. Similarly, in "The Place of Being in the Poetry of George Oppen," Chilton finds that in this poem Oppen's "sense of abstraction becomes more evocative of Heideggerian thinking" (MP 111), and thus moves away "from the particulars of his perception [...] towards perceiving the 'what-is in totality'" (MP 112). Likewise, Burt Kimmelman focuses on "Psalm" in "George Oppen and Martin Heidegger: The Philosophy and Poetry of *Gelassenheit*, and the Language of Faith," an essay celebrating "Oppen as the philosophical poet and Heidegger as the poetic philosopher" (Kimmelman 2009, 10). Chilton's idea, elaborated on by Kimmelman, is that Oppen's sense of awe derives from, or is crucially connected to, Heidegger's notion of astonishment. But apart from offering a sample of quotations from Heidegger and juxtaposing them alongside Oppen's poem, the case is hardly convincing, since neither awe nor astonishment can be said to be copyrighted concepts, notions, ideas or indeed feelings, although they are distinctive trademarks in Heidegger's vocabulary. Moreover, because the poem articulates a tension between a psalm and a cry, it cannot be said to reflect the idea of language alone, or ideas about language. What Nicholls is doing is moving away from what the poem may mean for Oppen, to make Heidegger yet a little more inescapable. Agreed, Oppen is immediately quoted by Nicholls as saying that he is "making that Heideggerian gesture of 'pointing'" (TP 101)—but at what? Not at Heidegger, who in turn vehemently refuses Rilke's notion of the Open as being connected to animality, the unconscious, or the absence of language, as critics have shown. In a note to paragraph 15 of *Hölderlin's Hymn "The Ister,"* Heidegger speaks again of "this profoundly untrue word of Rilke's" (Heidegger 1996, 91). Heidegger concludes his note with this damning statement: "This by way of an aside, because the thoughtless lumping together of my thinking with Rilke's poetry has already become a cliché" (Heidegger 1996, 91). Oppen neglects, or is presumably unaware, of the essential difference between Rilke and Heidegger regarding the meaning of the Open. Oppen's use of Rilke obeys his own logic. However, when painting a critical portrait of the influences at play in his work, one can no longer disregard the contradictions in the very evidence meant to illuminate the work. Heidegger does often discuss Rilke, as Jean-François Mattei notes, but in *Ister*, in *Parmenides* and in "What Are Poets For," this is what Heidegger writes:

> What Rilke, especially in the eighth of his Duino elegies, calls "the open" has only the sound and the vocalization in common with what the thinking of the essence of *aletheia* conceives in the word "open." A brief elucidation of what Rilke says about the "open" can help us consider more steadfastly the "open" as thought within the essential domain of *aletheia*, by decisively setting it off against the words of Rilke. (Heidegger 1992, 152)

Or, more explicitly:

> What is necessary is only an unequivocal indication of how Rilke's word about the "open" is distinct in all respects from the "open" as essentially connected to *aletheia* and to thoughtful questioning. (Heidegger 1992, 153)

Angrier still:

> There is, of course, a gaping abyss between what Rilke names the open and "the open" in the sense of the unconcealedness of beings. The "open" that dwells in *aletheia* lets beings emerge and come to presence as beings. Man alone sees this open. [...] The animal, on the contrary, does not glimpse or see into, and certainly does not behold, the open in the sense of the unconcealedness of the unconcealed. (Heidegger 1992, 159)

Despite such declarations on Heidegger's part, Nicholls writes that "Heidegger's 'saying' brings things into being by naming them and thus drawing them into what he calls (after Rilke) the 'open' or the 'clearing'" (TP 105), or again "that it is 'The Open which lets poetry happen'" (TP 105). Quoting from Agamben's *Language and Death* to underline the ontological dimension of words, now no longer content-based but now immersed in "the pure fact of their utterance" (TP 102), Nicholls neglects Agamben's *The Open: Man and Animal* (2004), which devotes its thirteenth section to a comparison between Heidegger's position and Rilke's. The reasons why many critical texts assimilate Rilke and Heidegger's opposed conceptions of the Open are presented most convincingly by Anthony Stephens in "Cutting Poets to Size: Heidegger, Hölderlin, Rilke" when he points out quite disarmingly that "Rilke simply had not aspired to have a stable concept of 'the Open'" (Stephens 2007). Much of the debate rests, as Heideggerian scholarship has shown, and as Stephens summarizes, on Heidegger's own evolution:

> The agenda of the "history of Being" that exalts the late Hölderlin and denigrates Rilke is very revealing of Heidegger's compulsive behaviour. Taking advantage of the twentieth anniversary of Rilke's death in 1946 to resolve a spurious debate on the true

> nature of "the Open" at Rilke's expense and in Hölderlin's (and thus implicitly his own) favour is, in one sense, a reversed reenactment of the political battles he lost in 1933–34. (Stephens 2007)

What is even more seldom questioned is the critical value of Heidegger's poetics. Writing from a specifically literary perspective, Stephens declares:

> In point of fact, what Heidegger claims as his 'discoveries' with regard to the relation of poetic language to the world of objects and common experience had already been anticipated in print by Rilke in his essays on aesthetics between 1898 and 1903 (Stephens 1976: 94–114), and Rilke, essentially, had done no more than draw his own original conclusions from the questions already posed by French Symbolism. Heidegger appears to have been blissfully ignorant of them—a *sine qua non* of his denigration of Rilke. Had Heidegger taken the trouble to read Mallarmé, then he could have scarcely presented his essentially old-fashioned poetics with the panache he does. But then, he had, quite arbitrarily, selected Hölderlin's latest poetry as the apogee of Western poetic achievement, and in this template there was no room for what European poetry had accomplished since Baudelaire. The hagiography that has attached itself to Heidegger's poetics has no defense but wilful ignorance. (Stephens 2007)

Such willful ignorance is what leads to the type of "lumping together" of philosophers and poets which, in this case, misrepresents both poet and philosopher. Some critics even make Oppen completely secondary to Heidegger, using his poems as ornaments for concepts. In "The Pre-Position Of: Being, Seeing and Knowing in George Oppen's Poetry" (1991), Paul Naylor first offers the following disclaimer: "I do not mean to imply, however, that Oppen's poetry is merely Heidegger done over in modernist verse. Oppen seems to identify Heidegger as more of a fellow traveller along a similar 'path' than as a philosophical mentor" (Naylor 1991, 102). But despite such precautions, Naylor then writes: "For Heidegger 'Being' is best referred to deictically, as that which is 'there.' Heidegger, then, uses deictic pronouns and prepositions not so much to refer to specific entities but to the context in which entities appear, which is, as I now want to argue, precisely the way Oppen uses them" (Naylor 1991, 105). Thus, in Naylor's argument, not only has Heidegger come to provide the framework one needs to read Oppen, but Heidegger is even promoted as the source of Oppen's own syntax. Naturally, Heidegger's discussion of what "there" means never properly makes it into Naylor's analysis: tackling the "Da" in "Dasein," which is to say the "there" in the "Being-There," cannot be done allusively. All of Heidegger's work would have to be drawn in. Naylor simply concludes that "deictic pronouns and prepositional phrases are parts of grammar and, as such, refer only to other parts of grammar" (Naylor 1991, 114), which he paraphrases by saying that "if language is, as Heidegger contends, the 'house of Being,' and if humans do 'dwell' in that house as in a home, then language is the first and foremost place to locate the referent of 'there' or 'that'" (Naylor 1991, 114). But what of Heidegger's own language, his syntax, his particular habits of nominalization? Can Heidegger's growing preference for deixis, in his later work, be paired so easily with Oppen's own deictic concerns? When Oppen repeats words such as "poem" or "words," is it really the same as Heidegger repeating the words "speech" or "language"? Instead of substantial answers to these legitimate questions, the reader must accept Heidegger's authority, without any sense of context and almost to the point of pastiche—all of which seems reminiscent of Bourdieu's remarks about "[t]he effects of Heideggerian language" such as "the *flabby rhetoric of the homily*, a variation on a sacred theme functioning as the melody for the harmonics of an unending and unremitting commentary" (Bourdieu 1991, 96). Morphologically speaking, Heidegger's concepts have been carefully assembled in German. Translators have long obsessed over them and they have been at the center of a great many debates to determine their echoes within German language and German history in the twentieth century—but none of this matters, it seems. While the distinction between Heidegger's language and Heidegger's use of the notion of language calls for careful investigation, the greatest possible confusion persists when it comes to welcoming the reader, with incredible flippancy, inside "the house of Being." As far as the reader knows when dealing with such accounts, there might as well never have been any scholarship on Heidegger. Indeed, when it comes to reading Heidegger into Oppen, it seems scholarship is only a one-way street. Sourcing Oppen's primary poetics, the poem becomes secondary to the source.

Nonetheless, if one looks at Oppen's poems for instances of the primitive, one finds, as in Rilke's poem, that the figure of the child is central. In fact, children or childhood exemplify the shift I am arguing for, away from philosophical outsourcing and toward acknowledging the primitive as a heightened form of historicization in Oppen's work. My point is that in Oppen's poetry, children are primarily signs of struggle, not symbols of the concept of consciousness. Since Oppen's poems are indeed tales of witnessing, one might surmise that children would be these perfect instances of witnessing. But as manifestations of a reality they do not mirror but embody, stand for and endure, children are inseparably connected with suffering and conflict. In the singular, childhood refers to Oppen's own youth in a few of his poems. But elsewhere, these are the children of the Great Depression, which demand the poet's care. Figuratively, and by virtue of biographical association, they are the poet and his wife, youths who escaped the adult world they refused not to change. They are the young men and women of the 1960s, Oppen's daughter's generation, in whom Oppen would recognize some of his own generation's concerns.

The role of the primitive in Oppen's poetry having often been approached through Oppen's use of Blake, one can learn a great deal about Oppen's historicization of the primitive through the image of children by looking at two specific poems in which Oppen opens a dialogue with Blake. Compare, for instance, Oppen's third poem from "Some San Francisco Poems," entitled "'And Their Winter and Night in Disguise'," and Blake's "Nurse's Song," in *Songs of Experience*, from which Oppen borrows his title. In Blake's two-stanza poem, the nurse "turns green and pale" when she reminisces about "the days of [her] youth" after hearing "the voices of children [...] on the green," and then proceeds to coax them into coming home with the life-denying moral: "Your life and your day are wasted in play, / And your winter and night in disguise" (Blake 1979, 47). In Oppen's poem, the California setting transposes Blake's "green" into a dilapidated scene. The "strip of beach" caught "between the service station and a deserted shack" shows "a discarded super-market cart in the ditch" (NCP 224). Called "the edge of a nation" (NCP 224), that beach resonates with "something like shouting along the highway": the westward advance of the nation, implicitly compared to the sea's ebb and flow upon the beach, could coalesce into a bright—if critical—picture of early 1970s California as Oppen's own Walden pond past "the long fast highway over the California mountains" (NCP 224). Yet with only cars speeding past with the roar of faceless shouts, this seascape paints a tragic picture. No sign here of Blake's vengeful prophetic proverbs, but a series of problematic statements, beginning "It is impossible the world should be either good or bad" (NCP 224), which culminate in:

> It is as remarkable in one case as the other
> As against this
>
> We have suffered fear, we know something of fear
> And of humiliation mounting to horror (NCP 224)

This world and the "world above the edge of the foxhole" (NCP 224) suddenly combine into a single place at the edge of this beach where, in the second half of the poem, "Dead men crowd us / Lean over us," "grovelling," so much so that "We will choke on each other" (NCP 224–5). Blake's melancholy and oppressive nurse is certainly absent from Oppen's suffocating burial scene in an otherwise emptied landscape, yet the transposition is remarkably powerful. Paraphrasing "Nurse's Song," one could say that the voices of children become, in Oppen's poem, the voices of his younger fellow soldiers, who make him turn "green and pale" to this day still when remembering the waste of their youth in war. Blake's word, "disguise," comes to represent the unbearable denial of the horror and trauma of war, because of the pressure of which "Minds may crack // But not for what is discovered // Unless that everyone knew / And kept silent // Our minds are split" (NCP 225). Immediate associations of childhood with rejuvenation, origin or innocence, as opposed to experience, have therefore little to do with Oppen's work or his use of Blake.

A similar point can be made about Oppen's well-known references to Blake in "Myth of the Blaze," a poem which again returns to the foxhole and evokes childhood. In "Of Being Numerous" Oppen had already alluded in a similar context to Thomas Hardy's Christmas poem, "The Oxen," speaking of "Farm animals, / Draft animals, beasts for slaughter" (NCP 174–5). In this poem's bestiary, Blake's "Tyger" serves first as a reference to the dreaded German tiger tanks, as they were called, against which Oppen's anti-tank unit had fought (Hoffman 2013, 56–57), and as an indirect reference to the furnace experienced during the fierce shelling the men endured in that foxhole. The terrifying analogy between the name "Tyger," for Blake's poem, and the name "tiger," for the German tank, provoke the insurmountable stutter in the poem, which repeats the word "tiger" in various spellings as if to try and tame it. The celebration of the tiger is therefore tainted with the slaughter of the lamb, which the reference, in the last line of the poem, to "each side of the knife" (NCP 249), suggests rather explicitly: the two sides of the knife evoke the dual image of a loving God and a terrifying God who asks for the sacrifice of Isaac who is figuratively as innocent as the lamb which he believes is to be sacrificed. Oppen does not comment explicitly on the story of Abraham and Isaac, yet its presence is a compelling possibility, which another important reference to Blake in Oppen makes quite inescapable. In "The Occurrences," from *Seascape: Needle's Eye*, one reads:

> [...] the forge flames the pulse
> Of infant
> Sorrows at the crux (NCP 212)

Oppen's plural—when Blake uses a singular—expands the resonance of that sorrow, almost making a verb out of the noun "sorrow." As for the pulsating flames from the forge, they evoke "The Tyger" far more than the sulking child from "Infant Sorrow," while the Christian "crux" so close to the flames reminds one of "A Little Boy Lost," sent to the stake by the priest. In the middle of these competing subtexts, Oppen's poem places the sacrificial children within the flames as the "burnt offering" from Genesis 22:2. The poem registers this holocaust, writing, "It will have happened to that other / The survivor   The survivor / To him it happened" (NCP 212), directly evoking the fate of a Holocaust survivor. So that if Oppen's statement, in his notes, that "Blake's Tyger [is] in the small words. They burn. The nouns are the visible universe, the night sky burning" (FM 153), places naming at the center of the poem, this does not suggest a celebration of creation through some variation on the poet's Adamic powers, despite the poem's emphasis on the "names the names the 'little' // adventurous / words a mountain the cliff // a wave are taxonomy" (NCP 248). Words or nouns are indeed, in "Myth of the Blaze," predominantly referred to as "names"—"what names / (but my name) // and my lover's name to speak // into the eyes of the Tyger," and at the end of the poem, "the names / of the Tyger   to speak / to the eyes // of the Tiger" (NCP 249). The poem's naming process accounts for much of the poem's topic, which begins with the need "to know to know in my life to know // what I have said to myself" (NCP 247)—to know, therefore, and be able to name. But in this genesis, *ars poetica* and war memory are one, and thus challenge the poet's naming abilities. As Oppen puts it in "The Book of Job," the previous poem in the collection, "what is the form / to say it there is something / to name" (NCP 240). Here the poet can only name names, as with Wyatt's and Reznikoff's intact and resilient lines, which appear nowhere in Oppen's poem. Or, when old memories are triggered by this moment of silent terror—"I'd cried / and remembered / boyhood degradation other / degradations and this crime [...]" (NCP 247)—the poet can only offer the word "crime." The poem seems torn between the capacity and the incapacity to name anything, which reflects explicitly on the use of Blake's poem. If in his children's book of songs Blake constantly dramatizes the act of naming, he does not do so epistemologically but rather, either allegorically or metaphorically, as a means of questioning how value is assigned, which plays an important part within the framework of his social and political critique. Oppen's poem, on the other hand, dramatizes the function of poetry by staging a conflict between the mnemonic properties of poems and the commemorative aim of this poem, in a way that calls into question the feasibility of the nomination process. In the context of "Myth of the Blaze," the primitive therefore implies a reduction of the poet's art to its most primitive tools through an analogy with an experience of primitive fear. If children's specific linguistic position is referenced in the poem in the etymological sense of infants who stand on the threshold of language, it is without any hint of the ineffable, but only inasmuch as "boyhood" evokes humiliations and subsequent "degradations" which the poet still struggles to articulate. A similar historical embeddedness is apparent in "Return," in which the experience of a child learning to say "welcome" (NCP 48) only makes sense within the very revealing context of the Oppens' return to the United States from political exile in Mexico and taking stock of their lives.

Through the same leaves and stem image that can be found in "Eclogue," the word children, in "Return," reads as a variation on the people, especially when Oppen writes,

Mary, we turn to the children
As they will turn to the children
Wanting so much to have created happiness
As if a stem to the leaves—(NCP 48)

In a letter to Harvey Shapiro, Oppen elaborates on this notion of turning "to the children," which suggests an implicit allegory:

> Perhaps Mary and I searched for 'trouble' and for the problems of children, a child's world - - a parent's world (which is the same thing) Not that Mary and I were unhappy, but that we were not The Happy Ending -- which is an end. And so we looked for the children Or The Workers or - - something beyond the Happy Ending which was, in a way, an end. (SL 308)

The parallel clearly enough connects "the children" and "The Workers," including the workers' children. But Oppen does not pit that world against another, less innocent one. Both worlds are said to be "the same thing," in that they are "beyond the Happy Ending," which is to say beyond the comfort another life-choice might have entailed. Children therefore stand for "'trouble'," if not for struggle, as they do in the epigraph from *Seascape: Needle's Eye*:

So with artists. How pleasurable
to imagine that, if only they gave
up their art, the children would be
healed, would live.
Irving Younger in *The Nation* (NCP 223)

In this context, children sound synonymous with either the people or the poor. Oppen may therefore be said to appropriate Wordsworth's and Blake's well documented metaphorical use of the children as political allegories—in Wordsworth and Blake, as allegories of revolutionary violence (Rowland)—although only up to a point. For the vision of the "Children of the early / Countryside" (NCP 123) in "Penobscot" as well the many other occurrences of the word "children" in Oppen's work, mostly convey a sense of exile and loss, and not the hope for change. The children from section 34 from "Of Being Numerous" (NCP 184) seem elemental, almost generic figures of the celebration of life, until these unified "voices of men and women" rapidly break down and Oppen evokes the cruel plight of women as the source of life, with "life seeming to depend on women, burdened and / desperate / As they are" (NCP 185). In "Historic Pun," the children who "appear / In the parks" suggest a desired, but ultimately foreign, harmony. In "Stranger's Child," Oppen contrasts the nimbleness of youth with mineral indifference (NCP 58). Even the children in "California" (NCP 83) and "Sunnyside Child" (NCP 84), which can be said to stand as if at the edge of civilization, do not embody any form of escape, and mock how "How the Romantic stood in nature" (NCP 83). In the end, if in Oppen's *Daybook V* one reads, among disconnected notes, about "Wordsworth's proof of immortality, the spirit of the very young child the spirit born in him" (SP 213), it should be apparent that Oppen's work confronts this thinking, rather than it embraces it. In Book V of *The Prelude*, Wordsworth paints a picture of the ills caused by too early an education, prompted by "these too industrious times": "'Tis a child—no child, / But a dwarf man!" ready to "read lectures upon innocence!" (Wordsworth 1995, 186). But Oppen writes:

> A generation's mark.
> It intervenes. My child,
> Not now a child, our child (NCP 55)

The poet's negation registers the inaccessibility of a time lying beyond the subject's own chronological reach. Whereas Wordsworth's repetition conceptualizes childhood into the political notion required by his philosophical views on education, in Oppen the historicization of childhood is both strict and literal. It forbids the poem from breaking into the expected generalizations, including the staging of a poet's birth to language. As examples of "gendered power" or "class privilege" (Davidson 2011, 108), children in "Boy's Room" or "the children of the middle class. // 'The pure products of America—'" (NCP 118) from "A Language of New York" always point to specific circumstances. What those circumstances are often recalls the most cruel pictures, as with the fifth section of "Route," which tells of a man's dilemma upon learning "he was about to be drafted" (NCP 196)—"They thought of tattooing the children's names and addresses on their chests so that perhaps they could be found after the war. But they thought that perhaps the tattooing would be cut out of the children…" (NCP 196)—that resonates with Oppen's own decision to join the army and his fears of having left his family behind. More often than not in fact, children are evoked in relation to death and destruction. The conclusion of the penultimate poem in "Some San Francisco Poems," the dedication of "The Book of Job and A Draft of a Poem to Praise the Paths of the Living" and that whole poem, as well as the poem "Semite" (NCP 252) all contain vivid passages calling on the reader to mourn the death of children.

These examples show that because Oppen's notion of the primitive derives from his exploration of the fate and figure of children, Oppen conceives the primitive as secondary, in the sense that it is a position at which the poet has arrived after the facts. Discussing Hugh Kenner's phrase that it took twenty-five years for him to write the next poem, Oppen explains the paradox according to which the primitive has become the conclusion to his own personal trajectory:

> [...] I am sure he did not mean merely that I needed time - - - He was aware that I needed to know, to see, to test, and be there - - - - I am sure that he did [...] And that he knew, the fact that he knew, itself had meaning. a sad meaning. In view of all the blood-shed Which means that poetry might sometime ---- you know I do not *want* to put forward this kind of self-aggrandizement of the poet - - - but it means that poetry might sometime be primary. (SL 341–342)

In these lines, Oppen does not argue for what is primary or primitive as a type of resource but as a destination, and thus as the remainder of what one has seen and known. Oppen's sense of what it means to "be primary," is colored by the meaning of what it took, to paraphrase Kenner's sentence, to write the next poem. Oppen writes, "in view of all the blood-shed," and that "view" cannot be abstracted from the poems.

Note

1. Quotations from Rilke are from the 1977 New Directions reprint of the Leishman translation published by Hogarth Press in 1960, which Oppen owned (FM 73).

References

Agamben, Giorgio. 1993. *Infancy and History: Essays on the Destruction of Experience*. Translated by Liz Heron. London: Verso.

———. 2006. *Language and Death: The Place of Negativity*. Translated by Karen E. Pinkus and Michael Hardt. Twin Cities: University of Minnesota Press.

———. 2004. *The Open: Man and Animal*. Translated by Kevin Attell. Stanford: Stanford University Press.

Blake, William. 1979. *Blake's Poetry and Designs*. Edited by Mary Lynn Johnson and John E. Grant. New York: W. W. Norton & Company.

Bourdieu, Pierre. 1991. *The Political Ontology of Martin Heidegger*. Translated by Peter Collier. Stanford: Stanford University Press.

Davidson, Michael. 2011. *On the Outskirts of Form: Practicing Cultural Poetics*. Middletown, CT: Wesleyan University Press.

Finkelstein, Norman. 1993. *The Utopian Moment in Contemporary American Poetry*. Lewisburg, PA: Bucknell University Press.

———. 2001. *Not One of Them in Place: Modern Poetry and Jewish American Identity.* Albany, NY: SUNY Press.

———. 2005. "The Sacred and the Real in *The Tablets* of Armand Schwerner." *American Literary History* 17: 259–279.

Heidegger, Martin. 1996. *Hölderlin's Hymn "The Ister."* Translated by William McNeil and Julia Davis. Bloomington: Indiana University Press.

———. 1992. *Parmenides.* Translated by André Schuwer and Richard Rojcewicz. Bloomington: Indiana University Press.

Kimmelman, Burt. "George Oppen and Martin Heidegger: The Philosophy and Poetry of Gelassenheit, and the Language of Faith." http://jacketmagazine.com/37/kimmelman-oppen-heidegger.shtml

Mattéi, Jean-François. 2004. "L'Ouvert chez Rilke et Heidegger." *Noesis* 7, http://noesis.revues.org/index28.html

Naylor, Paul. 1991. "The Pre-Position of Being, Seing, and Knowing in George Oppen's Poetry." *Contemporary Literature*, 32/1: 100–15.

Rilke, Rainer Maria. 1960. *Selected Works, II. Poetry.* Translated by J. B. Leishman. London: Hogarth Press.

———. 1977. *Possibility of Being: A Selection of Poems.* Translated by J. B. Leishman. New York: New Directions.

Schwerner, Armand. 1999. *The Tablets.* Orono, Maine: The National Poetry Foundation.

———. 1999. *Selected Shorter Poems.* San Diego: Junction Press.

Stephens, Anthony. "Cutting Poets to Size—Heidegger, Hölderlin, Rilke." http://jacketmagazine.com/32/stephens-heidegger.html

Watkin, William. 2010. *The Literary Agamben. Adventures in Logopoiesis.* London: Continuum International Publishing.

Weinfield, Henry. 2009. *The Music of Thought in the Poetry of George Oppen and William Bronk.* Iowa City: University of Iowa Press.

Conclusion

To Heal the Diction

A letter Oppen wrote to British poet Anthony Barnett epitomizes best the several threads running through this book:

> Dear Antony,
>
> fragile and lucid   as against strong and opaque - -
> I'm on your side
>
> and the poem's lines intertwine   All intertwining is a record
> of pain? perhaps it is   but in the end it is not 'weakness'
> is it
>
> fragile and lucid: light not darkness.
> a mirror: which gives something back
>
> 'if any man's work burn, he shall suffer loss; yet his life
> shall be saved,   but so as by fire   "
> (which is from Ecclesiastes)[1]

How easy it would be to start jumping to conclusions regarding Oppen's emphasis here on transparency and reflection (remnant of Objectivist concerns, turn to phenomenology, indication of solipsistic reflectiveness, realistic stance?), on apocalyptic imagery (political allusion, ontological preoccupation, spiritual evolution?), or on formal processes (innovative foregrounding of syntax, suggestively political poetics?). But whereas critics have tended to focus separately on "the cosmopolitan/European Oppen and the metaphysical/philosophical one," the "American Oppen," the "political/internationalist Oppen" or the "spiritual Oppen" (DuPlessis 2015, xviii), according to each's own preexisting agenda, this book was designed to show how all these aspects intertwine. To do so required, correspondingly, that one understand how "the poem's lines intertwine" exactly, and if and why, indeed, "All intertwining is a record of pain." The lines from Oppen's poem, "A mirror / Like our lives" (NCP 233)—from the tenth section of "Some San Francisco Poems," "But So As By Fire" (NCP 232–233), published around the time this letter was written in 1973—also evoke a similar kind of intertwining, through Oppen's very paradoxical gesture of pointing at the world outside oneself while also including oneself in it. The plural, "our," beckons to the reader as a co-witness of what has been endured, much like the syntax of Oppen's poetry, and his late poetry most vividly, pluralizes the reader's perspectives to include the reader as the co-performer of the meaning explored in the poem, in the hope that through this intertwining, a common sense will emerge out of which the commonplace might be recovered. However, for this endeavor to succeed, one must find a way to resist the temptation to make Oppen's lines "strong" by making them "opaque," and accept that the materials at hand will be forever "lucid" because they are "fragile."

To use Oppen's words from "The Book of Job and a Draft of a Poem to Praise the Paths of the Living," what this "pain" refers to, what is at stake, is this:

> tragedy 'seeking a statement
> of an experience of our own' (NCP 244)

Looking back on the book of Job, which tells of a similar search, one finds surprising analogies between Job's story and Oppen's. For example, Oppen's critics might be compared to Job's three friends, as they look for interpretive reassurance and want to confess Oppen's poems like Job's comforters confessing him for the sins he did not commit, thus clouding the truth which the whirlwind will inevitably reclaim and place beyond one's reach. I have shown how "tragedy," how the "experience of our own" that is put forward in the poem, fades away when doctrine circumvents the necessary preliminary resolution of a poem's composition—the active "seeking a statement"—to impose a single mindset onto the poem's structure. This impatience to label, this urge to supplement a poem's silences with ready-made comments stems from an understandable uneasiness when confronted with unsettling questions. One might then also make the case that Job's and his friends' initial silence over seven days, seeking a statement of the tragedy that has befallen Job, is an apt reminder of the importance of silence in Oppen's poetics. Listening to that search for a statement requires one to adopt the necessary critical silence that will allow one to trace the process by which one can arrive at that statement. The reason why this injunction does not take the poems toward solipsistic isolation or the ineffable is because in that silence lies the possibility of a recovery of the commonplace, for if Job's plight is his own, and by analogy, humanity's, Oppen's sense of tragedy is meant to be shared from the start.

Consider how, looking through Oppen's poems, tragedy always accompanies the mention of the commonplace. In "The Occurrences," one reads:

> Limited air   drafts
> In the treasure house moving and the movements of the living
> Things fall   something balanced   Move
> With all one's force
> Into the commonplace that pierces or erodes
>
> The mind's structure but nothing
> Incredible happens
> It will have happened to that other
> The survivor   The survivor
> To him it happened (NCP 212)

Oppen's choice to combine "pierces" with "erodes" indicates that one's awareness of the commonplace requires that the "living / Things" that are moving break through to the "mind's structure"—a possible description of the workings of consciousness—but it also implies that these things eventually break that structure down through erosion, as if phenomenological epiphanies proved lethal in the end. Consciousness itself is "but nothing," and cannot lay claim to the commonplace except as a bland expression of business as usual, when "nothing / Incredible happens." However, the commonplace cannot be said to gravitate around the exceptional "survivor" either—that survivor to whom "it happened"—for he is, by definition, "that other," forever unreachable. The commonplace then stands exactly in between these two extremes, and invites the reader to consider Oppen's lines in a different light, as they now suggest that the "mind's structure" is eroded by the nothing that happens until the incredible pierces through, and that other, the survivor, is welcomed back into a new and different commonplace. In other words, since the commonplace can never remain unchanged, because of erosion, it must pierce or be pierced by the "it" that "happened" and pierce our "mind's structure" in return.

Like "The Occurrences," "Of Hours" features flashes of Oppen's war experience, and pits the commonplace against forces of destruction:

Old friend   old poet
Tho you'd walked

Familiar streets
And glittered with change the circle

Destroyed its content
Persists   the common

Place   image
The initial light (NCP 217)

Here Oppen is not simply praising early Williams over Pound's later *Cantos*—Pound, whom it has been said the poem addresses as "Old friend" and "old poet"—although Oppen invites Pound to remember the "initial light" of the image, which could stand for the facts which could have saved Pound from the perils of "twisting" one's "voice" (NCP 219) for the benefit of fascist propaganda. Setting the word commonplace across two lines as "the common // Place," Oppen creates a chiasmus which seems to suggest first that the commonplace persists though the image—that one recognizes the commonplace in the image—but then also implies that the image's place or its role has now become a matter of prosody. Read this time as a verb, "Place" evokes the composing needed to produce persisting images and such a thing as "the common." When Oppen writes that "Destroyed, its content / Persists," he is therefore suggesting that the ideological content of the image—Pound's ideogram is the implicit target here—even if it "glittered with change," cannot endure, but that the image as perception, those "Familiar streets" where "you'd walked," these do remain. However, no familiar domestic scene, not even those same streets, are exempt from loss, as the following lines from "Of Being Numerous" make quite clear:

We want to say

'Common sense'
And cannot. We stand on

That denial
Of death that paved the cities [...] (NCP 178)

In the first passage, the commonplace could prevent erosion by accepting to be pierced through and through, and thus to be made to include what otherwise challenged its own coherence. In the second one, the commonplace becomes a process within the composition, an equivalent to the composition and perhaps even an analogy for the composition. These lines now pick up those two apparently separate threads. They ask if the commonplace can open itself to that "denial / Of death," and turn this denial into acceptance, into a piercing common sense affirmation. But they also ask how that shift might happen linguistically, since the very phrase seems impossible to utter. To be able once more to say "Common sense"—which the poem cannot, which is why it uses quotation marks around the words—it seems one needs another language altogether. In "The Book of Job," Oppen repeats the same dilemma:

> in the commonplace the last words
> survivors, will be tame
> will stand near our feet
> what shall we say [...] (NCP 242)

Bearing in mind that one cannot do justice to such a long and complex poem as Oppen's "The Book of Job" with a small quotation, it is worth noting that the commonplace is depicted here as an exchange taking place between us and the words of the survivor, now personified as "last words // survivors." Oppen's image a few lines above, "the words // piled on each other lean / on each other dance" (NCP 242), is even more troubling, because of the vision of bodies, instead of words, thus "piled" and leaning on each other and dancing. The survival of words—of their capacity to mean—depends on one's capacity to engage with them at that level, as survivors of a lost commonplace, however grotesquely morbid this may seem. Another example would be the final occurrence of the phrase among Oppen's *New Collected Poems*, in "The Poem":

> to save the commonplace save myself Tyger
> Tyger still burning in me burning
> in the night sky burning
> in us the light (NCP 270)

Oppen's *Primitive*, where this poem appears, like *Myth of the Blaze*, has been read at times as arguing for the reconciliation of creative and destructive energies. Because "the commonplace" in these lines extends to "myself," which in turn reaches out to Blake's mythical "Tyger," while "me" becomes "the night sky" and then "us," it has been read as hinting at a new American sublime. But Oppen's search for the commonplace cannot be said to end in a kind of poetic theodicy, which would vindicate the breakdown of language on its way to pure awe. On the contrary, "Tyger" is one of Oppen's surviving last words, one of the words that may be summoned to rebuild language's commonplace. As the name for an animal, it reaches back to the principles of Adamic taxonomy. As a title, it refers to a poetic tradition. As a quotation, it has special significance for Oppen's personal history, who spoke of the salutary powers of lines from poems remembered in moments of crisis during the war. As a noun, it echoes world history and, as previously discussed, the German "tiger" tanks. Saving the commonplace therefore does not mean keeping it intact, paradoxically, but already recognizing it as a product of survival in the words of the poem.

The question of the sublime is nonetheless a legitimate one. Oppen spoke of "another and overwhelming force" akin to "awe" (SL 231) in another letter to Michael Heller, to quote but one instance when Oppen commented on such preoccupations. This brings one back full circle to the book of Job. Bearing in mind Oppen's secularized sense of awe, one thinks of Oppen's view that God's answer, in the book of Job, was proof that a statement of truth could summon the whirlwind, that utter sincerity might achieve absolute disclosure, as Nicholls has very adequately shown from his examination of Oppen's notes (FM 166–169). It does not mean that poet or critic might substitute themselves to God in this scenario, and be the whirlwind's prophet, thus harnessing that power, but that articulating one's plight is itself revelatory enough. However, bearing I mind the behavior of Job's comforters, if the commonplace is broken in the sense that no intersubjective consensus is capable of cementing some kind of common sense in the face of disaster, how could the singular expression of disaster somehow repair the commonplace without any recourse to God in Oppen's poetry? Needless to say, Oppen does not resort to the lyrical I as the seat of a recovered universality, nor is he satisfied with turning the matter over to philosophy as a substitutive purveyor of meaning, contrary to critical belief. The question seems unanswerable, until one considers Oppen's "poetry of statement" (NCP 228). As statement, the poem sets the stage where the commonplace may be recovered. Instead of the whirlwind interrupting and making Job acknowledge his own inadequacy before the immeasurable, Oppen's poems rely on repeated dislocations, which welcome and in fact replicate a whirlwind-like disruption. Oppen's unorthodox take on the book of Job is even more remarkable in context. It has been established that at the time of "the emergence of the modern concept of literature as its own sphere of human creativity expressing most profoundly the relation of the human to transcendent questions" (Larrimore 2013, 103–4), the book of Job played an important role. Between the eighteenth and nineteenth centuries, when efforts were being made to read the Bible as "inspired literature" (Larrimore 2013, 103), in the hope that, since "the Bible poetry could be poetry, poetry could be sacred" (Larrimore 2013, 104), the book of Job was found to combine the beauty and power which epitomized "biblical" poetry—a purposefully vague classification which defied genre codifications in favor of a supposedly rawer or purer condition of language. Oppen's endeavor cannot be said to originate within that tradition. Rather than exaltation, elevation, or mystery, Oppen seems to have been attracted to Job's story for its truthfulness. This is where a "poetry of statement" comes into play, for that truthfulness is a matter of composition. Interestingly enough, Robert Lowth, the eighteenth century English scholar famous for having attempted to analyze biblical Hebrew first and foremost for its composition—especially the notion of parallelism, or symmetrical synthesis, as seen earlier—had paid particular attention to patterns of syntactical disjunction in Job (Larrimore 2013, 104). Naturally, Blake's *Illustrations of the Book of Job*, and indeed Blake's poetry, were of greater importance to Oppen than obscure advances in biblical scholarship, which were unknown to him. But the fact remains that the appeal of the book of Job depends largely on matters of composition, namely on its portrayal of the very drama of expression. Caught between his wish to stop arguing with his friends and entrust his words directly onto God ("Oh that my words were now written! oh that they were printed in a book! That they were graven with an iron pen and lead in the rock for ever!" Job 19: 23–24), and his humble reply to God after God's speech ("therefore have I uttered that I understood not; things too wonderful for me, which I knew not" Job 42: 3), Job's language shows that he is torn between the need to achieve the recognition that would sanction the truthfulness of his claims, and the recognition that he must accept how relative that truth really is. In Oppen, I believe this tension becomes a poetic credo. The statement must be put forth and "printed in a book," but because it may contain "things too wonderful," it must also break down, for its integrity does not lie in "rock," "lead," or "iron pen." It lies rather in the "bond" Oppen speaks of in "Semite":

> what art and anti-art to lead us by the sharpness
>
> of its definitions connected
> to all other things this is the bond
>
> sung to all distances (NCP 251)

These few lines illustrate every step I have taken so far. Because "the bond" can be "sung to all distances," including the syntactical distances that the song stretches across, the first step in understanding this bond of song is prosody. Since "the sharpness" of "definitions" assumes a leading role, it follows that it was necessary to restore the importance of Oppen's perceptions and images within his poetics. If his poetic "art" and "antiart" all at once is "connected / to all other things," it means that context is of primary importance, and that context should never be neglected in favor of protective abstractions or borrowed interpretations, because the song's sharp definitions are by essence meant to encompass the things that stand outside of it.

It may seem odd, even wrongheaded, to look for Oppen's final word on the commonplace in "Semite", since notions of Jewish identity or ethnicity were never the basis of a strict sense of community for Oppen. In fact, one might read the poem exclusively as an *ars poetica*, for if these "distances" connect immediately afterward in the poem with Reznikoff's diasporic distances, it does seem that it is the poem, and not the connections attached to its title, that makes up "the bond." In the poem's final stanza—"in the open the moving / edge and one / is I" (NCP 253)—that bond becomes apparent in all its syntactic, or prosodic, clarity. Since "edge" reaches back to the "sharpness" of "definitions"—one of the definitions of the word "edge" is "sharpness"—this implies that the distance over which the song must carry is the line break, for an edge is a place where something both begins and ends, like so many lines in Oppen's poems. One may even consider other, less obvious possibilities, and say that "edge and one" also offers a sound-image of the poet as the "edging one," as well as, perhaps, the "aging one." Or one could focus on the very last line, and how it opens onto the same uncertainties which had been suggested by Oppen's last line in "Historic Pun," "Semite: to find a way for myself" (NCP 189). In that poem, Oppen asked that we "Find a word for ourselves / Or we will have nothing, neither faith nor will" (NCP 189). That word is not so much the "I" in the last line here, picking up the title "Semite," but the word "bond," hidden in the last line of "Semite." Indeed, the whole line, "is I," can be said to refer to the well-known Hebrew phrase *hineni*, found in Genesis, but also in Exodus, Samuel or Isaiah, often translated as "here I am," sometimes "it is I," as in Isaiah 52:6. This much-commented statement, rewritten and truncated across two lines by Oppen as "one / is I," opens onto a vision of near anonymity—"I" is any "one." Yet the usual sense of commitment attached to the phrase, as in Isaiah's "Here am I, send me!" (Isaiah 6: 8) or Abraham's "Here I am" (Genesis 22: 11), is not all lost. That *hineni* may be the answer to the question asked earlier in the poem: "what is a word a name at the / limits // of devotion / to life" (NCP 252), that "word for ourselves" from "Historic Pun." Oppen's poem "Semite," his only poem that features a direct reference to the death camps, through the image of the murder of children, may be said to replay these biblical tests of commitment. That word or name "at the / limits // of devotion / to life," on that "open" and "moving / edge," is no impersonal, indifferent and interchangeable "one" or "I," but one *as* I.

Two words are capitalized by Oppen in "Semite," each time conspicuously, at the end of a line: "stripped naked Think" and "the hangman / comes to all dinners

Aim" (NCP 252). "Think" and "Aim," or: "Wars that are just? A simpler question: In the event, / will you or will you not want to kill a German" (NCP 196). Since "one / is I," how can one, how can I, both think and aim? From "distances" to "limits" down to the final "edge," Oppen's poem pits this "bond"—this broken bond of commonality in the most basic human sense—against the prevailing "deception," suffering and guilt that seems to overcome the poem. The requirements of "poems precise," of a poetry of "the low sky," "sung from the windows" by "women" in the "cities," of the simple "sun's light // on the sills" (NCP 251), all these "narrow / end" familiar touches, should help bridge our distances and bring us closer, if only inside that one poem. No heavens but a low sky, no direct contemplation that is not framed by actual window sills, no vague light but the sun's exact position. Still, in that domestic picture of the poem "born // of a planet the size // of a table top," one knows that the table is set for "the hangman" who "comes to all dinners," like "murder // comes to our dinners" (NCP 252). The low sky, once an image of nearness, drops to the level of "the foxhole" and its "overwhelming earth" that "rises" (NCP 251–2), and opens onto the rising, central sequence of adverbs and adjectives driven by Oppen's "terrible knowledge": "tragically / pitifully," "deceived," "betrayed / demeaned thrown away shamed / degraded // stripped naked" (NCP 252). One goes, from sharpness and precision, to nakedness and harm, or from Reznikoff and Oppen's "childish" preoccupations for simple things (SL 85) to "the children / the guards laughing" (NCP 252), or from "devotion / to life" to the "knowledge // of deception" (NCP 252).

Once that dynamic has been fully understood, as I have tried to do repeatedly in these pages, it seems little can be added to the statement. Because it is decisive, it feels definitive, as though coming to terms with the loss of the commonplace implied that one must eventually accept the loss and learn to let go. There is, however, something to be gained from all this, as Oppen suggests to Frederic Will in the following confession: "I doubt I'll really tell anyone very much: the thing may be largely vanity after all. Still, the statement, what statement one can make, has value to me -- O, has tremendous value, overwhelming value, as you know . ." (SL 161). One hesitates before choosing such sobering lines to feature prominently at the end of one's own book. They perfectly describe, however, the dilemma I have addressed: how to acknowledge at once the limitations of one's knowledge and the value of a statement of truth. Oppen meant for poetry to be of use, as when he wrote to Cid Corman, in 1960, "I have a belief that some of the poems, as they complete themselves, heal the diction" (SL 40–41). If "the diction," because it is not poetic diction but everyone's diction, stands for the commonplace that is language, then there is the value one can find in a statement, and there lies the sense of recovery in a poem.

Note

1. Unpublished letter to Anthony Barnett, March 12, 1973, courtesy of Anthony Barnett. The reference to "Ecclesiastes," if true to the spirit of these words, is wrong. In a letter to Diane Meyer (SL 185), Oppen mentions the actual source, 1 Corinthians 3:15 (NCP 400). Oppen puts quotes around the word 'weakness,' perhaps from a previous letter Barnett had sent, which would have included Barnett's *Fragile & Lucid* (1973), which reads:

   You are not fragile.
   I believe
   you are not fragile
   and do not believe
   in this lucidity,
   pronouncement of this fragility.

   I am not lucid.
   You believe
   I am not lucid
   and do not believe
   in this fragility,
   pronouncement of this lucidity. (Barnett 2012, 83)

   Barnett revisits his correspondence with Oppen in "'Leaving Again in Rags': Parts of a Lost Letter from George Oppen." *Snow* 2: 152–157.

References

Barnett, Anthony. 2012. *Poems &*. Lewes: Allardyce Book ABP.
Barnett, Anthony and Brinton, Ian, eds. *Snow* 2 (Fall 2013–Spring 2014).
DuPlessis, Rachel Blau, ed. 2015. *The Oppens Remembered: Poetry, Politics, and Friendship*. Albuquerque: University of New Mexico Press.
Larrimore, Mark. 2013. *The Book of Job, A Biography*. Princeton: Princeton University Press.

Index

A

B

C

D

E

F

G

H

I

J

K

L

M

N

P

R

S

T

W

Z

O